American Parishes

CATHOLIC PRACTICE IN NORTH AMERICA

American Parishes

REMAKING LOCAL CATHOLICISM

Gary J. Adler Jr., Tricia C. Bruce,
and Brian Starks, Editors

FORDHAM UNIVERSITY PRESS
New York 2019

Visit us online at www.fordhampress.com.

Library of Congress Control Number: 2019937394

Printed in the United States of America

21 20 19   5 4 3 2 1

First edition

In memory of Mary Ellen Konieczny (d. 2018).
Gifted member, leader, and observer of parishes.
Early supporter of this book.
Parishioner at the eternal banquet.

Contents

American Parishes

Introduction

What Is a Parish? Why Look at Catholic Parishes?

GARY J. ADLER JR., TRICIA C. BRUCE,
AND BRIAN STARKS

On Sunday, November 16, 2014, Holy Cross parish in San Jose, California, celebrated Mass just as it had for nearly a century. Originally founded as a mission to serve Italian immigrants, the parish had by then also welcomed a mix of Vietnamese, Filipino, and Latino Catholics into its changing environment. Reflecting the parish's mission to be a "diverse multi-cultural community of believers" (Holy Cross Church n.d.), Masses on that day were held in Spanish, English, and Italian. Like more than 17,000 US parishes in a nation of nearly 75 million Catholics (CARA n.d.), Holy Cross served as a community and a place for local Catholics to practice their faith together.

But that mid-November day at Holy Cross was different: later that afternoon, flames engulfed the church building and burned it to the ground. Soot covered the remains of a parish history of Masses, coffee hours, choir rehearsals, committee meetings, weddings, baptisms, and funerals. Firefighters worked to salvage the heavy Italian crucifix from the ashes. But while the church building was destroyed, Holy Cross's parish community was resilient. Financial donations, diocesan support, and hours of parishioner planning meant that Holy Cross would rise again. By Easter 2017, parishioners moved from their makeshift worship hall into a new church, celebrating Mass and living out their Catholicism locally, together once again.

What Is a Parish?

Is a parish a community? A territory? A local branch of a hierarchical institution? The answer to all these questions is yes. In the view of social science, parishes lie at the intersection of three distinct social forces: community, geography, and authority.

The devastating fire at Holy Cross may have challenged a community and destroyed a building, but the parish remained, mandated to serve a specific geographic locale within the worldwide Roman Catholic Church. All parishes, in a sense, continually rebuild as communities and organizations responding to changing external environments. Just as Holy Cross adapted to its changing ethnic-racial contexts for nearly a century, all American parishes—each a part of an interconnected US Church—attest to the remaking of local Catholicism.

It is impossible to understand how American parishes (re)make local Catholicism without understanding the way that social organization, social context, and Catholic authority influence them all. A parish is the most local unit in the hierarchical Roman Catholic Church. Parishes are not autonomous communities. They belong to a larger geographic network of parishes (a diocese), led by a bishop, following the Catholic Code of Canon Law:

> Can. 515 §1. A parish is a certain community of the Christian faithful stably constituted in a particular church, whose pastoral care is entrusted to a pastor (*parochus*) as its proper pastor (*pastor*) under the authority of the diocesan bishop.
>
> §2 The diocesan bishop alone can establish, suppress or alter parishes. He is not to establish, suppress or notably alter them unless he has consulted the council of priests.
>
> §3 A lawfully established parish has juridical personality by virtue of the law itself.

These codes highlight the importance of community, geography, and authority. Parishes are comprised of people ("a certain community of the Christian faithful"). They belong to "a particular church" in a specific locale, meaning a diocese. And they are subject to authority: parishes are led by a pastor, whose authority is rooted in relation to the local bishop. Formally, only a bishop can create or change the status of a parish as an organization.

But what motivates changes to local parishes? The logic behind the formation or restructuring of a given parish is not just theological but sociological. More than the address of a specific building, parishes encapsulate a territory carved out from a larger diocese governed by a local bishop. In theory, every inch of the globe belongs to a geographic parish. This means that every individual Catholic "belongs" to a parish, his or her attendance and participation notwithstanding. In the most basic sense, Catholics need not register as parishioners anywhere—where they live places them in a parish. A more densely populated area may necessitate more parishes, each containing smaller geographic territories. Still other parishes, called "personal parishes," are defined by purpose rather than territory (e.g., a personal parish for Vietnamese Catholics, or one devoted to the Traditional Latin Mass) (see Bruce 2017). But even these parishes fall within the wider geography and jurisdiction of a diocese.

Beyond delineating a territory, however, a parish almost immediately supersedes geography. Catholic parishes achieve unique identities by gathering specific communities of Catholics in a physical church structure over the course of time. The community of Catholics gathered in a parish is not the same as the geographic footprint of a parish. At times, parish-as-geography and parish-as-community overlap, such as when ethnic neighborhoods were identified by parish name among early twentieth-century Euro-American Catholic enclaves (McGreevy 1998). At other times, geography and community only loosely relate, such as when parishes draw self-selected parishioners together around particular preferences or purposes (Bruce 2017; Konieczny 2013). At still other times, geography and community conflict, such as when some local Catholics feel excluded (Cimino 2013; Sullivan 2012), when demographic transition leads to community conflict (Gamm 2008), or when population decline leads to parish closure (Bruce 2016; Loveland and Ksander 2014).[1]

A parish, in short, is not solely the product of divine sources but also social ones. By seeing parishes as a simultaneous product of community, geography, and authority, we can better grasp their diversity and complexity. The tools of sociology help us do just that. Our aim in the essays ahead is to reinvigorate the way that Catholics and researchers alike see and understand parishes.

---

1. Technically, parishes are not "closed" but "suppressed" and their territory reassigned.

(Re)Introducing a Sociology of Catholic Parishes

This book brings the lens of sociology to the Catholic parish. Sociology is the study of society—how communities, identities, resources, social contexts, traditions, and meanings intersect to shape individuals' and social groups' lived experiences. The pages ahead bring together new voices, data, methods, and questions to pave a path for a sociological reengagement with Catholic parishes.

Seeing Catholic parishes in a sociological perspective is not an entirely new enterprise, of course. One rather infamous example of early parish studies comes from Harvard-trained sociologist Fr. Joseph Fichter, SJ. His dogged sociological research about one parish and its parishioners revealed surprising differences between the teachings of the Catholic Church, Catholics' stated beliefs, and parishioners' lived behaviors (Fichter 1951). Not all Catholics attended weekly Mass, his research revealed, and not all believed the eternal truths that parish priests were preaching. This got Fr. Fichter into some trouble with his religious superiors, who likely hoped for more overlap between ideal and reality. The result was that only the first volume in his four-book series Southern Parish was published. The rest were suppressed. Clearly, applying the insights of sociology to the inner workings of Catholic parishes is not always a welcome enterprise.

Since Fr. Fichter's day, the relationship between sociology and religion has shifted, as priests and laypeople alike have pursued a social scientific understanding of Catholicism. The tools of social science, legitimized by Vatican II, are now more common in Catholic organizational and intellectual life.[2] Parishes—like many businesses, hospitals, and government agencies—now use planning surveys, elicit different forms of feedback, evaluate programs, and assess financial strategies. Despite these accommodating changes, however, we see so much unrealized potential for researching parishes and all they entail. Our understanding of how social science could and should engage with the parish develops from scholar-

---

2. Second Vatican Council documents explicitly discuss the importance of social science. *Gaudium et Spes*, for instance, notes that "in pastoral care, sufficient use must be made not only of theological principles, but also of the findings of the secular sciences, especially of psychology and sociology, so that the faithful may be brought to a more adequate and mature life of faith" (Pope Paul VI 1965; see also Gannon 1967).

ship done by each of us, as social scientists and Catholics. It also arises from our shared recognition of three problematic characteristics in current parish-related research.

First, parishes are poorly understood as a distinct level of analysis. Sociologists tend to look past the "meso-"—meaning the middle, organizational—level of Catholicism. They instead jump immediately into assessments of big picture ("macro-") Catholic landscapes or individual ("micro-") Catholic behaviors, without connecting these topics to the actual parish environments that organize individuals and shape the Catholic Church. The relative absence of parishes in both observation and analysis leads to reductionism at best, sheer invisibility at worst. Carol Ann MacGregor (2018), a sociologist specializing in Catholic schools, calls parishes the "missing middle" unit of analysis in research on American Catholicism. Among parish-attending Catholics, a lack of awareness about the power of parishes as structures can lead them to treat their own experiences as just "the way things are." The late sociologist Pierre Bourdieu (1977) referred to this commonsense view of the world as *doxa*: a feature of social stability that inhibits awareness as well as creative response to social change.[3] Limited awareness about parish processes among Catholics who themselves attend, support, or leave parishes can lead to passive participation or unresponsive leadership. Increased parish knowledge (and the tools to acquire it) empowers Catholics to be active shapers of their communities.

Second, many sociologists *are* working to build scholarship that attends to the parish, but this work is frequently overlooked. Too often, "parish studies" tilt toward an atheoretical description of trends in parish life (especially through individual attitude polls). Trends are interesting and useful but limited in what they reveal. The late sociologist Mary Ellen Konieczny reflected on this problem of parochialism, noting that much parish research shares the problem of other denominationally isolated research: it fails "to consider the larger theoretical significance of its empirical findings" (2018, 16). Too often, statistics and trend lines showcase parish data apart from a broader context. Such an approach uses the *methods* of sociology without conceptual elaboration or theoretical interpretation—that is, what the findings *mean* for the public, whether

---

3. The myth that Catholic dogma has not changed—and cannot—is a relevant example.

Catholic, sociological, or otherwise. Part of this is because many parish studies operate as sociology-on-demand, for a client.[4] In Fr. Fichter's day, this benefactor/beneficiary bind led to suspicion and suppression of research. In our day, it can lead to disinterest outside of a narrow audience.

This book, by contrast, elevates and celebrates innovative work done by scholars—many early in their career—who, through close observation and theoretical interpretation, see parishes as places to study processes that are wider and more universal than the parish setting alone. This kind of scholarship, as the essays of our book show, can reveal fascinating insights into a range of sociological topics. Just as parishes are not isolated from the social world, parish-focused research can engage with concepts, topics, and questions of broader interest to sociologists, Catholics, and non-Catholics alike.

The third problematic characteristic of current parish-related research is its close overlap with its sociological neighbor, the field of congregational studies. This more generalized area of study lends a robust set of theoretical and methodological tools but is insufficient by itself to understand Catholic parishes in particular. The field of congregational studies (see Wind and Lewis 1994; Ammerman et al. 1998) was born more than four decades ago of the purposeful efforts of (mostly) Protestant scholars to shift observers' gazes from the individual or denomination level to the local, organizational level of the congregation. Many data offices in various denominations now do this well, enhancing the health of local church communities and providing knowledge on membership, leadership, diversity, ritual, networks, conflict, politics, charity, and activism work in congregations. The longevity of congregational studies research, its rising status within sociology, and its connection with religious communities are all impressive. And yet, while there is much to be learned from congregational studies, Catholic parishes, as we shall see, differ in meaningful ways from other congregations, Protestant or otherwise.[5] We are wary of ceding parish studies to this generic, shared field.

In the remainder of this Introduction, we introduce concepts and themes that can assist in a renewed social scientific study of parishes, one

4. For a discussion of this common problem with applied research, see Burawoy 2005.

5. In this volume, one of the leaders of congregational studies, Nancy Ammerman, turns her focus toward parishes.

that sees parishes as the intersection point of local people and cultural processes, embedded in a field of social forces. Each parish—each intersection point—is shaped by the interests of religious authorities; rules of Catholic hierarchical polity; models of voluntary association in congregations and broader society; environmental resources; and social change in equality, family, and politics. How these forces permeate parishes and to what extent they intermix with local processes should drive our understanding of how parishes organize and remake Catholicism.

We highlight four themes that sociological research on parishes should attend to: (1) the role parishes play between Catholics and Catholicism; (2) the spectrum of active ("core") parish involvement to less active ("periphery") parish involvement among American Catholics; (3) the role of power and process in parish life; and (4) the parish as a form of organization amid multiple organizational fields. These guiding themes build on existing research as well as in-person conversations we shepherded among contributors sharing early drafts of their volume essays. After highlighting each theme, we synthesize them into what we call an "embedded field approach" for the sociological study of parishes. This approach, which we develop in greater detail in the Conclusion, was not a theoretical starting point for the research contained in this book. Instead, it was the inductive product of empirically driven conversations among the volume contributors and ourselves, with an eye toward the productive directions that new research might take. This approach suggests the beginning of a renewed sociological conversation about parishes, a yet-unfinished one.

Between Catholics and Catholicism

Perhaps unsurprisingly, the gaze of generations of scholars examining Catholics and Catholicism has tended to veer upward—focused on elite Catholic hierarchy and the official Church's role in public life—or downward—focused on the attitudes and behaviors of everyday lay Catholics. Gazing "downward" at individual lay Catholics paints a sociological portrait of contemporary American Catholicism that is highly autonomous, moderately parish engaged, committed to the common good and to the poor, increasingly Hispanic/Latino, in disagreement with official teachings on sexuality, and generally skeptical of institutions and their leaders. An "upward" gaze toward the official Church and its leaders reveals an American Catholicism characterized by distinctive pro-life and pro-justice commitments, priest shortages, abuse scandals, and vocal engagement with political issues.

These are truths, but only partial truths. In order to see "lived religion" among Catholics at a micro-level or "big picture" Catholicism at a macro-level, one must also look to Catholicism and Catholics at the meso-level—most notably, in parishes. Parishes mediate between individual Catholics' lived experience of Catholicism and the global, shared, universal tradition of the Roman Catholic Church. Without a gaze toward Catholicism "straight on"—seeing Catholics in and through parishes—we are missing the full picture. This corrective brings a corollary implication: researchers need to ask what parishes can and cannot tell us about individual Catholics and about the Catholic Church.

It may help to offer a potentially clichéd but nonetheless apropos metaphor: individual snowflakes fall to the ground in seemingly disconnected, autonomous ways. Collectively, they gather to form mounds and layers and snow drifts. When we admire a snowy landscape on the whole, sometimes we forget both the individual flakes and the collective process of their transformation into a wintry scene. But each layer forms the whole: the individuals, the spawned collectives, and the broad entirety of the snowfall. Sociologically, we must appreciate this same dynamic in American Catholicism.

Parishes mediate the multilayered expression of Catholicism, sitting between official Church polity and Catholics' own religious meaning-making (Starks 2013). To become a Catholic means entering "the Church" through a local church (Yamane 2014). Parishes are places for local groupings of Catholics to work out what Catholicism means to them theologically, emotionally, altruistically, economically, and politically. In parishes, Catholics live out their faith in community. Parish communities, in turn, shape individual Catholics' perceptions of morality and the good (Konieczny 2013). A parish is more than a sum of the individual Catholics therein, particularly since parishes tend be large and often heterogeneous (Chaves and Anderson 2014; Edwards, Christerson, and Emerson 2013). Through ongoing cultural work in shared worship and religious socialization, parishes produce local organizational cultures that feel "natural," until one visits a parish where the same things are done differently (Baggett 2009).

A focus on parishes remedies the intensely individual-focused understanding of American Catholics that has emerged within the sociology of religion especially since Vatican II. Without an understanding of the parish environment, wherein most lay Catholic religious activity occurs— even if for only an hour every week or so—it is difficult to make sense of how Catholicism influences the attitudes, opinions, imaginations, and behaviors of individual Catholics. A focus on parishes also corrects the analytic lens that too often interprets Catholics only through observing Church hierarchy. Parishes mediate between a Catholic hierarchical organization and individual Catholic agency.

Parishes also help reveal how organized Catholics perpetuate (and challenge) a religious tradition in ways that produce distinctive religious identities. Things happen in parishes that don't happen in other Catholic settings—for example, at homes, at Catholic hospitals, at Catholic charities, or at retreat centers. Because of this, parishes are central to questions about Catholicism as a religious tradition, including those regarding its internal disagreement, continuity, and change. These questions are reducible neither to individual Catholics nor to hierarchical pronouncements. In short, parishes provide a necessary window into understanding Catholics, Catholicism, and the Catholic Church.

Core and Periphery: Catholic Individuals and Communities in One Tradition

Parish-related behavior has long served as an essential proxy for the strength of one's religious identity. As Mark Gray notes in his essay, individual Catholics' relationship to the Church is typically assessed along a spectrum from highly active and involved to nominally active or uninvolved. As such, a minority of Catholics constitute the "core" of parishes in terms of Mass attendance and participation; a plurality constitute the "periphery" at the margins (or absent altogether). Per Gray's account in this volume, "American Catholicism has seen its core weaken and its periphery grow in the last seventy years."

Similar findings from the Pew Research Center's Religious Landscape study suggest that just 16 percent of Catholics exhibit "high" involvement in their parishes, as measured by membership, frequency of attendance at worship services, and frequency of attendance at small group religious activities (Pew Research Center 2015a). This puts Catholics near the bottom of all Christian denominations, ahead of only Episcopalians in low levels of "high" involvement. But even more notable is the vast swath of Catholics that Pew labels as having "medium" levels of involvement: a full 70 percent of American Catholics—a proportion larger than nearly all other Christian denominations in the report. This conveys two things. First, as an empirical reality, the average Catholic may be rather low intensity in his or her parish involvement. Second, social scientists may not be capturing the full spectrum of Catholics' parish connections.

Ironically, whether one is counted as "core" or "periphery" or marked at "high," "medium," or "low" levels of involvement, the parish still operates as *the* point of access to sacramental life for individual Catholics. Baptism, First Communion, confirmation, marriage, and funeral rites all happen at the parish—and usually *only* at the parish. For lay Catholics, the parish acts as a gatekeeper to the Eucharist, to formal religious socialization, and to traditional rites of passage. Life cycle transitions, community involvement, and personal change are all partially organized in parishes. Individual parish participation, though, obscures the drastic variance in *how* Catholics interact with parishes. Parishes may be "sacramental stations" that allow for anonymous free riding, close-knit communities that feel exclusive to newcomers and outsiders, or something in-between. Understanding how these diverse patterns arise, what they mean for parish functioning, and what they portend for the future of Catholicism is crucial.

But to what extent does parish involvement still accurately measure Catholics' levels of commitment in an era when fewer Catholics regularly attend and participate in parishes? Whereas more than half of Catholics attended Mass at least weekly in the mid-1960s, only a quarter do today (CARA n.d.). And how do we understand the one-in-ten American adults who do not self-identify as Catholic religiously but nonetheless see themselves as Catholic in some other way—a third of whom attend Mass at least once a year (Pew Research Center 2015b; Bruce 2018)? While we are convinced of the importance of parishes in the future of the American Catholic Church, it is clear that Mass attendance does not solely capture or organize Catholic life. This empirical truth actually helps turn sociological attention to the many *non*-sacramental ways that parishes are used (in schooling, as food pantries, for community organizing, etc.) and the many non-Catholic groups that use them (Cub Scouts, Alcoholics Anonymous, Bread for the World, etc.). If we limit our curiosity to how many people attend the core ritual of Catholic parishes—the Mass—we miss all the other ways that parish engagement shapes individuals.

We can also apply lessons from the core/periphery split to parishes themselves: namely, which parishes capture the attention of scholars and commentators and which escape it? Some images of "parish" emerge as central and highly visible in the US Church, all the more so given their resonance with dominant social statuses and privileges. The Basilica of the National Shrine of the Immaculate Conception in Washington, DC, for example, dominates in physical size as the largest in the country; St. Matthew parish in Charlotte, North Carolina, dominates in sheer number of parishioners (upward of 34,000). The "suburban parish" trope depicts a cross section of upwardly mobile Catholics raising families on the edges of large metropolitan areas; the "urban parish" evokes ethnic, immigrant-serving parish communities. These categories are neither exhaustive nor representative. Marking characteristics of "immigrant parishes" or "suburban parishes" can be helpful but does not sufficiently make sense of the diversity of parish forms (Konieczny 2018). What can we learn by examining rural parishes, some of which are experiencing economic transformation, outflows of long-time residents, and inflows of ethnic migrants (Nabhan-Warren, 2015)? Or predominantly Latino parishes, such as those examined in the *National Survey of Leadership in Latino Parishes and Congregations* (Stevens-Arroyo et al. 2003) or *Hispanic Ministry in Catholic Parishes* (Ospino 2014)? So many parishes—arguably those evincing the most vitality—may be rendered invisible due to their economic, racial, regional, or other characteristics. All American parishes are a part of the Catholic Church in the United States; research should better engage and reflect their diversity.[6]

---

6. The minimal incorporation of these studies into a sociological stream of research suggests that (a) the attention and conceptual categories of researchers can be difficult to shift and (b) some methodological approaches—for example, data with comparatively low response rates and sample sizes—will limit reception among sociologists.

Power and Process in Parish Life

Unlike some congregations or other venues of religious community, parishes are not fully autonomous spaces. Legally, parishes belong to a polity that constrains aspects of leadership, resources, membership activity, and ritual life. Decisions to retain or oust a pastor, for example, do not reside directly in the hands of parishioners. Recommendations made by pastoral councils are consultative, not binding. A parish can be merged, suppressed, or relocated into another building without attendees' consent—or even amid their protest (Seitz 2011). While being Catholic may be infused with an ethos of individualism, particularly in the American context, being a Catholic parish is not.

Power works through parishes in material and symbolic ways, with both local and translocal dimensions. The power exercised in parishes is especially formidable because it finds legitimacy in the multiple modes of authority identified by social theorist Max Weber long ago: traditional (rooted in ideas about how it's "always" been done, like the all-male hierarchy), charismatic (derived from powerful personalities), and especially legal-rational (codified in rules, like canon law). Despite the oft-remarked disregard of authority by individual Catholics in personal matters, power in the parish is usually perceived as authoritative (D'Antonio, Dillon, and Gautier 2013). Religious authority in Catholic parishes stipulates acceptable liturgical practice and rules of sacramental compliance. Allocation of roles, positions, and statuses in Catholic parishes—open to some but not others—originates from theological understandings and Vatican-controlled teaching. While models of parish leadership have been an intensive area of inquiry for scholars focused on pastoral practice (Clark and Gast 2017; Wallace 1992), this research speaks also to long-running sociological debates about organizational gatekeepers, overwork, and egalitarian leadership structures (Kanter 1993; Rothschild-Whitt 1979). Further, dioceses prescribe what parishes can and cannot do, including credentialing volunteers, mandating the reading of certain pulpit messages, and collecting an annual "tax."

If many aspects of parish life are relatively circumscribed by translocal rules, much of what happens inside a parish on a regular basis is about the negotiation of local power. A sociology of parishes necessarily draws attention to *whose* voices carry power in parish life: the laity, lay staff, and ordained leadership. Membership openness does not always translate to equal treatment or access to leadership positions (Adler 2012). When and how is power shared? Who is asking for space, time, and funds, and how are those resources allocated across parish groups? Who gets to decide the necessary conditions for speaking and acting as a parish? How are service times decided? (This last one is more serious than it may seem, affecting everything from priests' schedules, to morning traffic flows, to children's Sunday School schedules, to the brunch rush in local restaurants.) Parish decision-making is mutually configured, reconfigured, abandoned, and contested.

Case studies can reveal the complex dynamics of intraparish decision-making, as well as instances when external authorities attempt to exert influence (and how this is received). Bishops may ban certain lay groups from meeting in diocesan parishes (Bruce 2011), or pastors may treat pro-life groups as one among a wide array of ministries so as to tamp down internal polarization (Munson 2010). Parishes show us negotiations (or impositions) of both formal and informal power, emphasizing the inter-relations of a diverse Catholic laity and an exclusively male ordained Church leadership.

Parishes in a Society of Organizations

Finally, it is helpful to see parishes in comparison to other organizations, particularly religious organizations, in this era of living through associations (Perrow 1991). Doing so poses the questions, What is the parish? and Where is the parish? among numerous scholarly assessments of Americans' organizational engagement.

Operating in the unique religious setting of the United States, parish organizations are objects of interest to a range of non-Catholic authorities and parties. Construction of a parish building, for example, must satisfy building codes as well as the architectural and aesthetic tastes of the community. As religious entities, parishes indirectly reduce federal government revenue, are accorded special status to receive donations, and remain tax exempt. Parishes also shape local communities in ways beyond religious purposes; they provide education, offer social services, entertain through bingo and beer gardens, and link businesses with local consumers. They fit into organizational fields of education, charity, politics, activism, commerce, and more.

For students of organizations, parishes should be interesting places (Hinings and Raynard 2017). Are they different from other types of organizations? For example, how might parishes—known for their relative size, anonymity, and similarity across geographical locales—compare to large, anonymous exercise studio chains? Do Catholic beliefs influence the reception of bureaucratic authority or the diffusion of organizational innovation? For example, how is the deployment of new products and processes in parishes similar to or different from the processes of a global corporation? The Catholic Church regularly changes its song books and educational curricula and even recently rolled out a massive retranslation of its English liturgy, rewording long-memorized prayers. These changes adhere only if received on the local level. Do adherence and resistance work differently in Catholic parishes than in other organizations?

For those interested in religious organizations in particular, parish similarity or exceptionality is a key theme. Our contention is that parishes echo the broader organizational field depicted by congregational studies but that parishes' unique characteristics warrant specialized study. Sociologist James Cavendish argues that parishes are distinct from congregations in two meaningful ways: their "location within a highly centralized authority structure" and the complicated way that parishes allow subgroups to coexist within the same organization (2018, 8). Compared to more autonomous congregations from less centralized denominations, for example, Catholic parishes inhabit a type of polity that limits self-governance and resource distribution. Limiting sacramental authority to ordination—alongside declining numbers of the ordained—generates larger parishes, especially when compared to the average size of their Protestant congregational counterparts. Multiple Masses at a single parish can produce multiple parish communities using the same space but (perhaps) not meaningfully interacting. These distinctive characteristics trace back to the constitutive logic of parishes as territorially designated, not born of voluntary association alone. Parishes' unique qualities can skew sociologists' generic measures of diversity, involvement, and religious commitment if applied uniformly across all religious organizations.

Toward a New Sociology of Catholic Parishes: An Embedded Field Approach

The approach that we are describing brings sociology—its central questions, methods, theories, and observations of human behavior—to Catholic parishes. It treats the parish as the most localized, officially sanctioned organizational base of Catholicism: where Catholic religious socialization most frequently occurs, where members with varying religious statuses (lay, ordained, theologically trained, vowed religious) interact, where formal organization meets idiosyncratic community-building, and where Catholic religious life plays out in American society. Parishes are interactive, permeable, and exceptional spaces.

We can only know the extent, meaning, and importance of each of these aspects, however, through rigorous methodology based in the right comparisons. This requires what we call an "embedded field approach" to the sociological study of parishes. Parishes are embedded in an authoritative structure, in their local contexts, in a longstanding Catholic tradition, and in concentric circles of social life.[7] Essential to any sociological study of a Catholic parish, then, is attention to the elements we have described: parishes' constitutive qualities, their correlation to individual Catholics' behaviors and to hierarchical structures of Catholicism, their composition of core and periphery Catholics, their positionality among the full population of Catholic parishes, their internal processes for distributing or limiting power, and the varied organizational fields within which they sit.

Parishes produce and are the products of society. They offer data and points of analysis for studies of religion, race, ritual life, organizations, activism, education, family, and so forth—and not solely among Catholics. They demonstrate how core social processes of integration, authority, and inequality occur in and through organizations, alongside or in tension with the rituals and teachings of faith. Parishes reverberate throughout organizational, cultural, and social milieus far beyond themselves, and their networks can spread—quite literally—to every inch of the globe.

---

7. In the sociological study of organizations, institutional and field approaches have helped bridge levels of analysis and theorize contextual influences. See, for example, Armstrong and Bernstein 2008; Martin 2003; Mohr and Friedland 2008; Becker 1999; and Wilde et al. 2010.

We hope that this volume and approach will reach a dual audience of sociologists and Catholics, both leaders and laity. Occasionally, as mentioned at the outset, these audiences overlap. The aforementioned priest-sociologist Joseph Fichter later wrote of his own parish-studying ordeal that he had, at the time, "held the firm—if naïve—conviction that the pastor would be satisfied, even proud of his parish, when he saw the results in book form" (1973, 58). We retain a similar optimism that—even amidst complexity and historic examples to the contrary—social scientists can forge mutually enriching partnerships with others interested in and concerned with the future of Catholicism in the United States.

The Essays Ahead

The research highlighted in this volume was conducted by individual scholars whose intellectual interest about parishes, or processes that run through parishes, led them to undertake multiyear projects. Each applied to participate in a selective seminar of The American Parish Project convened by the book's editors and hosted by the Institute for Advanced Catholic Studies at the University of Southern California in summer 2015, with funding support from the Louisville Institute. Authors bring a range of vantage points—as current Catholics (including one priest), former Catholics, and observers of Catholicism from other standpoints. Though the contributing scholars overlap in their intentionally sociological orientation to the study of parishes, their disciplinary training, institutional locations, and career stages vary. Collectively, their writing brings depth, breadth, and historical comparison through both qualitative and quantitative analyses.

The essays that follow trace the aforementioned themes of a renewed sociology of Catholic parishes through an array of methods: case studies, meta analyses, historical-comparative work, survey research, and practical application. The remainder of Part I, "Seeing Parishes through a Sociological Lens," sets parish studies in temporal and contextual space. In Chapter 1, "A Brief History of the Sociology of Parishes in the United States," Tricia Bruce, one of the editors of this volume, maps the origins and trajectory of American sociologists' exploration of parishes from its contentious start to its largely applied orientation today. Bruce's historiography reveals an indelible link between parish studies and the institutional Catholic Church, at times pitting "the Church" apart from—even against—"the academy." With parish research often in service of other aims, Bruce asks whether there are now *any* contemporary sociological studies that set the Catholic parish at their center.

The next essay, "Studying Parishes: Lessons and New Directions from the Study of Congregations" comes from a leader in the field of congregational studies. Nancy Ammerman's many publications include *Congregation and Community* (1996), *Studying Congregations: A New Handbook Paperback* (1998), and numerous definitive arguments in the sociology of congregations. Here, she asks the fundamental question of what makes Catholic parishes distinctive (or not). Situating the study of parishes within the comparative and lively congregational studies tradition, Ammerman suggests useful transferable methodological and theoretical tools for analysis. At the same time, she posits that the large size of parishes (as compared to their Protestant counterparts) generates underexplored questions about local religion.

Part II presents a national portrait of parish trends in the United States. Coeditor Gary Adler's essay, "The Shifting Landscape of US Catholic Parishes, 1998–2012," draws on data from the National Congregations Study to offer a big picture look at US parishes. It helps readers understand parishes as organizations, highlighting what has remained the same and what has changed in basics such as average size, staffing, political activity, and membership over twenty years. Adler models the study of religious organizations more generally, suggesting how surveys can provide an opportunity to ask and answer numerous questions about parishes.

Next, Mark Gray, a senior research associate at the Center for Applied Research in the Apostolate (CARA) of Georgetown University, assesses CARA data over time to account for how Catholics have moved from the core to the periphery. His essay, "Stable Transformation: Catholic Parishioners in the United States," shows how baptisms, registration, and Mass attendance patterns reveal that many Catholics do not attend or participate in parishes at all, while others at the "core" are highly involved. Gray traces meaningful differences between these periphery and core Catholics.

Part III brings into focus race, class, and diversity in parish life. This set of essays examines how power and privilege are often unevenly distributed across racial, economic, and ordination status in parishes. Different expressions of Catholicism generate different cultural constructions of the parish community. Brett Hoover, for example, describes what he calls "shared parishes." His essay, "Power in the Parish," shows ethnographically how three parishes in Southern California negotiate a mixed community of white, Hispanic, black, and Asian parishioners. Here, we learn that language and culture can create fault lines between racial and ethnic identities and that lay leaders' pastoral work is circumscribed by deference. Parishes are places where the power dynamics of the broader society are realized in day-to-day interactions.

We encounter another set of parishes—this time on the East Coast— through Tia Pratt's essay, "Liturgy as Identity Work in Predominantly African American Parishes." Pratt critiques the literature on Catholic parishes as well as that on African American religion for failing to sufficiently include black Catholics. She remedies this by discussing the cultural and identity work that black Catholics do through Catholic liturgy. Pratt articulates a typology of black Catholic liturgical styles, ranging from the "traditionalist liturgy style," to the "spirited liturgy style," to the "gospel liturgy style," challenging narrow conceptions of black Catholicism along the way.

Next, Mary Jo Bane—whose work has been agenda setting in the arena of poverty and inequality—paints a demographic portrait of American Catholic parish composition. As the United States grows increasingly diverse racially and the gap between the rich and the poor grows, Bane asks whether the heterogeneity of American Catholics manifests itself in diverse parish communities. In short, her answer is no; parishes remain highly segregated, on average, and are fairly homogenous communities. Bane grapples with the implications of this empirical reality, along with potential solutions.

Noting that patterns of parish attendance and participation differ across generations, the authors in Part IV consider young Catholics. Kathleen Garces-Foley draws our attention to an important moment in the life course: young adulthood (Catholics in their twenties and thirties). Her essay, "Parishes as Homes and Hubs" considers modern modalities of parish participation fueled by delayed marriage, higher educational attainment, and shifting gender roles. In Garces-Foley's analysis, drawn from ethnographic observation in the Washington, DC, area, young adult Catholics rarely register with a parish, instead engaging with the Church through diocesan, parish, or parachurch organizations. Their collective Catholic experience is often transient and hypersegmented generationally. Garces-Foley's essay challenges the use of parish attachment as the sole measure of institutional commitment.

"Preparing to Say 'I Do'" hones in on another important life-course moment: preparation for a sacramental Catholic marriage. Courtney Irby, whose dissertation examined marriage preparation across multiple religious traditions, focuses here on how Catholics have institutionalized—for better or worse—lay leadership and "therapeutic culture" into marriage preparation. Irby showcases how collective meaning-making in parishes can cut across ordained and lay statuses as well as traditional lines of authority in the Church.

The volume concludes with Part V, "The Practice and Future of a Sociology of Catholic Parishes." It continues a legacy present at the origins of sociological parish studies: priests studying parishes. One essay in this section embraces a conversational and practitioner-oriented approach; we'll meet John A. Coleman, SJ, a trained, well-published sociologist and Jesuit pastor in Northern California. "A Sociologist Looks at His Own Parish" models the kind of inquiry raised by previous essays, applying them in a practical way to a single parish to which the author belongs. Through lived experience and his dual role as sociologist and parish priest, Fr. Coleman shares in a personal way his own application of the embedded field approach to the study of Catholic parishes. The essay poses numerous questions and tools for applied sociological parish studies.

Finally, a concluding essay extends the embedded field approach to studying parishes and summarizes what we have learned, what questions remain, and what this means for future studies of American parishes enlivened by the perspective of sociology. It advocates for the reappearance of parishes (the "missing middle") in studies of American Catholicism, suggesting ways to enhance scholars' access to and analysis of parishes. We outline how an embedded field approach to studying parishes changes the study of Catholicism, distilling suggestions for future parish research.

Altogether, we hope that *American Parishes: Remaking Local Catholicism* spawns meaningful, methodologically sound, and theoretically robust studies of Catholic parishes for years to come.

References

Adler, Gary. 2012. "An Opening in the Congregational Closet? Boundary-Bridging Culture and Membership Privileges for Gays and Lesbians in Christian Religious Congregations." *Social Problems* 59 (2): 177–206.

Ammerman, Nancy T., Jackson W. Carroll, Carl S. Dudley, and William McKinney, eds. 1998. *Studying Congregations: A New Handbook*. Nashville, Tenn.: Abingdon Press.

Armstrong, Elizabeth A., and Mary Bernstein. 2008. "Culture, Power, and Institutions: A Multi-Institutional Politics Approach to Social Movements." *Sociological Theory* 26 (1): 74–98.

Baggett, Jerome P. 2009. *Sense of the Faithful: How American Catholics Live Their Faith*. New York: Oxford University Press.

Becker, Penny Edgell. 1999. *Congregations in Conflict: Cultural Models of Local Religious Life*. Cambridge: Cambridge University Press.

Bourdieu, Pierre. (1972) 1977. *Outline of a Theory of Practice*. Translated by Richard Nice. Volume 16. Cambridge: Cambridge University Press.

Bruce, Tricia C. 2011. *Faithful Revolution: How Voice of the Faithful Is Changing the Church*. New York: Oxford University Press.

———. 2016. "Preserving Catholic Space and Place in 'The Rome of the West.'" In *Spiritualizing the City: Agency and Resilience of the Urbanesque Habitat*, edited by Victoria Hegner and Peter Jan Margry. London: Routledge.

———. 2017. *Parish and Place: Making Room for Diversity in the American Catholic Church*. New York: Oxford University Press.

———. 2018. "Cultural Catholics in the United States." In *The Changing Faces of Catholicism*, edited by Solange Lefebvre and Alfonso Pérez-Agote, pp. 83–106. Leiden: Brill.

Burawoy, Michael. 2005. "For Public Sociology." *American Sociological Review* 70 (1): 4–28.

CARA (Center for Applied Research in the Apostolate). n.d. "Frequently Requested Church Statistics." Accessed 2018 from http://cara.georgetown .edu/caraservices/requestedchurchstats.html.

Cavendish, James. 2018. "Why Should Social Scientists Care about Catholic Parishes Today?" *American Catholic Studies* 129 (1): 1–27.

Chaves, Mark, and Shawna L. Anderson. 2014. "Changing American Congregations: Findings from the Third Wave of the National Congregations Study." *Journal for the Scientific Study of Religion* 53 (4): 676–86.

Cimino, Richard. 2013. "Filling Niches and Pews in Williamsburg and Greenpoint: The Religious Ecology of Gentrification." In *Ecologies of Faith in New York City: The Evolution of Religious Institutions*, edited by Richard Cimino, Nadia A. Mian, and Weishan Huang, pp. 55–80. Bloomington: Indiana University Press.

Clark, William A., and Daniel Gast, eds. 2017. *Collaborative Parish Leadership: Contexts, Models, Theology.* Lanham, Md.: Lexington Books.

D'Antonio, William, Michele Dillon, and Mary Gautier. 2013. *American Catholics in Transition.* New York: Rowman & Littlefield Publishers.

Edwards, Korie, Brad Christerson, and Michael Emerson. 2013. "Race, Religious Organizations, and Integration." *Annual Review of Sociology* 39: 211–28.

Fichter, Joseph H. 1951. *The Dynamics of a City Church.* Southern Parish, vol. 1. Chicago: University of Chicago Press.

———. 1973. *One-Man Research: Reminiscences of a Catholic Sociologist.* New York: John Wiley & Sons.

Gamm, Gerald. 2008. *Urban Exodus: Why the Jews Left Boston and the Catholics Stayed.* Cambridge, Mass.: Harvard University Press.

Gannon, Francis. 1967. "Bridging the Research Gap: CARA, Response to Vatican II." *Review of Religious Research* 9 (1): 3–10.

Hinings, C.R. and Mia Raynard. 2017. "Organizational Form, Structure, and Religious Organizations." In *Religion and Organization Theory*, edited by Paul Tracey, Nelson Phillips, and Michael Lounsbury, pp. 159–86. West Yorkshire, UK: Emerald Publishing Group.

Holy Cross Church. n.d. "Mission Statement." Accessed 2018. http://www.holycrosssj.com.

Kanter, Rosabeth Moss. 1993. *Men and Women of the Corporation.* New York: Basic Books.

Konieczny, Mary. Ellen. 2013. *The Spirit's Tether: Family, Work, and Religion among American Catholics.* New York: Oxford University Press.

———. 2018. "Studying Catholic Parishes: Moving Beyond the Parochial." *American Catholic Studies* 129 (1): 14–21.

Loveland, Matthew T., and Margret Ksander. 2014. "Shepherds and Sheep: Parish Reconfiguration, Authority, and Activism in a Catholic Diocese." *Review of Religious Research* 56 (3): 443–65.

MacGregor, Carol Ann. 2018. "The Parish as the 'Missing Middle' Unit of Analysis in Catholic Studies." *American Catholic Studies* 129 (1): 22–27.

Martin, John Levi. 2003. "What is Field Theory?" *American Journal of Sociology* 109 (1): 1–49.

McGreevy, John. 1998. *Parish Boundaries: The Catholic Encounter with Race in the Twentieth-Century Urban North.* Chicago: University of Chicago Press.

Mohr, John, and Roger Friedland. 2008. "Theorizing the Institution: Foundations, Duality, and Data." *Theory and Society* 37: 421–25.

Munson, Ziad W. 2010. *The Making of Pro-Life activists: How Social Movement Mobilization Works.* Chicago: University of Chicago Press.

Nabhan-Warren, Kristy. 2015. "Cornbelt Catholicism: Hispanic Ministry in Iowa and the Future of American Catholicism." Paper presented at the Seminar of the Sociology of the Catholic Parish. Los Angeles, Calif.

Ospino, Hosffman. 2014. *Hispanic Ministry in Catholic Parishes: A Summary Report of Findings from the National Study of Catholic Parishes with Hispanic Ministry*. Boston: Boston College School of Theology and Ministry. http://www.bc.edu/content/dam/files/schools/stm/pdf/2014/HispanicMinistryinCatholicParishes_2.pdf.

Perrow, Charles. 1991. "A Society of Organizations." *Theory and Society* 20 (6): 725–62.

Pew Research Center. 2015a. *America's Changing Religious Landscape*. Washington, DC: Pew Research Center. http://www.pewforum.org/2015/05/12/americas-changing-religious-landscape/.

———. 2015b. *U.S. Catholics Open to Non-Traditional Families*. Washington, DC: Pew Research Center. http://www.pewforum.org/2015/09/02/u-s-catholics-open-to-non-traditional-families/.

Pope Paul VI. 1965. *Pastoral Constitution on the Church in the Modern World: Gaudium Et Spes*. http://www.vatican.va/archive/hist_councils/ii_vatican_council/documents/vat-ii_const_19651207_gaudium-et-spes_en.html.

Rothschild-Whitt, Joyce. 1979. "The Collectivist Organization: An Alternative to Rational-Bureaucratic Models." *American Sociological Review* 44, 509–27.

Seitz, John C. 2011. *No Closure: Catholic Practice and Boston's Parish Shutdowns*. Cambridge, Mass.: Harvard University Press.

Starks, Brian. 2013. "Exploring Religious Self-Identification among US Catholics: Traditionals, Moderates, and Liberals." *Sociology of Religion* 74, 4.

Stevens-Arroyo, Anthony, Anneris Goris, Ariela Keysar, Irene Quiles, Andras Tapolcai, Dorothy Craig, and Christina Spinuso. 2003. *The National Survey of Leadership in Latino Parishes and Congregations*. Brooklyn, NY: Program for the Analysis of Religion among Latinas/os (PARAL).

Sullivan, Susan Crawford. 2012. *Living Faith: Everyday Religion and Mothers in Poverty*. Chicago: University of Chicago Press.

Wallace, Ruth. 1992. *They Call Her Pastor: A New Role for Catholic Women*. Albany: State University of New York Press.

Wind, James P., and James W. Lewis, eds. 1994. *American Congregations, Volume II: New Perspectives in the Study of Congregations*. Chicago: University of Chicago Press.

Wilde, Melissa, Kristin Geraty, Shelley Nelson, and Emily Bowman. 2010. "Religious Economy or Organizational Field? Predicting Bishops' Votes at the Second Vatican Council." *American Sociological Review* 75 (4): 586–606.

Yamane, David. 2014. *Becoming Catholic: Finding Rome in the American Religious Landscape*. New York: Oxford University Press.

Part I: Seeing Parishes through a Sociological Lens

Anyone who has ever put on a pair of prescription glasses for the first time is familiar with that feeling of seeing things anew. Suddenly, you notice the leaves on trees, numbers on license plates, and countless details that you hadn't even realized you'd been missing.

The sociological imagination is like that, too. Our task in the pages ahead is to help readers see Catholic parishes, Catholicism, and the many facets of society that they interact with through a new lens. We began the Introduction by explaining what a parish is and introducing a new way of looking at parishes sociologically. Chapter 1 provides a history of other studies that have looked at parishes sociologically, and Chapter 2 situates the study of parishes within the context of studies of all religious congregations.

Suggested Additional Readings

Ammerman, Nancy T. 1997. *Congregation and Community*. New Brunswick, N.J.: Rutgers University Press.

Ammerman, Nancy T., Jackson W. Carroll, Carl S. Dudley, and William McKinney, eds. 1998. *Studying Congregations: A New Handbook*. Nashville, Tenn.: Abingdon Press.

Baggett, Jerome P. 2009. *Sense of the Faithful: How American Catholics Live Their Faith*. New York: Oxford University Press.

Bruce, Tricia C. 2017. *Parish and Place: Making Room for Diversity in the American Catholic Church*. New York: Oxford University Press.

———. 2018. "Forum: Studying Parishes in Studies of American Catholicism." *American Catholic Studies* 129 (1): 1–26.

Gamm, Gerald. 2008. *Urban Exodus: Why the Jews Left Boston and the Catholics Stayed*. Cambridge, Mass.: Harvard University Press.

Wind, James P. and James W. Lewis, eds. 1994. *American Congregations (Vol 2): New Perspectives in the Study of Congregations*. Chicago: University of Chicago Press.

1   A Brief History of the Sociology of Parishes in the United States

TRICIA C. BRUCE

Not long before American Catholics' Mass attendance peaked in the 1950s, sociologist-priest Francis J. Friedel remarked in his address to the American Catholic Sociological Society (ACSS) that the parish resides among the most fertile "fields of research that lie open to the Catholic sociologist" (1942, 132). Parishes, after all, were the hubs and incubators of Catholic life in a predominantly Protestant America, filling both religious and social functions among an ethnically diverse Catholic populace. But the young ACSS and its corresponding journal had produced little by way of research on the Catholic parish. Graduate programs likewise evidenced scant study of parishes. Sociological examination would, in Friedel's estimation, "be of tremendous value to a parish."

That this agenda-setting assertion would come from a Catholic priest-sociologist and apologist of the faith set the tone for sociological research on American Catholic parishes. Then and now, the sociology of parishes posed a "dual-constituency value proposition": good for the academy, good for the Church. Sociologists could benefit from understanding social life as manifested in and through the parish; Catholics could benefit from a sociological assessment of their most integral organization. Not surprisingly, it was Catholic sociologists who were mostly likely to heed this call—and to endure the consequences that accompany a scholarly look at one's own tribe.

The trajectory of parish studies—from its early years, to its interface with changes introduced by Vatican II, to its current state—constitutes the focus of this essay. I confine my examination to studies with a fairly explicit focus on parishes, although of course studies about many varieties of Catholic experience likewise intersect parishes.[1] As goes the parish,

1. Readers can look to Cavendish (2007) for a historical appraisal of sociology and American Catholicism overall and to Bruce (2018) for an expanded forum on the imperative of studying parishes in American Catholicism.

so (often) goes Catholicism. Here, I generally limit my purview to studies conducted by sociologists (or in some cases, social historians) who employ the methods of social science, exempting those by theologians, journalists, or researchers from other disciplinary vantage points. This bracketing carries the explicit agenda of seeing—and foreseeing—what distinguishes the sociological study of the Catholic parish in particular. The essay proceeds chronologically, examining parish studies during three periods: (1) before the Second Vatican Council (roughly 1940–1961); (2) Vatican II and subsequent decades (1962–1989); and (3) the most recent quarter century (1990 to the present).

Parish Studies before Vatican II

An American sociology of the parish emerged alongside an American sociology of religion in the postwar era. Embattled and isolated in their own discipline, sociologists of Catholicism at the time found themselves defending their parochial focus as often as their empirical methodology. The parish (and Catholicism, and even religion) required justification as an arena worthy of sociological attention (see Smith et al. 2013). Sociologists did so by advancing the idea that the parish constitutes the basic unit of social organization in the Catholic Church. "It is unnecessary to recall to Catholic sociologists that the parish is the primary community for Catholics," wrote Archbishop Edwin V. O'Hara in a 1945 issue of the *American Catholic Sociological Review* (23). From family to schooling to social mobility, parishes coalesced Catholics and operated as key sites for institution building. Nevertheless, O'Hara's pitch ran counter to the slow pace of research being conducted on parishes at the time.

The sociological study of the parish developed largely as a study of parish "problems," revealing deep pastoral roots. Friedel (1942), for example, contended that the burgeoning field could reveal data on topics such as interfaith marriage, childrearing, education, and disaffiliation. Parishes had problems; sociologists could name them. This orientation stemmed jointly from the positionality of researchers (mostly priests or other religious), and the view of sociology as a novel scientific tool for unpacking social realities. Professors offered classes in Parish Problems at the Catholic University of America and the University of Notre Dame. Publications frequently concluded with impassioned assessments of parish weaknesses and troubling areas worthy of attention. Far from a neutral enterprise (especially for Catholic "insiders" whose own training would have been paid by Church funds), sociology was principally a skillset in service of a greater Catholic good.

Scholarship in the 1940s, for example, produced a handful of parish case studies highlighting themes such as the influx of new immigrant attendees, blended church communities, Catholic youth, and concerns about defection from the faith. The tone used to present parish findings in these early publications is decidedly practitioner-oriented. For example, Brother Gerald J. Schnepp's 1942 article, which, in the course of examining tensions in a mixed Irish, German, and "American" parish, expresses sincere concern over parishioners' average fertility rate of 2.1 children per family, deemed too low to "assure future strength for the Church in America" (160). Studies at the time posed the questions and set an agenda imbued with intentionality and praxis. A sociology of the parish should *better* the parish.

The 1950s introduced a more strident claim to a formal sociology of the parish as a defined field. Writing in 1950, John Donovan of Fordham University lamented the "remarkable fact that despite the organizational role which the parish plays in the total structure of the Catholic Church and in the religious and social life of its members, no attempt to describe or analyze it in the scientific terminology of the social sciences exists" (66). Heeding the call personally, he suggested that thinking of the parish primarily as a *place* obscured its realities as a *social organization* with statuses and roles. His argument resonated during an era of sociology dominated by functionalism and its emphasis on "systems within systems" (Parsons 1937). Donovan further articulated the primacy of the *institutional character* of the parish: parishes cannot exist autonomously, apart from the Church. Accordingly, he devised a brief definition:

> The Catholic parish must be conceived of as a real social group composed of the Catholic clergy, religious and laity within certain territorial boundaries who share a unity founded on common religious beliefs and who participate in socio-religious relationship[s] institutionally defined by the parent organization of the Church. (Donovan 1950, 69)

Parishes, in other words, were more than the sum of their parishioners and different than autonomous congregations. His was an attempt to articulate a grand theory of "the parish"—a Weberian ideal type, operational across all contexts of pre–Vatican II American Catholicism.

A 1951 symposium and resulting volume titled *The Sociology of the Parish* signaled an optimistic trajectory for sociological parish studies. Editors C. J. Nuesse and Thomas J. Harte (both professors of sociology at the Catholic University of America) critiqued prior attempts as "the products of individual interest rather than of concerted effort" (1951, 12). Empirical studies of the parish—both statistical and descriptive—were key to understanding what happens in parishes. The book's chapters consider parishes' historical development, organization, methods of research, and pastoral implications. Contributors' attention to the dynamics of race, setting, structure, and methodological technique would have enduring relevance were it not for the book's near-extinct status today.

The influence of *The Sociology of the Parish* might have been greater had it not come on the heels of another now-infamous book. Sociologist-priest Joseph H. Fichter published the first volume of his Southern Parish series, *Dynamics of a City Church*, in 1951. It represented the first book-length sociological look at a Catholic parish, its data stemming from a yearlong field study of a single New Orleans parish. Fr. Fichter sought to understand "in what ways, and to what extent, does the informal practice of Catholicism differ from the formal expectations of the official church" (1973, 32). The parish offered a natural place to explore how closely official Church teachings overlapped with lived behavior. Granted permission from the local bishop (in New Orleans) as well as the pastor, Fichter and ten research assistants set out to conduct extensive field research, interviews, and surveys. "They were everywhere, watching everything, talking with everyone," Fichter later recounted (1973, 39).

Southern Parish revealed that Catholics' lived behaviors did *not* always align with official Catholic teaching. Further, parishioners' compliance with institutional rules generally mirrored their frequency of Mass attendance. Mass attendance acted as a proxy for strength of Catholic identity, setting a precedent for what is now commonplace in assessments of Catholic identity. Fichter developed a typology of commitment, with points along the spectrum from nuclear ("the most active participants and the most faithful believers"); to modal ("the normal 'practicing' Catholics easily identifiable as parishioners"); to marginal ("conforming to a bare, arbitrary minimum"); to dormant ("who have 'given up' Catholicism, but have not joined another denomination") Catholics (1953, 22). The sociology of the parish had divulged Catholics' deviance from the norms of the Church.

The revelation of a less-than-perfect overlap between precepts and behavior incensed the pastor of the parish Fichter studied. Sociology had thus far been framed as scholarship in service of parish betterment, especially when conducted by priest-sociologists. Southern Parish appeared to threaten this dominant paradigm, even as it relayed empirical findings drawn from scientific research. The perceived disjuncture between social science and parish betterment led Fichter's Jesuit provincial to permanently suppress the subsequent volumes (two through four) of Southern Parish. Fichter recounts the saga in detail in his book *One-Man Research* (1973). He reveals a highly politicized arena, all the more so given that the vast majority of parish studies were conducted by priests, brothers, and to a lesser extent, sisters and laypeople. The weight of episcopal oversight was even backed by canon law (see Morris 1989). Early parish sociologists—in particular, those whose personal vows tied them to their topic of study in ways others' positions did not—encountered limits to scholarly freedom and pastoral reception.

Tensions between sound scholarship and perceived fidelity to the Church contaminated an otherwise promising research trajectory for the sociology of the parish. Setting up sociology as a problem-naming science concurrently set up sociology (and sociologists) as problem generating. Social science did not map neatly onto parish betterment. The discipline's postwar narrowing to a positivist orientation (Steinmetz 2008) seemed incompatible with pastoral sociology. Furthermore, with parish research being done almost wholly by those *in* the Church and framed with an applied orientation *to* the Church, studies were often isolated from broader disciplinary conversations. Protected spaces such as the ACSS safeguarded "religious sociology" from general sociology, while exacerbating outsiders' skepticism (Reed 1982). Set up as a dual-constituency value proposition, neither the Church nor the academy seemed to value sociological studies of the parish.

Even so, an early sociology of parishes successfully pioneered the notion that parishes are places where Catholics live out juxtapositions between authority and individualism—juxtapositions that have come to characterize Catholicism in modernity. One measure debuted in early studies, for example, compares census data in a given parish territory to the number of regular Mass attendees reported by parishes. Discrepancies signaled "leakage" (a now-antiquated term) or "dormant" Catholicism. Today, similar measures are used to calculate proportions of Catholics not attending Mass. Early parish studies suggest that understanding the social role of the parish means not confining analysis only to those who actively attend.

Parish Studies after Vatican II

Early sociological studies of the parish foreshadowed (perhaps even encouraged) broader conversations about Catholicism in modernity and social science in pastoral application. The Second Vatican Council (1962–1965) set into motion new forms of worship, leadership, and organizational structure, reorienting the sociology of Catholicism in meaningful ways. Bishops and pastoral leaders could innovate, critique, and experiment; Catholic laity could offer greater input in pastoral affairs. Subsequent declines in ordinations and religious life intensified these parish-level changes.

Vatican II affirmed a mutually beneficial relationship between social science and the Church. Its documents asserted "a right to information about affairs which affect men individually or collectively," conveyed as truthfully and completely "as charity and justice allow" (Pope Paul VI 1963). Putting prior tensions in sharp relief, the Second Vatican Council advanced the idea that "in pastoral care, sufficient use must be made not only of theological principles, but also of the findings of the secular sciences, so that the faithful may be brought to a more adequate and mature life of faith" (Pope Paul VI 1965). Empirical studies of parishes conducted by sociologists could be valued rather than feared. Religious insiders trained in sociology found a newly defensible space for their inquiries.

Exemplifying this, many dioceses established offices for pastoral research. Parish studies found new fervor under the guise of "pastoral planning." A new Center for Applied Research in the Apostolate (CARA) channeled donations to meet Church leaders' research needs starting in 1964 (Gannon 1967). Vatican II motivated a plethora of studies to test how the council was making a difference in American Catholic practice. New voices chimed in to research this question, diversifying the primarily priest-driven positionality of earlier parish studies.

Methodological advances in sociology likewise beckoned new approaches to parish studies. Large-*n* surveys (i.e., those with a large sample size) and computer-aided methodologies shifted some scholars' attention from parishes to broad populations of Catholics (see Donovan 1967 and the trendsetting work of sociologist-priest Andrew Greeley by way of example). Rather than examining the parish as the unit of analysis, studies began using parishes as a means of accessing individual Catholics' behavior. Large surveys of priests and parishioners (e.g., Fichter 1963) illuminated relationships between pastor and people, absent an exploration of their shared organizational parish contexts. Studies in the mid-1970s considered the parish through the changing roles of Catholic clergy, motivated by a burgeoning sociological field of occupations and role performance. Priest-and-parishioner studies also signaled the transition from a highly priest-centric pre–Vatican II parish model to a more lay-centered post–Vatican II parish model (see, for example, Castelli and Gremillion 1987).

Nonetheless, the parish itself still constituted a focal point in some sociologists' attempts to understand Catholic life. Young and Hughes (1965), for example, presented a model for parish analysis integrating organizational theory and the tandem influence of Church and society. Karcher, Robinson, and Balswick (1972) tested the post–Vatican II applicability of Fichter's parishioner typology, finding that new expectations bred new models of parish participation. Jesuit priest and sociologist Thomas P. Sweetser wrote *The Catholic Parish* in 1974, profiling ten Chicago-area parishes in the wake of Vatican II. Sweetser summarized clergy reactions to the council's implemented changes, polling attitudes toward "guitar Mass with contemporary hymns" and perceptions of parishioner morality. He found evidence of declining parish involvement among Catholics of all ages, concluding that:

> The dominant pattern that is emerging is that Catholics are inclined to make up their own minds, not only in their involvement in parish life, but in their value orientations as well. The Church and the parish are still their guide but not their sole authority. The American Catholic Church, in other words, is becoming a voluntary Church much like the Protestant tradition of membership. (Sweetser 1974, 79)

Sweetser's finding is consistent with patterns of Catholic identity observed by others in subsequent years. Parishes opened a window into changes in Catholics and Catholicism in a post–Vatican II era. The study of parishes could work hand in hand with the study of broad demographic trends.

In 1980, fifteen years after the close of the council, the United States' bishops encouraged parish studies with their publication of "The Parish: A People, A Mission, A Structure." The corollary resurgence of research into the parish was marked most notably by the Notre Dame Study of Catholic Parish Life, conducted throughout that decade. As the principle investigators on this project described it:

> The Notre Dame Study of Catholic Parish Life is an interdisciplinary endeavor to understand better the American parish of the 1980s as a dynamic community. Many elements of parish life are addressed: organization, staffing, leadership, priorities, and their interrelations; liturgies and sacramental preparation; programs and participation; beliefs, values, expectations, and practices; historical, ethnographic, sociological, and religio-cultural contexts. The Study is proceeding in three phases, 1981 to 1988. (Leege and Gremillion n.d., 2–3)

The Notre Dame study offered a thorough and multidisciplinary look at Catholic parishes in the United States, drawn from a multiphased representative sample of parishes nationally. It studied parish-connected Catholics, accessing American Catholicism through parishes rather than through religious self-identification on general population surveys. This generated a portrait of the Church and of American Catholics that placed Catholics' communal orientation at its center.

The Notre Dame Study of Catholic Parish Life identified the constituent elements of parish life as follows:

> Parishes are composed of members who participate actively in programs organized and directed by leaders who now include many laity side by side with clergy and religious. The liturgy as reformed by Vatican II is now central to parish spirituality and community experience; public devotions such as novenas and the rosary have greatly declined. Other parish activities have expanded, with specialized ministries to the aged and the divorced, for social action, and with great emphasis on religious education of adults and their training for

ministry and community leadership. Several teachings closely identified with the Vatican magisterium are quietly ignored or openly re-
jected by significant numbers of parish-connected Catholics,
specifically for example, concerning birth control and remarriage
after divorce. (Gremillion and Leege n.d., 8)

Its expansiveness and methodology set a new precedent for large-scale,
multistage, multilevel parish assessment.

Findings from the Notre Dame Study of Catholic Parish Life were published in a series of fifteen reports between 1984 and 1989 and used in
numerous articles and books. Among them are social historian Jay Dolan's
edited two-volume set *The American Catholic Parish* (1987) and Jim Castelli and Joseph Gremillion's *The Emerging Parish* (1987). One of the lega-
cies of the Notre Dame Study of Catholic Parish Life—realized most
pointedly in Dolan's series—is that of regionalism. Whereas early studies
of parishes attempted to establish a single "ideal type" of parish, comparable to all parishes, Dolan and his collaborators emphasized the imperative of taking regional variation into account. Their collection of studies,
rooted in local parish communities, proclaimed "a new departure" whereby
"henceforth . . . no history of American Catholicism can be complete
without the comparative regional dimension" (Dolan 1987, 4–5).

Parish studies during this period also moved ahead by looking back,
as social historians published rich accounts of immigrant parishes during
US Catholicism's early years. While a focus on immigration and ethnic
relations had characterized a handful of early parish studies, this later
work by Jay Dolan, Robert Orsi, and others elevated the depth, history, and
qualitative contextualization of a socio-historical parish analysis. Advances
in scholarship on this front provided a needed—albeit belated—
understanding of American Catholics' institution building via parishes,
organized largely along ethnic lines. Parishes constituted Catholic micro-
cosms inhabiting a predominantly Protestant American milieu. The idea
of the parish as an immigrant haven resonated for sociologists examining
contemporary iterations of immigrant congregations in the post-1965 era
of the United States.

Also in the 1980s, the comparative field of congregational studies coalesced to subsume Catholic parishes as one variety of local religious
organization among many (Stokes and Roozen 1991). New funding from

the Lilly Endowment invigorated a broad research agenda on North American religion. Interdisciplinary conversations among a predominantly Protestant committee led to the creation of a "Project Team for Congregational Studies" and eventual *Handbook for Congregational Studies* (Carroll et al. 1986). This scholarship helped articulate an inclusive methodology, driving set of questions, and theoretical home for studying parishes as congregations. How well parishes fit this rubric (then or now) remains an under-studied question, contemplated in this volume by leading congregational researcher Nancy Ammerman and in the Conclusion by coeditors Gary Alder, Brian Starks, and me.

The years surrounding Vatican II took a nascent, politicized, and uniform-seeking study of parishes into adolescence. The sociology of parishes matured with increased reciprocity by the academy and the Church, attention to regional distinction, and historical-comparative contextualization. New parish studies showcased compatibility with broad trend analyses of American Catholicism and American Catholics. The sociological study of the parish reached its then-apex in the Notre Dame Study of Catholic Parish Life. Nevertheless, Church-academy and insider-outsider tensions persisted. As Andrew Greeley wrote in 1989 of sociologists studying Catholicism: "As far as the Church is concerned we don't even begin to exist" (397).

Parish Studies from 1990 to the Present

The most recent quarter century introduced both continuity and novelty into the trajectory of sociological parish studies. Tensions at the nexus of dual—and dueling—constituencies (Church and academy) persist. Increases in racial and other forms of diversity across American Catholicism further dismantle a single, grand theory of the parish. Changes to US cities and rampant diocesan restructuring necessitate altered paradigms for understanding local Catholic life. Today's parishes make readily transparent the gap between a uniform parish experience and the lived realities of contemporary American Catholicism. Sociological studies of the parish have kept up in some ways, but not all.

Scholars into the 1990s and even 2000s continued to publish works using data from the 1980s Notre Dame Study of Catholic Parish Life. The study's unparalleled scope lent an arguably outsized (and now rather outdated) influence on parish studies for decades. In 2004, the Institute for Church Life at Notre Dame floated the idea of a renewed study of parish life, some twenty-five years after the original. In tandem with this process, Davidson and Fournier compiled a meta-analysis of parish studies conducted in the interim, noting their attention to structural, human resource, symbolic, and political dimensions of Catholic parishes. But despite pointing out a number of limitations in extant research, Davidson and Fournier concluded that there was "no need for Notre Dame to replicate the Parish Life Study at this time" (2006, 76).

The closest proxy to a Catholic-specific, national-scope study in recent years comes from the bounty of data generated through the mostly commissioned work of CARA at Georgetown University. *Catholic Parishes of the 21st Century* (Zech et al. 2017) summarizes findings from a multistaged CARA study of 5,549 parishes. It identifies trends affecting parishes since the Notre Dame study: declining vocations; higher concentrations of Catholics in the South, West, and suburbs; increased growth from immigration; further aftereffects of Vatican II; and declining sacramental participation. While the study's low response rates limit its generalizability, its accessible reporting lends itself well to pastoral use. For example, the recent volume *Collaborative Parish Leadership* (Clark and Gast 2017) uses CARA data to introduce its comparative case studies of pastoral ministry. CARA's parish data is frequently cited among non-sociologists and journalistic accounts of American Catholicism.

My own book, *Parish and Place: Making Room for Diversity in the American Catholic Church* (Bruce 2017), uses a sociological lens to examine parish structures in the United States. Integrating a national survey of dioceses, sixty-two in-depth leader interviews, and field data from sixty-eight parishes in twelve dioceses, the book focuses on the phenomenon of "personal parishes" organized by special purpose rather than territory. Many American bishops have renewed the model of the personal parish to serve specialized communities on the basis of ethnicity or liturgical preference. *Parish and Place* details how parish decision-making works from the top, as Church leaders respond to grassroots change in American Catholics' parish-going behavior.

Most new wide-scale studies, however, include Catholic parishes among a larger, interreligious sample of congregations. Leading the trend in broad, comparative assessments is the National Congregations Study (NCS).

Spearheaded by Mark Chaves in 1998, the NCS generated a nationally representative sample of congregations. Catholic parishes comprise the largest proportion of congregations included in the NCS sample, at nearly a quarter of the total. While only about 6 percent of all US congregations are Roman Catholic, their larger average size led to a higher proportion of them being named by religious attendees polled by the General Social Survey (GSS), from which the NCS draws its sample. Multiple waves of NCS data (summarized most recently in Chaves and Anderson 2014) shine light on the social character, demographics, and leadership of Catholic parishes. Gary Adler's essay in this volume utilizes NCS to unpack contemporary trends in parishes as a distinctive subset of congregations. Most NCS publications, however, do not disaggregate parishes from other religious congregations.

The 2000–2001 Program for the Analysis of Religion among Latinas/os (PARAL) Study of Latino Faith Communities likewise invokes a comparative frame in its examination of Latino-serving US congregations (Stevens-Arroyo et al. 2003). Its report on 496 Catholic parishes and 387 Protestant congregations summarized twelve dimensions: size, growth, worship, ethnicity, finances, government funds, ecumenicalism, social justice, Latino faith, sermons, ritual, and conflict. Nevertheless, these insights remain underutilized by sociologists of religion. PARAL data were not made available on the popular repository the Association of Religion Data Archive (www.thearda.com), and *Sociological Abstracts* lists no articles that use this data.[2] This is a missed opportunity for sustained scholarship on parishes as an arena of study, especially among Latino Catholics.

While generic congregational research offers useful comparative context, it necessarily identifies a shared rubric using the lowest common denominator. Similar limitations characterize the pan-denominational congregational studies literature that has matured in recent years. As religious studies scholar Michael Carroll writes in *American Catholics in the Protestant Imagination* (2007), much of the framing that scholars of religion bring to the history and characterization of Catholicism remains deeply embedded in a Protestant cultural approach.

---

2. The same is true of CARA datasets, which rarely appear in data archives due to their proprietary nature.

Another theme in more-recent parish studies is the hyperlocalized, qualitative case study approach. Jerome Baggett's 2009 *Sense of the Faithful*, for example, zooms in on six northern California parishes. Through field observation and interviews, the book describes how everyday Catholics make sense of their lives. Catholics consume and reappropriate a shared cultural tradition within parishes. Likewise, Mary Ellen Konieczny's book *The Spirit's Tether* (2013) takes us inside two parishes to understand meaning-making and moral awareness. David Yamane (2014) uses a few parishes to answer questions about conversion. Still others offer micro-level looks at conflict and community (e.g., Wittberg 2012; Loveland and Ksander 2014). By narrowing analysis to a few strategically selected parishes, these kinds of studies provide a depth and validity frequently lacking in broad statistical analyses.

Where parish case studies offer a home base for observation and assessment, their theoretical focus is usually not about the parish *qua* parish, but about the parish as an entry point to other arenas of sociology. Baggett, for example, openly theorizes about culture, not parishes. Konieczny makes claims about cultural conflict and the family. Yamane stays within the realm of initiation. Most do not posit particular claims about the parish nor contribute explicitly to a sociology of parishes (the fruitfulness of their work in that regard notwithstanding). The same can be said of most recent studies in parish leadership (e.g., Wallace 2000; Schoenherr 2002; Hoge and Wenger 2003; Gautier, Perl, and Fichter 2012), whose conclusions transcend the organizational space of the parish itself.[3]

This theme echoes across other recent scholarship; parishes act as entry points to examinations of myriad (non-parish) facets of social life. Whereas sociologists' early parish studies were marked by their apartness (both self-selected and imposed by external factors), more recent studies are marked by the near opposite: parishes are one component among many in crosscutting examinations of social life. Just as American Catholics have entered the mainstream, so too have American parish studies donned camouflage to disguise (or at least mitigate) their distinctiveness. Inroads to parish studies' acceptance and perceived value in the discipline may come at the expense of parochialism.

3. Clark and Gast 2017 present a useful exception.

A number of urban studies, for example, include Catholic parishes. Reflecting post-1965 demographic shifts, suburbanization, and diocesan restructuring from limited financial and priest resources, American cities have witnessed substantial change in how Catholics organize and make place. Sociologists have contemplated some (though arguably not enough) of these changes, among them Orsi (1999), Livezey (2000), Cimino, Mian, and Huang (2013), Numrich and Wedam (2015), Bruce (2016), and Martinez (2017). Most take the city as the primary unit of analysis and congregations (Catholic or otherwise) as the dependent—or occasionally independent—variable of change.

Parishes likewise appear in scholars' contemporary considerations of race relations. John McGreevy (1998), for example, authored an account of cultural and urban change in the twentieth-century urban North with Catholic parishes at the center. *Latino Catholicism* (Matovina 2011) explores the changing face of parishes as they incorporate an increasingly Latino demographic. Brett Hoover (2014) considers Latinos' and whites' experience in "shared" parishes, a theme he expands on in this volume. Hosffman Ospino (2014) offers a comprehensive portrait of parishes ministering to Hispanics.

Recent studies of immigration also feature parishes as supporting actors in first-generation immigrants' cultural adaptations to the US (among them Warner and Wittner 1998; Kniss and Numrich 2007; Stepick, Rey, and Mahler 2009; and Alba, Raboteau, and DeWind 2009). Works by Garces-Foley (2009), Ninh (2014), and Cherry (2014) are among a handful of city-centered and ethnic group–centered studies of Asian American Catholics adapting, and adapting to, local Catholic parishes. Work by social historians (e.g., Mitchell 1998; Dolan 2002) has aided sociologists in conceptualizing parishes' roles in building immigrants' social capital.

Nevertheless, today's parish studies generally underrepresent the ethnoracial variance of American Catholicism. Hispanic/Latino Catholics, for example, now comprise some 40 percent of the total Catholic population but substantially less among sociologists' parish studies. Predominantly black parishes and black Catholics in multiracial parishes receive little to no attention. The few studies that do exist generally consider black Catholics in comparison to whites (e.g., Cavendish, Welch, and Leege 1998 and Cavendish 2000). Tia Noelle Pratt's essay in this volume begins to remedy this.

Moreover, nearly all voices behind Catholic parish studies are white, even those researching and writing about nonwhite Catholic spaces. While new scholarship has helped destabilize an assumed white-European (usually Irish) parish default, it rarely comes from scholars of color uniquely positioned to articulate the diversity of Catholic experiences. Contemporary work on parishes widens the voices telling and stories told but not yet in a way that mirrors American Catholics' own demographic profile.

All told, much of the research of the last twenty-five years has not been driven by the parish as the leading story. Catholic parishes are embedded within broader empirical and theoretical narratives—whether about congregations in general or another intersecting realm of sociology. To a greater or lesser extent, depending on the treatment therein, theorizing about parishes *qua* parishes is latent, masked, or erased as a meaningful marker of community and difference. One could justifiably ask, then, if there are really *any* contemporary studies that look at the Catholic parish as the central driving question, with consequential sociological import. Situating parishes as a locus of data does not equate to situating them as a locus of analysis.

The contemporary landscape of parish studies signals an enduring, now-ironic exchange between parish studies for and by the Church and those for and by the academy. Early parish studies unabashedly positioned themselves as pastorally oriented, most by Church actors. The cost was a lackluster reception by both Church and academy. More recent studies, by contrast, seem destined to either an applied, pastoral orientation (often by nature of their commissioned origins) or an academic space with an arms-length distance from pastoral application to sway a still-skeptical sociological audience. Perhaps a day will come when the dual-constituency value proposition of parish studies does not pit one constituency against the other. Parish studies can bring value to both.

Conclusion

The trajectory of sociological studies on Catholic parishes from roughly 1940 to today—three-quarters of a century—can hardly be described as a smooth, prolific, ever-more-robust, or theoretically maturing path. The following plea from the 1951 symposium on the sociological study of the parish carries near equal import today:

> The immediate need is for more empirical studies of American parishes. Until sufficient factual material is presented in the form of statistical analyses or of descriptions of parish structure and functioning, knowledge of what is happening within parochial boundaries will remain rudimentary. Research reported in the past has been based upon census procedures or social surveys. While these approaches have yielded results of interest and use, newer studies should be designed to test hypotheses bearing upon sociological theory. . . . One purpose for the present symposium is to call attention to the need for sociologically oriented investigations. (Nuesse and Harte 1951, 12–13)

While sociological parish studies have advanced since the mid-twentieth century, this work remains unfinished.

Nearly all scholars of the parish—then and now—acknowledge the constitutional element of authority in their work. Many express this in their analyses, stymied by imperfect attempts to apply a more autonomous or generalized theory of congregations. As literature across three-quarters of a century iterates, the parish espouses a definitional quality linked to the institutional Catholic Church. Acknowledging this core connectivity acknowledges that institutions—structures—influence the direction of parishes and of parish research. Catholic priests spearheaded American parish studies. Catholic leaders suppressed Southern Parish. Vatican II reawakened parish research. The US Bishops' statement on parishes motivated the Notre Dame Study of Catholic Parish Life. Sponsored research enabled much of CARA's contemporary parish data. Publications on parish leadership, community, authority, and size all mushroom from restructuring in and by the institutional Church. As Richard Juliani reminds us, the three dimensions of priest, parish, and people—evoking the institutional, biographical, and sociocultural—"cannot easily be separated from one another, nor should they be" (2007, 309). Ignoring this means ignoring a key element of what makes a parish a parish.

The future of sociological studies of the parish may rest on the willingness of both the academy and the Church to accept a dual-constituency value proposition: parish studies *can* be simultaneously good for the academy and good for the Church. This would mean facing fears articulated by sociologist Carol Ann MacGregor in a recent forum: "Will data make parishes look bad? Does sharing data with non-Catholics and external researchers mean relinquishing control over messaging? Who would frame the significance of the data to the church and to the world?" But "overcoming this fear," MacGregor says, "can open the door to the production of cumulative knowledge, fresh perspectives, and insights into solutions for problems the twenty-first century church faces" (Bruce 2018, 26). This constitutes the next step in sociological studies of American parishes.

To what extent is the study of Catholic parishes actually the study of American Catholicism and American Catholics? One cannot sufficiently assess US Catholicism without assessing Catholics' participation in and relationship (if any) to their local parish. Changes in parishes reveal changes in Catholics' behavior, identity, and meaning-making within local ecologies. Embedding parishes within broader social categories (or fields, as elaborated on in the Conclusion to this volume) does not render meaningless parishes' distinctive attributes. At the same time, sociologists must ask what strands of Catholicism and the American Catholic experience are made visible through studying parishes and which (or whose) are left obscured or even erased. The storyteller shapes the stories told. While the study of Catholic parishes is an American Catholic story, it is not an exhaustive one.

Fichter concluded *Dynamics of a City Church*—the first and only volume in the Southern Parish series to be published—with the observation that "a parish is what people are" (1951, 271). The sociology of parishes can tell us what people are.

References

Alba, Richard D., Albert J. Raboteau, and Josh DeWind, eds. 2009. *Immigration and Religion in America: Comparative and Historical Perspectives.* New York: New York University Press.

Bruce, Tricia C. 2016. "Preserving Catholic Space and Place in 'The Rome of the West.'" In *Spiritualizing the City: Agency and Resilience of the Urbanesque Habitat*, edited by Victoria Hegner and Peter Jan Margry. London: Routledge.

———. 2017. *Parish and Place: Making Room for Diversity in the American Catholic Church.* New York: Oxford University Press.

———. 2018. "Forum: Studying Parishes in Studies of American Catholicism." *American Catholic Studies* 129 (1): 1–26.

Carroll, Jackson W., Carl S. Dudley, and William McKinney. 1986. *Handbook for Congregational Studies.* Nashville, Tenn.: Abingdon Press.

Carroll, Michael P. 2007. *American Catholics in the Protestant Imagination: Rethinking the Academic Study of Religion*. Baltimore: Johns Hopkins University Press.

Castelli, Jim, and Joseph B. Gremillion. 1987. *The Emerging Parish: The Notre Dame Study of Catholic Life Since Vatican II*. San Francisco: Harper & Row.

Cavendish, James C. 2000. "Church-Based Community Activism: A Comparison of Black and White Catholic Congregations." *Journal for the Scientific Study of Religion*, 39, no. 1 (March): 64–77.

———. 2007. "The Sociological Study of American Catholicism: Past, Present, and Future." In *American Sociology of Religion: Histories*, edited by Anthony J. Blasi, pp. 151–176. Boston: Brill.

Cavendish, James C., Michael R. Welch, and David C. Leege. 1998. "Social Network Theory and Predictors of Religiosity for Black and White Catholics: Evidence of a 'Black Sacred Cosmos'?" *Journal for the Scientific Study of Religion* 37, no. 3 (September): 397–410.

Chaves, Mark, and Shawna L. Anderson. 2014. "Changing American Congregations: Findings from the Third Wave of the National Congregations Study." *Journal for the Scientific Study of Religion*, 53 (4): 676–86.

Cherry, Stephen M. 2014. *Faith, Family, and Filipino American Community Life*. New Brunswick, N.J.: Rutgers University Press.

Cimino, Richard, Nadia Mian, and Weishan Huang. 2013. *Ecologies of Faith in New York City: The Evolution of Religious Institutions*. Bloomington: Indiana University Press.

Clark, William A., and Daniel Gast, eds. 2017. *Collaborative Parish Leadership: Contexts, Models, Theology*. Lanham, Md.: Lexington Books.

Davidson, James D., and Suzanne C. Fournier. 2006. "Recent Research on Catholic Parishes: A Research Note." *Review of Religious Research* 48, no. 1 (September): 72–81.

Dolan, Jay P., ed. 1987. *The American Catholic Parish: A History from 1850 to the Present*. New York: Paulist Press.

Dolan, Jay P. 1994. "Patterns of Leadership in the Congregation." In *American Congregations*, edited by James P. Wind and James W. Lewis, pp. 225–56. Chicago: University of Chicago Press.

———. 2002. *In Search of an American Catholicism*. New York: Oxford University Press.

Donovan, John D. 1950. "The Sociologist Looks at the Parish." *The American Catholic Sociological Review* 11 (2): 66–73.

———. 1967. "Sociology of the Parish." In *New Catholic Encyclopedia* vol. 10: 1019–1020.

Fichter, Joseph H. 1951. *The Dynamics of a City Church*. Southern Parish, vol. 1. Chicago: University of Chicago Press.

———. 1953. "The Marginal Catholic: An Institutional Approach." *Social Forces* 32 (2): 167–73.

———. 1963. "A Comparative View of the Parish Priest." *Archives de sociologie des religions* 8 (16): 44–48.

———. 1973. *One-Man Research: Reminiscences of a Catholic Sociologist.* New York: John Wiley & Sons.

Friedel, Francis J. 1942. "Catholic Sociological Research." *The American Catholic Sociological Review* 3 (3): 129–36.

Garces-Foley, Kathleen. 2009. "From the Melting Pot to the Multicultural Table: Filipino Catholics in Los Angeles." *American Catholic Studies* 120 (1): 27–53.

Gannon, Francis X. 1967. "Bridging the Research Gap: CARA, Response to Vatican II." *Review of Religious Research* 9 (1): 3–10.

Gautier, Mary L., Paul M. Perl, and Stephen J. Fichter. 2012. *Same Call, Different Men: The Evolution of the Priesthood Since Vatican II.* Collegeville, Minn.: Liturgical Press.

Greeley, Andrew. 1989. "Sociology and the Catholic Church: Four Decades of Bitter Memories." *Sociological Analysis* 50 (4): 393–97.

Gremillion, Joseph, and David C. Leege. n.d. "Post-Vatican II Parish Life in the United States: Review and Preview." *Notre Dame Study of Catholic Parish Life, Report No. 1.* Accessed 2018. https://mcgrath.nd.edu/assets/39500/report15 .pdf.

Hoge, Dean R., and Jacqueline E. Wenger. 2003. *Evolving Visions of the Priesthood: Changes from Vatican II to the Turn of the New Century.* Collegeville, Minn.: Liturgical Press.

Hoover, Brett C. 2014. *The Shared Parish: Latinos, Anglos, and the Future of US Catholicism.* New York: New York University Press.

Juliani, Richard N. 2007. *Priest, Parish, and People: Saving the Faith in Philadelphia's "Little Italy."* Notre Dame, Ind.: University of Notre Dame Press.

Karcher, Barbara C., Ira E. Robinson, and Jack O. Balswick. 1972. "Fichter's Typology and Changing Meanings in the Catholic Church." *Sociological Analysis* 33 (3): 166–76.

Kniss, Fred, and Paul Numrich. 2007. *Sacred Assemblies and Civic Engagement: How Religion Matters for America's Newest Immigrants.* New Brunswick, N.J.: Rutgers University Press.

Konieczny, Mary Ellen. 2013. *The Spirit's Tether: Family, Work, and Religion among American Catholics.* New York: Oxford University Press.

Lane, Ralph, Jr. 1996. "The Sociology of the Parish: Fichter's Work and Beyond." *Sociology of Religion* 57 (4): 345–49.

Leege, David C., and Joseph Gremillion. n.d. *The U.S. Parish Twenty Years after Vatican II: An Introduction to the Study.* Notre Dame Study of Catholic Parish

Life, Report No. 1. Accessed 2018. https://mcgrath.nd.edu/assets/39486
/report1.pdf.

Livezey, Lowell, ed. 2000. *Public Religion and Urban Transformation: Faith in the
City*. New York: New York University Press.

Loveland, Matthew T., and Margret Ksander. 2014. "Shepherds and Sheep:
Parish Reconfiguration, Authority, and Activism in a Catholic Diocese."
Review of Religious Research 56 (3): 443–65.

Martinez, Juan. 2017. "'This Is an Italian Church with a Large Hispanic
Population': Factors and Strategies in White Ethno-Religious Place Making."
City and Community 16 (4): 399–420.

Matovina, Timothy. 2011. *Latino Catholicism: Transformation in America's
Largest Church*. Princeton, N.J.: Princeton University Press.

McGreevy, John T. 1998. *Parish Boundaries: The Catholic Encounter with Race
in the Twentieth-Century Urban North*. Chicago: University of Chicago Press.

Mitchell, Brian C. 1988. "Introduction." In *Building the American Catholic City:
Parishes and Institutions*, edited by Brian C. Mitchell, pp. i–xvii. New York:
Garland Publishing.

Morris, Loretta M. 1989. "Secular Transcendence: From ACSS to ASR."
Sociological Analysis, 50 (4): 329–49.

Ninh, Thien-Huong T. 2014. "Colored Faith: Vietnamese American Catholics
Struggle for Equality Within Their Multicultural Church." *Amerasia Journal*
40: 81–96.

Nuesse, C. J. and Thomas J. Harte, ed. 1951. *The Sociology of the Parish: A Survey
of the Parish in Its Constants and Variables*. Milwaukee, Wis..: Bruce Publishing.

Numrich, Paul D., and Elfriede Wedam. 2015. *Religion and Community in the
New Urban America*. New York: Oxford University Press.

O'Hara, Edwin V. 1945. "Returned Veterans in the Parish." *The American
Catholic Sociological Review* 6 (1): 23–25.

Orsi, Robert A., ed. 1999. *Gods of the City: Religion and the American Urban
Landscape*. Bloomington, Ind.: Indiana University Press.

Ospino, Hosffman. 2014. *Hispanic Ministry in Catholic Parishes: A Summary
Report of Findings from the National Study of Catholic Parishes with Hispanic
Ministry*. Boston: Boston College School of Theology and Ministry. http://
www.bc.edu/content/dam/files/schools/stm/pdf/2014/HispanicMinistryinC
atholicParishes_2.pdf.

Parsons, Talcott. 1937. *The Structure of Social Action*. New York: McGraw-Hill.

Reed, Myer S., Jr. 1982. "After the Alliance: The Sociology of Religion in the
United States from 1925 to 1949." *Sociological Analysis* 43 (3): 189–204.

Pope Paul VI. 1963. *Decree on the Media of Social Communications: Inter Mirifica*.
http://www.vatican.va/archive/hist_councils/ii_vatican_council/documents
/vat-ii_decree_19631204_inter-mirifica_en.html.

————. 1965. *Pastoral Constitution on the Church in the Modern World: Gaudium Et Spes*. http://www.vatican.va/archive/hist_councils/ii_vatican_council /documents/vat-ii_const_19651207_gaudium-et-spes_en.html.

Schnepp, Gerald J., 1942. "Nationality and Leakage." *The American Catholic Sociological Review* 3 (3): 154–63.

Schoenherr, Richard A. 2002. *Goodbye Father: The Celibate Male Priesthood and the Future of the Catholic Church*. New York: Oxford University Press.

Smith, Christian, Brandon Vaidyanathan, Nancy Tatom Ammerman, José Casanova, Hilary Davidson, Elaine Howard Ecklund, John H. Evans, Philip S. Gorski, Mary Ellen Konieczny, Jason A. Springs, Jenny Trinitapoli, and Meredith Whitnah. 2013. "Roundtable on the Sociology of Religion: Twenty-Three Theses on the Status of Religion in American Sociology—A Mellon Working-Group Reflection." *Journal of the American Academy of Religion* 81 (4): 903–38.

Steinmetz, George. 2008. "American Sociology before and after World War II: The (Temporary) Settling of a Disciplinary Field." In *Sociology in America: A History*, edited by Craig Calhoun, pp. 314–66. Chicago: University of Chicago Press.

Stepick, Alex, Terry Rey, and Sarah J. Mahler, eds. 2009. *Churches and Charity in the Immigrant City: Religion, Immigration, and Civic Engagement in Miami*. New Brunswick, N.J.: Rutgers University Press.

Stevens-Arroyo, Anthony, Anneris Goris, Ariela Keysar, Irene Quiles, Andras Tapolcai, Dorothy Craig, and Christina Spinuso. 2003. *The National Survey of Leadership in Latino Parishes and Congregations*. Brooklyn, NY: Program for the Analysis of Religion among Latinas/os (PARAL). http://depthome .brooklyn.cuny.edu/risc/publications_survey.htm#parastudy.

Stokes, Allison, and David A. Roozen. 1991. "The Unfolding Story of Congregational Studies." In *Carriers of Faith: Lessons from Congregational Studies*, edited by Carl S. Dudley, Jackson W. Carroll, and James P. Wind, pp. 183–90. Louisville, Ky: Westminster John Knox Press.

Sweetser, Thomas P. 1974. *The Catholic Parish: Shifting Membership in a Changing Church*. Chicago: Center for the Scientific Study of Religion.

Wallace, Ruth A. 2000. "Women and Religion: The Transformation of Leadership Roles." *Journal for the Scientific Study of Religion* 39 (4): 496–508.

Warner, R. Stephen, and Judith G. Wittner, eds. 1998. *Gatherings in Diaspora: Religious Communities and the New Immigration*. Philadelphia: Temple University Press.

Wittberg, Patricia. 2012. "The Concept of 'Community' in Catholic Parishes." In *Religion, Spirituality and Everyday Practice*, edited by Giuseppe Giordan and William H. Swatos Jr., pp. 89–108. Dordrecht, Netherlands: Springer.

Yamane, David. 2014. *Becoming Catholic: Finding Rome in the American Religious Landscape*. New York: Oxford University Press.

Young, Barry, and John E. Hughes. 1965. "Organizational Theory and the Canonical Parish." *Sociological Analysis* 26 (2): 57–71.

Zech, Charles E., Mary L. Gautier, Mark M. Gray, Jonathon L. Wiggins, and Thomas P. Gaunt, SJ. 2017. *Catholic Parishes of the 21st Century*. New York: Oxford University Press.

Studying Parishes

Lessons and New Directions from the Study
of Congregations

NANCY T. AMMERMAN

Catholic parishes are distinctive organizations. They are both like other congregations and distinct in their cultures, understanding of authority, and definition of territory. Like other local religious groups, Catholic people who gather into a local organization for the purpose of worshipping, educating themselves and their children about religious faith and tradition, and working together for religious ends can be thought about as a "congregation" (Ammerman 2009). So borrowing tools and concepts developed over the past thirty years in the field of congregational studies can provide a useful resource to a revitalized study of American Catholic parishes. And as new work builds on that foundation, a fruitful new conversation can emerge among those who study all kinds of local religious communities.

In sociology, the study of congregations has arisen to encompass a category of organizations, even those—like parishes—that might not use the term for themselves. These organizations are nevertheless shaped by "institutional isomorphism," a process that treats organizations with similar functions and similar external cultural and regulatory pressures as occupying a "field" (DiMaggio and Powell 1983); in American culture, local multipurpose religious gatherings are such a field. The larger culture expects certain patterns in them—regular weekend gatherings for worship, programs for children, a recognized religious leader in charge. The law treats them in similar ways—tax exempt property, recognition of the power of the leaders to conduct weddings or to serve as chaplains, and the like. These larger cultural processes were the context in which sociologist R. Stephen Warner declared that the standard form of religious organizing in the United States is "de facto congregationalism" (Warner 1994). People voluntarily organize religious groups and expect to have a say in how things run. The congregations they form, in turn, provide protected spaces in which traditions are preserved and marginalized voices are heard.

It is within this sociological context that the field of congregational studies emerged, but its earliest proponents were advocates as well as researchers. They were interested in calling attention to congregations as important sites of study and developing tools for engaging in that study out of a conviction that local gatherings of people of faith were a thing of value (Carroll, Dudley, and McKinney 1986; Dudley 1983). In the ensuing years, the argument for paying attention to congregations was made on civic and social grounds, perhaps most notably by Robert Putnam and his colleagues (Putnam, Feldstein, and Cohen 2003). Congregations, this research noted, contribute to a wide range of measures of personal and social well-being (Lim and Putnam 2010). Still others have simply noted that one cannot understand the American political and social landscape without including the roughly 350,000 organizations to which perhaps 40 percent of the population has at least some passing connection and in which perhaps one in five can be found on a given weekend. Beyond social impact, the early congregational studies scholars also wanted denominations and theologians to pay attention, sometimes making their arguments on theological grounds. Today, in fact, there is a growing intersection between the theological field of ecclesiology and the sorts of ethnographic study undertaken among congregational studies scholars.[1] On a variety of grounds, then, congregational studies has grown as an engaged argument about the importance of a particular form of religious social organization.

Roman Catholics have not been absent from this conversation. While the earliest congregational studies were done in the Protestant context of the Institute for Social and Religious Research (Douglass and Brunner 1935), Catholics were early observers of parish life as well. Joseph Fichter's landmark study (1954) made its way into wide scholarly circulation, but other works on parishes by Catholic research offices were less well known.[2] In the 1980s, however, historians and religious studies scholars, such as Jay Dolan (1987) Gerald Gamm (1999), Jeffrey Burns (1994), John

1. On links to ecclesiology, see Browning 1991; Gustafson 1961; Nieman 2002; and Percy 2001.
2. See, for example, Murnion 1983; Sweetser 1983; or Bonn 1974.

McGreevy (1996), and Robert Orsi (1985), brought Catholic parish life to the larger conversation about religion in American culture. Tricia Bruce's essay in this volume reviews this trajectory of parish studies.

Still, the foci and primary engagements of the emerging congregational studies field that began to emerge in the 1980s were Protestant. The field began with a focus on white mainline Protestants, and many of its initial questions were shaped by Protestant assumptions. The congregation being studied was not a group of nuns or monks but a group of ordinary laypeople living secular lives. It was a congregation that fundamentally assumed voluntarism as an organizing principle in a way that Roman Catholicism did not. People would choose where to attend, choose (within some limits) how they would organize, expect laypeople to have leading roles, and expect them to contribute and distribute the resources to support the congregation. Proponents of congregational studies wrote about the dynamics of congregational life with a distinctly Protestant model in mind.

The field has, however, gradually grown to include work that focuses on a wide range of ethnic and religious traditions, including Catholicism. And over the same period, Catholicism itself has changed. Many aspects of local Catholic religious communities remain distinctive. Differences in authority remain, but voluntarism and choice are present, as well. What I will suggest in this essay is how many of the tools and questions developed in the larger study of congregations can be helpful in a revitalized study of American Catholic parishes.

Parishes as Producers of Culture

Much of my own work in congregational studies has emphasized the social processes of culture production (see also Wuthnow 1994). In *Studying Congregations*, I wrote, "Each gathering of people creates its own ways of doing things, its own ways of describing the world, its own tools and artifacts that produce its distinctive appearance. . . . Culture is who we are and the world we have created to live in. It is the predictable patterns of who does what and habitual strategies for telling the world about the things held most dear" (Ammerman 1998, 78). As much as a larger religious tradition may prescribe patterns of worship and decision-making, each local gathering will put its own stamp on those patterns. The larger

Church provides a rich store of symbols and rituals, but each parish uses those symbols in its own way and adds its own array of material, social, and theological "products" to the mix. As American parishes encounter an unprecedented array of changes, they often bump into these layers of local culture without quite knowing what is happening. Understanding parishes as producers and users of multiple cultures is often a critical practical necessity.

The study of the cultural world of a congregation begins with the recognition that people bring cultural toolkits with them into their local religious community.[3] Most obviously, perhaps, they bring language and ethnic traditions. The Roman Catholic Church historically recognized this fact by organizing national parishes in which the particularities of each new immigrant culture could flourish. Not only were native languages spoken, but favorite saints and festivals were honored. Today's more complicated parishes, however, rarely have such ethnic homogeneity (Gray et al. 2013). Even when they are functionally united by language, few assumptions about shared ethnic culture within those language communities are possible. That emphatically does not mean that ethnic culture does not matter, of course (Hoover 2014; Matovina 2012). Deep (and sometimes difficult) explorations of symbols, stories, rituals, and ordinary ways of doing things will take a parish far beyond an initial recognition that cultures are different. Tia Pratt's essay in this volume delves into the multidimensional cultural work of black Catholics in predominantly African American Catholic parishes. Understanding that there are many parish cultures may begin with documenting the ethnic traditions present, but it will not end there.

The cultural toolkits parishioners bring also include their experiences as participants in different educational, occupational, and social class worlds (Lamont 1992). Those larger cultural domains shape expectations and tastes in ways that show up throughout parish life. Different kinds of education shape far more than the skill level people bring to reading scripture. Education and other aspects of social class shape media and material consumption, as well as expectations about authority and participation. The college-educated professional not only listens to different sources of news and entertainment but expects to have a different voice in decision-

3. The notion of cultural toolkits is borrowed from Ann Swidler (1986).

making. The member who was educated in Catholic schools has a different cultural repertoire than the member who was not. The day laborer who has little energy for any of this has another set of cultural tools altogether. Understanding the cultures of a parish will require attention to these external cultural building blocks, and that is likely to require the full array of survey, observation, focus group, and interview methods that can be borrowed and adapted from congregational studies.

Those same tools can also be used to gain a window on the cultures that have been produced locally within the parish's own life. What are the patterned activities that mark the various cultures of parish life? What formal and informal activities give shape to the everyday interactions of parishioners? Even the most scripted gatherings, like a Mass, can reveal a great deal about a given group's culture. Who participates and in what ways, how the time is structured, and how the space is used—all are particular variations on the larger liturgical story being told. Music and movement tell their own story, as do sights and smells.[4] Careful observation over time can allow critical insights into the ties that bind a group together and the ways in which there are cultural variations and conflicts.

While Mass attendance may be the most common activity in most parishes, cultures are defined by activities that go far beyond those weekend gatherings. Culture is built in educational programs, service projects, informal gatherings, festivals, and even committee meetings. Those who participate may have stories about the past that they share. They may have created space that is customized as their own, perhaps with symbols of their own favorite saints. They may have expectations about how to greet each other and what parts of their lives they share. They will almost certainly have favorite foods and drinks. Any time a group interacts regularly around a common focus, it will develop common ways of doing things. We see in Chapter 9 of this volume how parishioners actively adapt culture through marriage preparation activities. While Catholic parishes may involve proportionately fewer of their members in activities beyond Mass

---

4. The growing literature on material and embodied religion is helpful here, although much of it ignores what happens within organized religious settings. Among those that do pay attention, see for example Konieczny 2009; McGuire 2007; Orsi 1996; and Vasquez 2010.

(Bane 2005), it is nevertheless useful to think about all the places in which parish cultures may be constructed.

Physical places themselves are also culturally defined. Every culture has its artifacts, and parishes are certainly no exception. Perhaps the relatively non-iconic nature of Protestantism led to the neglect of material culture in the earliest days of congregational studies, but that neglect is no longer so apparent. Even those studying the most austere Congregationalists or Quakers recognize that austerity is a material form of culture, too. In most Roman Catholic parishes, there is no such need to remind people that material things have meaning. The things that form the visual and tactile surroundings of the church building, no matter how modest, guide the interactions and experiences of those who gather there. Church architects often have specific liturgical specifications in mind, and those will have their effects, but people will use and interpret the space in their own ways. Among the most useful techniques for learning about a parish's culture, in fact, is an exploration of its physical space in the company of different kinds of guides. As each person tells stories about important places, the physical, social, and spiritual contours of the parish's many cultures may become apparent (Hoover 2014). Brett Hoover's essay in this volume walks us through the power dynamics that can emerge when multiple ethnic communities share common parish space.

Those stories are themselves a further window on the parish's cultures. In addition to examinations of activities and artifacts, cultures can be studied through the accounts people give of who they are. Some of those accounts will be the official histories and mission statements produced by those in charge. Some will draw on broader theologies and biblical narratives that attempt to capture and guide their way of life. Still others will be folktales about the defining moments and beloved characters that old-timers love to tell. When a parish community undertakes a timeline exercise, these are the stories that make the history come alive (Thumma 1998). But as parishes get more complex, merge, and welcome new populations, it may be harder to find those common folktales. There may be many different histories and even different versions of the official mission guiding the parish. The research tools aimed at uncovering congregational cultures may be even more important but less straightforward. It will be especially critical to look for the multiple stories, present in multiple parish cultures, and to utilize methods that allow those differing cultures to be discovered and heard.

Parishes in a Religious and Social Ecology

Congregational studies, from its beginning, insisted that congregations had to be understood in context. Faith communities gather in particular places and are always in relationship to those places. As neighborhoods changed, it was assumed, so would the congregation. As the needs of the neighborhood evolved, congregations should respond. For all their Protestant predispositions, the earliest forms of congregational studies had remarkably Catholic missional ecclesiologies—churches had particular obligations to their immediate locale (Dudley 1996; Roozen, McKinney, and Carroll 1984).

The resulting concepts and methods, then, stressed getting to know the people, places, and organizations of the immediate area in which a congregation was located. Congregational leaders were encouraged to take a walk, to meet local business owners, to connect with local schools. They were encouraged to utilize census data to discover the ethnic, income, and age diversity that might not readily be apparent. They were encouraged to learn the history of the community and meet its political leaders. Learning about context was both a matter of discerning needed ministries and finding potential recruits. People beyond the congregation were informants who could help the congregation envision its vocation.

As the proponents of congregational studies themselves became more diverse and studied a wider array of local faith communities, this picture of a single congregation related to a single place began to expand (Eiesland and Warner 1998). Congregational leaders knew that theirs was not the only faith community in a given place; people and places they cared about had other religious resources. It was still important to map the community, but now other congregations, service organizations, and public agencies entered the inventory. Leaders also knew that their congregants were not exclusively from a single neighborhood, so thinking about mapping populations and constituencies became more complicated than getting the local census data. Census and planning data for a whole region were called for. The study of context had become the study of the

organizational ecology of congregations. The field came to include attention to all the ways a single congregation both depended on and contributed to the environment in which it was located.

In the days when most Catholic parishes were geographically bounded
in practice as well as in definition, none of this seemed relevant. There
was little sense of being one Catholic option among many and little ur-
gency (or openness) to interaction with institutions beyond the Catholic
world. Parish leaders were deeply acquainted with the residents and businesses in their neighborhoods and knew the Catholic institutions on which
they could call. However, that sense of continuity and relative insularity
of place is taken for granted less today. Many parishioners choose their
places of worship, even if they are not supposed to. Dioceses alter the definition of the parish to which members thought they belonged (Bruce
2017). Parish lines get redrawn, and parishes merge. Not only do new populations move into a neighborhood, but an entire other parish's membership may enter the scene when that parish closes. The need to understand
parishes as part of a religious and organizational ecology has become urgent. At diocesan levels, people are often trying to think in exactly these
terms, but parish communities themselves need tools for asking the kinds
of ecological questions congregational studies has attempted to put
forward.

If Catholics are not entirely constrained by official Church geography
and parishes do not exist in an enclosed Catholic bubble, it is important
to understand how an overall ecology of parishes functions and how each
parish fits into the larger demographic and organizational environment.
We can think about both the resources a religious organization needs
to survive and the way it uniquely contributes to its environment, both
singly and in partnership with other contributors. We might ask, for
instance:

> What mental maps define parish boundaries for those who currently
>   attend, and what are the demographic, historical, and cultural
>   characteristics that define those maps? How do they compare to
>   the official church maps?
> What is the functioning "catchment area" from which the parish
>   draws participants and to which it is related as a service provider?
> What are the changes and challenges faced within that area?

What other religious organizations (congregations and others) exist
in that catchment area?

What religious organizations and networks beyond the immediate
area (such as Cursillo or charismatic renewal) supply influential
resources and ideas?

What defines this parish's niche in the catchment area? That is, what
is religiously and culturally distinctive about the parish, drawing
people to it? And what resources does it uniquely contribute to the
well-being of the area?

An ecological approach to parish life also calls for attention to the larger
cultural and organizational context. The presence of immigrants in a
neighborhood happens because there are larger economic and political
forces at work, and understanding parish life means paying attention to
those forces. The existence of parishes that are informally identified with
particular populations (gay Catholics, "social justice" Catholics, and the
like) happens in the context of larger cultural and institutional forces that
identify such populations and sustain niches in which they thrive. The absence of sufficient numbers of ordained leaders, likewise, requires attention to more than the immediate local context. The danger in moving to
those larger levels of analysis, of course, is that the particular local impact is lost. Local Catholic communities need research that helps them
see the larger cultural and political milieu in which they are doing their
work, but they also need attention to what that looks like in their own
particular locale. Drawing on the work of others for the big picture, local
parish researchers can create nuanced and multilayered pictures of the
ecology they are studying.

Taking an ecological approach also draws attention to resources of all
kinds. Just as plants and animals thrive or perish based on their ability to
find resources and adapt to what they find, so parishes thrive or perish
based in part on the available resources of people, money, infrastructure,
and legitimacy. When any of these is in short supply, competition may
ensue. When the nature of any of them changes, it is the adaptive group
that may thrive. Given the stresses in American Catholic life, there is am-
ple room to study these resource questions and the range of adaptive responses: What happens to a parish as it has to make do without funds it
had counted on? How do other area congregations respond to a declining

or merging parish? What strategies are available for reclaiming legitimacy that may have been damaged by scandal? What options are available for the use of excess building space? What assets are represented by the vitality of the human community itself? What new resources are represented by the networks to which members are connected? How is spiritual strength being nourished and put to work? Parishes are both dependent on the resources of the larger material and organizational environment and contributors to that environment. A careful look with an ecological eye may be especially energizing for the future.

Parishes as Dynamic Centers of Organizational Action

Converting a resource into action, however, requires power, and the many ways in which power is generated and used in congregations have been another focus of congregational study. Carl Dudley, one of the pioneers in the revival of congregational studies, talked about the importance of understanding process (Carroll, Dudley, and McKinney 1986). Included in that, for him, was a wide range of cultural and organizational factors, all affecting how a congregation "gets things done." My own sociological framework draws on the work of Rosabeth Kanter in the study of organizational leadership (Kanter, Stein, and Jick 1992). She defines power as the ability to get things done and points out that leadership is a matter of mobilizing the people, resources, and motivation to pursue an organization's goals. Leaders must communicate, persuade, connect, and empower so that work otherwise impossible gets done.

Thinking of power in this way may at first seem like another of those distinctly Protestant views of congregational life. After all, priests and parishes are lodged in a hierarchical Church that can command loyalty to prescribed programs without such deliberation and persuasion. Priests and bishops decide what should be done and how. While today's Catholic parishioners no longer just "pray, pay, and obey," there are still external constraints on what any group of laity can do. Nevertheless, we know that Catholic laity, no less than their Protestant counterparts, want to be engaged in deciding what happens, who their leaders are, and how money is raised and spent (D'Antonio, Davidson, and Hoge 1996). There are external authority structures that need to be understood in studying parishes—authorities that can, in fact, determine the future—but the people who gather have their own ways of getting things done within those constraints. Understanding the dynamics of power—how it is mobilized and exercised—is another critical part of understanding parish life.

Mobilizing power means understanding where the human resources are. Every task requires a variety of kinds of expertise, including the deep wisdom of those with long experience and empathic people skills. Understanding how things get done requires careful observation and intentional conversations that can help the researcher (or parish leader) see these points of leverage (or points of resistance). It also requires systematic inventories of the more visible skills supplied by education or occupational expertise. To the extent that all these capacities are visible to the parishioners themselves, they may perceive their own community as able to act in pursuit of its goals.

Whether those skills and capacities get mobilized in any given instance will also depend on the effectiveness of the communication channels in the parish. Studying the official channels of homily and newsletter and email lists is an essential starting point, but the student of parish communication will also look for the informal networks and for gaps in those networks. Returning to questions of culture, we might ask how communication flows along, and perhaps not between, various cultural subgroups in the parish. Who has enough information to be an effective contributor, and who does not? Who may be unpersuaded to act, at least in part because the task at hand is not seen as essential to the mission and identity of the portion of the parish's culture to which they are committed? Understanding parish culture is a necessary part of understanding where energy and commitment are most and least likely to be mobilized.

Parishioners who are engaged in collective work—planning programs and festivals, running a sodality, fixing up the building—will inevitably bring to that work their cultural assumptions about how people should work together. Everything from written agendas to the arrangement of chairs to the kind of beverages served at meetings will reflect the particular decision-making cultures that prevail in the various corners of the parish. Some will want elaborate record-keeping, while others will expect oral accounts. Some will want official rules and votes, while others will want consensus. Some will welcome, even provoke conflict, while others will elaborately avoid it. Some will expect that whatever they decide will actually happen, others will not. Observing collective work is another of the vital tools in the study of parish life.

Conflict is, of course, ubiquitous, and it is a critical site for observing parish life. Disagreements are likely to reveal both key values and key players. Finding out what people have argued about and the form those arguments took is likely to be very revealing of a parish's culture and how it gets things done. Finding out how those arguments have been resolved may also reveal imbalances in power. It may be more critical to find out which differences never get voiced. Suppressed differences are a window on one kind of power. Facilitating conversations about difference is another manifestation of power. And discovering that a group thinks it has no differences is probably a good indicator of a parish deeply resisting change. One of the most striking findings that emerged from the research I did on congregations in changing communities was the perfect correlation between conflict and adaptation (Ammerman 1997). Congregations that adapted had all experienced (and weathered) significant conflict. Congregations on the wane were uniformly peaceful.

Understanding parishes means understanding forms of leadership, expectations about how meetings run, ideas about money and responsibility, ways of originating innovations and bringing them to fruition, and methods of handling disagreement. It also means taking fully into account the way the Church's authority is understood and exercised. The foundation of authority is the legitimacy granted to that authority by those who live in relationship to it. When religious authorities can claim that legitimacy, they are also able to exercise a moral leadership based on shared commitments to a power beyond themselves. When the traditions and symbols of the Church are in the hands of such trusted authorities, they can be significant sources of power for accomplishing all the kinds of work in which a parish is engaged. Standing in their mediating role, priests have the capacity to invoke moral and spiritual power and to create a sacred narrative that empowers action. Students of parish life should pay close attention to how that power is used. What action does the Church's official symbolic power enable, and what does it forbid? Where is it essential, and what work gets done anyway? To argue that parishes have local norms for how they work is not to dismiss the importance of understanding the structures of Church authority within which that work is done.

The Distinctive Puzzles of Parishes

Students of Catholic life have turned their attention to a wide range of sociological and theological issues, often intertwined. As scholars turn their attention to a renewed program of parish studies, there is much to learn. As I have suggested above, the tools developed over the last thirty years in congregational studies can point to important questions to ask and useful ways to ask them. Despite the initial Protestant focus of the field, its methods and theories provide an important foundation on which to build. Attention to parish life can enrich our knowledge about how faith communities gather and organize, and it may reveal the need for new methods and theories. What I want to suggest in the remainder of this essay is one of the places where I think parish studies will face important methodological challenges, but with potential for significant new knowledge.

The single feature that immediately distinguishes parishes from other congregational forms is their typically large size. Compared to Protestant congregations, Catholic parishes are four times as likely to have at least 250 regular attendees and ten times as likely to have more than a thousand (Association of Religion Data Archives 2012). Indeed, the average parish has more than three thousand registered members. Studying such large organizations will pose methodological challenges, but it is the conceptual terrain I want to explore. The vast majority of the literature on very large congregations is concerned with Protestant megachurches (Thumma and Travis 2007), and it may provide few clues to the questions that need to be asked about Catholic "megachurches." This is an area where the study of parishes may genuinely plow new ground.

We know that very large organizations are likely to engender high levels of passive consumerism. When there are others around to be in charge, any given individual may feel less inclined to act. On the other hand, even those passive bodies are critical. Megachurches themselves depend on the presence of large numbers of worshippers to generate a sense of excitement and importance (Thumma 2000). But does a big crowd mean the same thing to a Catholic worshipper? Studying the experience of worship in the Catholic context can add immeasurably to the research literature on large churches, a literature dominated by emphasis on performance and production values. Sights and sounds may be foundational in a Catholic parish as well, but they may operate very differently from their use in an evangelical megachurch. Here there is a differently scripted combination of individual and collective engagement from the audience-performer interaction of most megachurches. The Mass's structure of actively responding together, listening quietly, and individually moving forward to receive the sacraments is a quite different set of activities and may mediate the large group experience differently.

We also know that the typical megachurch employs a vast array of small specialized study and ministry groups to complement the experience of worshipping in a crowd. We know a little about how those specialized groups relate to the whole, along with how delegated leadership and networking strategies are employed (Gladwell 2005; Wilford 2012). But we have virtually no data on what that looks like in a Catholic context. We do know that individual Catholics are far less likely than Protestants to be involved in any activity beyond worship (Bane 2005). To what extent is that just about size, or are there alternative systems at work? What role may be played, for example, by nonparish-based lay ecclesial movements, such as Cursillo (Nabhan-Warren 2013)? The structures through which very large parishes engage and mobilize their members is a question in need of additional answers.

Clerical authority and expectations about lay leadership are also at play, of course. To what extent are large-parish patterns due to the priest shortage, and to what extent can we look to an absence of the strong Protestant emphasis on lay leadership and participation? The reality of fewer priests has meant that laypeople (and women religious) are increasingly stepping into leadership roles, but will that mean a more comprehensive mobilization of members? We already know that women constitute a near majority of workers in official parish roles, as directors of religious education, liturgists, and more (Gray, Gautier, and Cidade 2010); we know that their presence is changing how Catholics think about leadership (Wallace 1992). Will that open the door to a transformation of large parishes into complex laity-led networks of cells? Or will Catholic sensibilities about authority and membership lead to different forms of parish life?

How very large Catholic parishes organize to balance large-group and small-group interactions is something parish studies can tell us about. Both size itself and the remnants of the more passive past mean that there may be distinct expectations about what it means to belong, and that may have implications for the degree to which members actively participate in producing their parish's culture and contributing their resources toward the community's work. The production of culture may have different dynamics in this context. How do parishioners in a very large parish relate to the stories, symbols, and material surroundings of their building? Under what circumstances does the parish community as a whole experience a sense of collective engagement? And who is understood to have the power to change things? If power is highly concentrated, what defines those lines of power?

A very large Catholic parish is also an interesting site for study because it is likely to have significant diversity within it. Evangelical megachurches, at least in their earlier manifestations, were likely to attract members along lines of similarity. But Catholic parishes today are often merged, and they are often in neighborhoods that include significant population turnover. A bishop may no longer encourage national ("personal") parishes but may insist that parishes take responsibility for all the diverse people within their boundaries (Bruce 2017). These large mixed populations provide an ideal opportunity to study how diversity is experienced and managed. We know that the experience of diversity is different when it is imposed from outside than when it is intentionally sought because of the congregation's own sense of mission (Emerson and Kim 2003). But how is that different in the context of a very large Catholic parish that may have the capacity (and inclination) to create homogeneous subunits within its own boundaries? Brett Hoover's work (2014) begins to provide answers to those questions, but there is much more work to be done at the intersection of size, diversity, authority, and tradition.

If large size is accompanied by a relative absence of small-group participation, that in turn may mean that the spiritual culture of the parish is less readily linked to the everyday life and practice of many participants. My own work suggests that arenas of spiritual conversation are the "plausibility structures" that sustain links between spiritual and mundane planes of reality (Ammerman 2014), and without opportunities for congregational conversation, those links may not happen. But the nature of the Catholic tradition suggests that such conversations may be carried on in places beyond organized parish programs. Traditionally, the entire geographic community was dominated by Catholic life, with everyday relationships sustaining the tradition. But in the current context, what structures and practices remain (or are being invented) to form a substitute "plausibility structure"? In what ways is the spiritual life of the Church being sustained and appropriated? What experiences and conversations within the parish are linked to what sorts of effects beyond the parish?

Finally, that suggests that there are interesting research questions to be raised about the place of large Catholic parishes in the organizational ecology. Protestant megachurches tend to have detrimental effects on the smaller congregations that attempt to compete with them (Chaves 2006; Eiesland 1997), but the Catholic ecology operates more as a "managed economy" than as a competitive market. Still, there is competition, as ex-Catholics join other religious groups (Pew Research Center 2009), immigrants participate in both Pentecostal storefronts and their local parish, and "Catholic" neighborhoods are dotted with other religious communities (Dahm 2004). Students of parish life will need to pay attention to that larger religious ecology, as well as to the way the parish relates to the many organizations that constitute its immediate context. The notion of relating to a particular geography remains, but the decline of national parishes means that the link between neighborhood, ethnicity, and congregation is no longer so clear (Bruce 2017). We know little about the patterns of organizational and cultural connection that prevail when the pragmatic definition of parish lines is more blurred. Does membership size mean that resources of space, people, and infrastructure are also widely used by others, and if so, by whom? Do demands on the parish itself and the relative paucity of personnel and resources deplete its ability to make outside connections? The nexus of relationships between the cultures and resources of parishes and the cultures and resources of the rest of the community is another fertile direction for future parish research.

Conclusion

Catholic parishes are laboratories for understanding many aspects of congregational life, not just the effects of size. The rapidly shifting realities created by mergers, closings, and immigration make parishes fertile ground for examining local religious culture. Students of organizational structure and power will find in parishes fascinating opportunities to observe the balance between official and unofficial authority that emerges where newly empowered lay leaders fill the priestly vacuum. The dynamics of scarcity and new forms of religious competition will fascinate those who study religious ecologies. And attention to how the effects of size are mediated by religious tradition will be a further addition to what we know about local communities of faith. None of these are dynamics unique to parishes, but many of them are distinctly shaped by Catholic tradition and theology. The tools of congregational studies—used with a distinctly Catholic sensibility—can yield important new insight into what nearly a quarter of the US population calls its parish home.

References

Ammerman, Nancy T. 1998. "Culture and Identity in the Congregation." In *Studying Congregations: A New Handbook*, edited by N. T. Ammerman, J. Carroll, C. Dudley, and W. McKinney, pp. 78–104. Nashville, Tenn.: Abingdon Press.

———. 2009. "Congregations: Local, Social, and Religious." In *Oxford Handbook of the Sociology of Religion*, edited by P. B. Clarke, pp. 562–80. Oxford: Oxford University Press.

———. 2014. "Modern Altars in Everyday Life." In *The Many Altars of Modernity*, edited by P. L. Berger, pp. 94–110. Boston: Walter De Gruyter.

Ammerman, Nancy Tatom. 1997. *Congregation and Community*. New Brunswick, N.J.: Rutgers University Press.

Association of Religion Data Archives. 2012. "Congregational Quickstats": National Congregations Study Cumulative Dataset. Retrieved May 24, 2015. http://www.thearda.com/ConQS/qs_295.asp.

Bane, Mary Jo. 2005. "The Catholic Puzzle: Parishes and Civic Lives." In *Taking Faith Seriously: Valuing and Evaluating Religion in American Democracy*, edited by M. J. Bane, B. Coffin, and R. Higgins, pp. 63–93. Cambridge, Mass.: Harvard University Press.

Bonn, Robert L., and Ruth T. Doyle. 1974. "Secularly Employed Clergymen: A Study in Occupational Role Recomposition." *Journal for the Scientific Study of Religion* 13 (3): 325–43. https://doi.org/10.2307/1384761.

Browning, Donald S. 1991. *A Fundamental Practical Theology*. Minneapolis, Minn.: Fortress.

Bruce, Tricia C. 2017. *Parish and Place: Making Room for Diversity in the American Catholic Church*. New York: Oxford University Press.

Burns, Jeffrey M. 1994. "Que Es Esto? The Transformation of St. Peter's Parish, San Francisco, 1913–1990." In *American Congregations: Portraits of Twelve Religious Communities*, edited by J. P. Wind and J. W. Lewis, pp. 396–463. Chicago: University of Chicago Press.

Carroll, Jackson W., Carl S. Dudley, and William McKinney. 1986. *Handbook for Congregational Studies*. Nashville, Tenn.: Abingdon Press.

Chaves, Mark. 2006. "All Creatures Great and Small: Megachurches in Context." *Review of Religious Research* 47 (4): 329–46.

Dahm, Charles W. 2004. *Parish Ministry in a Hispanic Community*. New York: Paulist Press.

D'Antonio, William V., James D. Davidson, and Dean R. Hoge. 1996. *Laity American and Catholic: Transforming the Church*. Kansas City, Mo.: Sheed & Ward.

DiMaggio, Paul J., and Walter W. Powell. 1983. "The Iron Cage Revisited: Institutional Isomorphism and Collective Rationality in Organizational Fields." *American Sociological Review* 48: 147–60.

Dolan, Jay P., ed. 1987. *The American Catholic Parish: A History from 1850 to the Present*. New York: Paulist Press.

Douglass, H. Paul, and Edmund de S. Brunner. 1935. *The Protestant Church as a Social Institution*. New York: Harper & Row.

Dudley, Carl S., ed. 1983. *Building Effective Ministry*. San Francisco: Harper & Row.

Dudley, Carl S. 1996. *Next Steps in Community Ministry*. Bethesda, Md.: Alban Institute.

Eiesland, Nancy L. 1997. "Contending with a Giant: The Impact of a Megachurch on Exurban Religious Institutions." In *Contemporary American Religion*, edited by P. E. Becker and N. L. Eiesland, pp. 191–220. Walnut Creek, Calif.: AltaMira Press.

Eiesland, Nancy L., and R. Stephen Warner. 1998. "Ecology: Seeing the Congregation in Context." In *Studying Congregations: A New Handbook*, edited by N. T. Ammerman, J. Carroll, C. Dudley, and W. McKinney, pp. 78–104. Nashville, Tenn.: Abingdon Press.

Emerson, Michael O., and Karen Chai Kim. 2003. "Multiracial Congregations: An Analysis of Their Development and a Typology." *Journal for the Scientific Study of Religion* 42 (2): 217–28.

Fichter, Joseph. 1954. *Social Relations in the Urban Parish*. Chicago: University of Chicago Press.

Gamm, Gerald. 1999. *Urban Exodus: Why the Jews Left Boston and the Catholics Stayed*. Cambridge, Mass.: Harvard University Press.

Gladwell, Malcolm. 2005. "The Cellular Church: How Rick Warren's Congregation Grew." *The New Yorker*, September 12, 2005, 60–67.

Gray, Mark, Melissa Cidade, Mary Gautier, and Thomas Grant. 2013. *Cultural Diversity in the Catholic Church in the United States*. Washington, DC: Center for Applied Research in the Apostolate at Georgetown University.

Gray, Mark, Mary Gautier, and Melissa Cidade. 2010. *The Changing Face of U.S. Catholic Parishes.* Emerging Models of Pastoral Leadership Project. Washington, DC: National Association for Lay Ministry.

Gustafson, James M. 1961. *Treasure in Earthen Vessels.* Chicago: University of Chicago Press.

Hoover, Brett C. 2014. *Shared Parish: Latinos, Anglos, and the Future of U.S. Catholicism.* New York: New York University Press.

Kanter, Rosabeth Moss, Barry A. Stein, and Todd D. Jick. 1992. *The Challenge of Organizational Change: How Companies Experience It and Leaders Guide It.* New York: Free Press.

Konieczny, Mary Ellen. 2009. "Sacred Places, Domestic Spaces: Material Culture, Church, and Home at Our Lady of the Assumption and St. Brigitta." *Journal for the Scientific Study of Religion* 48 (3): 419–42.

Lamont, Michele. 1992. *Money, Morals, and Manners.* Chicago: University of Chicago Press.

Lim, Chaeyoon, and Robert D. Putnam. 2010. "Religion, Social Networks, and Life Satisfaction." *American Sociological Review* 75 (6): 914–33.

Matovina, Timothy. 2012. *Latino Catholicism: The Transformation of America's Largest Church.* Princeton, N.J.: Princeton University Press.

McGreevy, John T. 1996. *Parish Boundaries: The Catholic Encounter with Race in the Twentieth-Century Urban North.* Chicago: University of Chicago Press.

McGuire, Meredith. 2007. "Embodied Practices: Negotiation and Resistance." In *Everyday Religion: Observing Modern Religious Lives,* edited by N. T. Ammerman, pp. 187–200. New York: Oxford University Press.

Murnion, Philip J. 1983. "Parish Life in the United States." Washington, DC: United States Catholic Conference.

Nabhan-Warren, Kristy. 2013. *The Cursillo Movement in America: Catholics, Protestants, and Fourth-Day Spirituality.* Chapel Hill: University of North Carolina Press.

Nieman, James. 2002. "Attending Locally: Theologies in Congregations." *International Journal of Practical Theology* 6 (2): 198–225.

Orsi, Robert A. 1985. *The Madonna of 115th Street: Faith and Community in Italian Harlem, 1880–1950.* New Haven, Conn.: Yale University Press.

———. 1996. *Thank You, St. Jude.* New Haven, Conn.: Yale University Press.

Percy, Martyn. 2001. *The Salt of the Earth: Religious Resilience in a Secular Age.* London: Sheffield Academic Press.

Pew Research Center. 2009. "Faith in Flux: Changes in Religious Affiliation in the U.S." Pew Forum on Religion and Public Life. Washington, DC: Pew Research Center. http://www.pewresearch.org/wp-content/uploads/sites/7/2009/04/fullreport.pdf.

Putnam, Robert D., Lewis M. Feldstein, and Donald J. Cohen. 2003. *Better Together: Restoring the American Community.* New York: Simon & Schuster.

Roozen, David A., William McKinney, and Jackson W. Carroll. 1984. *Varieties of Religious Presence.* New York: Pilgrim Press.

Sweetser, Thomas. 1983. *Successful Parishes: How They Meet the Challenge of Change.* San Francisco: Harper & Row.

Swidler, Ann. 1986. "Culture in Action: Symbols and Strategies." *American Sociological Review* 51, 273–86.

Thumma, Scott. 1998. "Methods for Congregational Study." In *Studying Congregations: A New Handbook,* edited by N. T. Ammerman, J. W. Carroll, C. S. Dudley, and W. McKinney, pp. 196–239. Nashville, Tenn.: Abingdon Press.

———. 2000. "Exploring the Megachurch Phenomena: Their Characteristics and Cultural Context". Retrieved December 19, 2000. http://hirr.hartsem .edu/bookshelf/thumma_article2.html.

Thumma, Scott, and Dave Travis. 2007. *Beyond Megachurch Myths.* San Francisco: Jossey-Bass.

Vasquez, Manual A. 2010. *More Than Belief: A Materialist Theory of Religion.* New York: Oxford University Press.

Wallace, Ruth. 1992. *They Call Her Pastor.* Albany: State University of New York Press.

Warner, R. Stephen. 1994. "The Place of the Congregation in the Contemporary American Religious Configuration." In *American Congregations: New Perspectives in the Study of Congregations,* edited by J. Wind and J. Lewis, pp. 54–99. Chicago: University of Chicago Press.

Wilford, Justin G. 2012. *Sacred Subdivisions: The Postsuburban Transformation of American Evangelicalism.* New York: New York University Press.

Wuthnow, Robert. 1994. *Producing the Sacred.* Urbana: University of Illinois Press.

Part II: Parish Trends

Sociologists pay close attention to patterns and trends over time. This allows for comparisons to see what is changing—and what remains the same. We learned in Part I that the tools to examine patterns and trends in Catholic parishes are many and have been refined over time. Part II shows us how using these tools can help us understand the contemporary scene of American parishes.

The two essays in this section use a multitude of quantitative data sources to assess parishes over time. Parishes offer a useful space from which to track patterns of Catholic behavior, affiliation, and attitudes. How has American Catholics' parish-going behavior changed in recent years? What do parishes look like in terms of leadership and parishioner composition? What differences can we observe between Catholics who attend a parish regularly and those who do not? These next essays help us answer these kinds of questions and more.

Suggested Additional Readings

Chaves, Mark. 2017. *American Religion: Contemporary Trends.* 2nd ed. Princeton, N.J.: Princeton University Press.

D'Antonio, William V., Michele Dillon, and Mary L. Gautier. 2013. *American Catholics in Transition.* Lanham, Md.: Rowman & Littlefield Publishers.

Pew Research Center. 2015. *U.S. Catholics Open to Non-Traditional Families.* Washington, DC: Pew Research Center. http://www.pewforum.org/2015/09/02/u-s-catholics-open-to-non-traditional-families/.

Zech, Charles E., Mary L. Gautier, Mark M. Gray, Jonathon L. Wiggins, and Thomas P. Gaunt. 2017. *Catholic Parishes of the 21st Century.* New York: Oxford University Press.

3   The Shifting Landscape of US Catholic Parishes, 1998–2012

GARY J. ADLER JR.

There are more than 17,000 Catholic parishes in the United States (Zech et al. 2017). What has changed among them in recent years? Tracking patterns of change is a crucial first step for knowing why change occurs and for understanding what that change means to the millions who practice Catholicism in thousands of churches each week.

This essay presents trends among Catholic parishes in the United States from a recent period: 1998 to 2012. Looking back, this period was a rather tumultuous time in both the Catholic community and the US. Three different popes served during these years. The period included major revelations about the sexual abuse of minors by Catholic clergy and its scandalous mismanagement by some Church leaders; the largest terrorist attack against civilians in US history; fast-growing social tolerance of same-sex marriage; and the Great Recession. Social scientists see this period as a time of meaningful change in American religious life. The church-going population grew older, while Americans overall reported lower rates of religious affiliation. Religious diversity increased, especially due to immigration, and religious tolerance increased as well. Amid these larger social trends—and sometimes in response to them—Catholic parishes experienced their own changes.

While there are many themes we could focus on, this essay highlights five key areas of parish change: organizational characteristics, member demographics, local parish culture, political activity, and membership boundaries. Before we focus on the trends, though, it's important to understand *how* we can measure such things.

How to See Trends among Catholic Parishes

Social trends can be captured in different ways, each with trade-offs for what we see and how we understand it. Imagine, for a moment, your smartphone's camera as a tool for capturing evidence about social trends. The video app could capture large amounts of information, but this would include extraneous footage (and quickly fill your memory card). You might use your phone's picture app to take a snapshot of one moment in time, but that wouldn't tell you much about whether that context was bound to change or stay the same. If you pieced together snapshots over time, you could get some sense of a trend (think of social media features that remind you what you were doing last year). But you would have to take the snapshots carefully and methodically. After all, *when* pictures are taken and *how* they are taken both affect whether the resulting collage is representative of the "big picture."

Translating from the world of digital photography to sociology, the best "app" for taking snapshots of social trends is a repeated social survey. Ideally, a survey would be repeated at regular intervals of time ("when"), using the same questions and question order ("how"). If done well and with a representative sample, the results would be generalizable to the population of interest and useful for tracking change. In other words, the collage of snapshots provided by repeated surveys would represent the big picture. In our case, a repeated survey of Catholic parishes would tell us a lot about trends in the population of Catholic parishes.

Surprisingly, there are not many national, contemporary surveys about US Catholic parishes. In 2006, Jim Davidson and Suzanne Fournier reviewed data sources that had emerged from growing interest about parishes and congregations in American life. The authors briefly mentioned the data source I use in this essay, the National Congregations Study (NCS), but few researchers have systematically taken advantage of it for its insight into Catholic parish life (for exceptions, see Bane 2005, Cavendish 2000, and Palmer-Boyes 2010).[1]

The NCS is an organizational survey with three waves (i.e., "snapshots") of data, having been fielded in 1998, 2006/07, and 2012 (Chaves and Anderson 2014).[2] Its sample of congregations was created from individuals who responded to the General Social Survey (GSS), which is the gold stan-

---

1. Mary Jo Bane in this volume uses the same data source for a provocative analysis of inequality among Catholic parishes.

2. Data were downloaded from the Association of Religion Data Archives at Pennsylvania State University (www.thearda.com).

dard of nationally representative surveys used to analyze social trends (Marsden 2012). Each respondent to the GSS was asked if he or she had attended a worship service in the previous year and whether he or she could provide a name of that congregation. Because the GSS is nationally representative, by the logic of hypernetwork sampling, the list of congregations nominated by individual survey respondents constitutes a nationally representative sample of congregations in the United States (Chaves et al. 1999). Each nominated congregation was subsequently contacted by phone to complete a survey with a key informant in the organization. Most surveys were completed by the head clergyperson of the congregation.

There are a number of reasons to use this data source for insight into Catholic parishes. First, the NCS produces a nationally representative sample of Catholic parishes, with enough cases to allow for statistical analysis.[3] Second, the NCS has a surprisingly high response rate: 80 percent in 1998, 78 percent in 2006, and 73 percent in 2012.[4] Higher response rates are important because they help ensure that information will not be systematically biased by the parishes that declined to participate. (In sociological terms, higher response rates reduce nonresponse bias.[5] Lots of RSVPs to your birthday party give a more representative picture of your social network than one RSVP from your best friend.) Third, the sampling strategy of the NCS avoids using official lists to build a sample of Catholic parishes. This is important because such sources are notorious for being incomplete, irregular, or out of date. Fourth, the NCS has been deployed three times (three waves), which means it has the minimum

3. In their review of parish data sources, Davidson and Fournier (2006) seem to imply that only 5 percent of the NCS *cases* are Catholic parishes. The 5 percent actually reflects the effect of a statistical weight used to represent the *proportion* of Catholic congregations among the population of all congregations in the United States. In reality, there are about 300 cases of Catholic parishes in each NCS wave, representing about 20 percent of all NCS cases.

4. When these rates are adjusted to include nonresponse by individuals within the GSS itself, the NCS response rate for 1998 is 60 percent, 58 percent for 2006, and 52 percent for 2012.

5. By contrast, the response rate for parish surveys conducted by CARA is about 15 percent (Zech et al. 2017). Brad Fulton's (2016) analysis of organizational research shows evidence that low response rates in organizational surveys (less than 34 percent) produce significant nonresponse bias, which affects the validity and representativeness of results.

number of data points required to draw some conclusions about trends. Finally, the NCS has two statistical weights that allow for different but complementary analyses. One weight provides a view of the "average parish" by adjusting for the size of congregations. A second weight allows us to look at Catholic parishes from the view of the "average attender." This "view from the pew" tells us what Catholic parishes are like for the average attender. From this view, larger parishes have more influence on the results, since more Mass attenders are in larger parishes. Accordingly, this view tells us how larger parishes may be different.

Alongside these strengths, the NCS also has a few drawbacks to keep in mind. First, the NCS is oriented toward *all* congregations. Some questions are asked differently than Catholics themselves might ask them. For example, Catholic leaders often refer to the number of registered families or number of sacraments fulfilled in a year, neither of which the NCS asks about. Second, the NCS is unable to tell us everything occurring within a parish. For example, the NCS asks only about the "main service" of a congregation. However, Catholic parishes have multiple Masses that are quite different, often along ethnic lines. Third, the information provided in the NCS comes from one key informant within a parish. Key informants are good at reporting some basic organizational and demographic information but are not infallible (Frenk et al. 2011; Fulton 2018; Schwadel and Dougherty 2010). Fourth and finally, the NCS does not ask about many other topics we might want to know about—like what the homilies covered, whether individual attendees felt welcome, or which artistic version of Mary the Mother of God adorns the side chapel. These are important questions about parish identity that we cannot know from the NCS.

Continuity in Catholic Parishes

Before turning our attention to what has changed, it's helpful to look at what has *not* changed. One of the remarkable stories of American religion in the second half of the twentieth century was continuity in religious beliefs and behaviors (Chaves 2011). With that tendency toward persistence in mind, what has stayed the same among Catholic parishes since the late 1990s? Table 1 shows aspects of Catholic parishes that did *not* experience significant change between 1998 and 2012.

Table 1. Parish continuity from 1998 to 2012

| | Average parish | | | Parish of the average attender | |
	1998	2012		1998	2012
Organization Composition					
Number of adults and children regularly participating (median)	300	400		1700	1600
Number of people affiliated in any way with parish (median)	500	1100	†	3500	4000
Full-time staff (median)	2	3		6	7
Part-time staff (median)	2	3		4	4
Services on weekend (median)	7	8		11	11
Regular adult participants that are female (%)	59	59		58	59
Regular adult participants under 35 years old (%)	29	28		30	29
Regular adult participants under $25K/year (%)	37	34		27	31
Regular adult participants that are black or African American (%)	6	4		6	6
Regular adult participants that are Asian or Pacific Islander (%)	3	3		5	5

†$p < .10$

Many demographic characteristics of parishes have not changed. The average parish has seen neither decrease nor increase in the percentage of adult female participants, young adult participants, poor participants, black participants, or Asian participants who regularly attend the parish. We can observe this continuity from both the view of the average parish and the view of the average attender.

Trends in parish size also suggest some continuity over time, although this story is rather complex. The first two rows in Table 1 show different ways of measuring the number of people connected to a parish: the number of regularly participating adults and children (a "restrictive" definition of parish size) and the number of people affiliated with the parish in any way (an "inclusive" definition of parish size). As described earlier, both numbers would have been estimated by key informants in parishes (e.g., the pastor). These ways of measuring parish size differ from the usual Catholic ways of measuring parish size, that is, counting all Catholics in a given geographic area as parish members (even if they never show up to Mass) or using registration lists maintained by parishes themselves. The measures I use provide a standardized way to collect data across a diverse landscape of parishes and thus are likely more accurate about the actual day-to-day presence of people in parishes.

Looking at the numbers reported for regularly participating adults and children over the period (restrictive definition) indicates that the median size of parishes has held steady.[6] In 2012, the average parish had four hundred adults and children that regularly participated, showing no statistically significant change. A full 1,100 people were affiliated in any way with the average parish (inclusive definition). The difference displayed in Table 1 in the number of affiliated people per parish between 1998 and 2012 seems quite large. However, this difference is not statistically significant by common standards. Given this, while there might have been change occurring, we should be careful before declaring so.

Another stable pattern over time is that the average Catholic attends a fairly large parish. You'll notice a big difference between the size of the average parish and the size of the parish of the average attender. The last two columns show the size of the parish that the average Catholic attended. No matter the period, the average Catholic went to Mass in a parish that was much bigger than the average parish. In 2012, the parish of the average attender had 1,600 regularly participating adults and children, with 4,000 affiliated in some way. This means that while more *parishes* are smaller, more *individuals* attend parishes that are larger.

One more area of continuity worth noting is in regard to parish staff. Counterintuitively, despite the decline in number of priests in the United States, Table 1 shows that there has been *no* significant change among parishes in the average number of paid full-time staff persons or paid part-time staff persons. The number of weekend worship services has also held

---

6. Because the size distribution of parishes is quite skewed, I use the median to describe the central tendency.

steady. What this means is that full- and part-time parish staffing levels may not have kept pace with declines in priest resources. This implies (potentially) that parishes today spread more responsibility across a smaller number of mostly lay parish leaders.

What Has Clearly Changed?

Most importantly, the NCS gives us a sense of what has *changed* in US Catholic parishes over time. Table 2 provides basic data on four areas: organizational characteristics, demographic composition, local parish culture, and political activity.

Organizational Composition: Older and More Hispanic

Compared to 1998, today's Catholic parishes look older and more racially diverse, among both priests and parishioners. Regarding the former, Table 2 confirms two much-discussed trends (Zech et al. 2017): the aging and changing racial composition of priests. Since 1998, the age of pastors at the average Catholic parish increased by six years, to fifty-eight years old. The racial composition of pastors also shifted dramatically over this time. In 1998, pastors were overwhelmingly white. By 2012, just 71 percent of parishes had a white pastor. This is a substantial decrease, visualized in Figure 1. Over the time period, the percent of parishes with a white pastor decreased by about a quarter. These changes are somewhat less dramatic when seen from the pew, where about 80 percent of average attenders are still in a parish with a white pastor. This suggests that the racial diversification of pastors has occurred more extensively among smaller parishes.

Lay Catholic parishioners, too, are now older and less likely to be white. The middle of Table 2 reflects this. If you were to compare photographs of the people in a parish in 1998 and in 2012, you might be able to notice the difference with your own eyes. The average Catholic parish in 2012 was comprised of older, more educated, and more Hispanic adult participants than in 1998. These changes are occurring in the average parish but are especially strong (and statistically significant) when looking at the parishes of the average attender.

The changing ethnic and racial makeup of parishes is especially notable. The "browning" of Catholicism in recent years amplifies the centuries-old

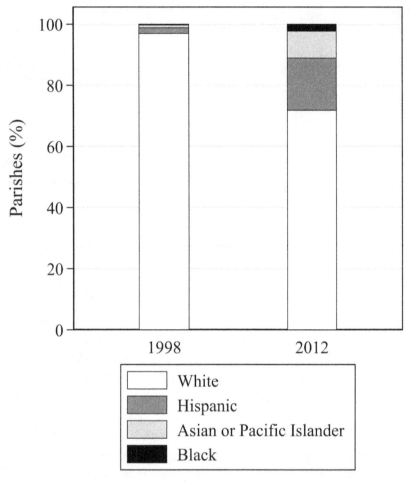

FIGURE 1. Head clergy race

presence of Hispanics in the geographic space of the United States (Matovina 2012).[7] An increasing Hispanic presence across the country has elevated racial diversity in Catholic parishes (Lichter and Johnson 2009). This growth, caused by changes in migration, trends in fertility, and differences in retention of religious identity, has translated into nearly three

7. I use the term "Hispanic" in line with the most recent research on Catholics (Ospino 2014) and the terminology of the National Congregations Study. This broad term refers to people of different nationalities and ethnicities who can trace lineage to geographic areas or countries originally colonized by the Spanish.

Table 2. Parish change from 1998 to 2012

	Mean					
	Parishes (org view)			Parishes (attender view)		
	1998	2012		1998	2012	
Organizational composition						
Age of head clergyperson	52	58	**	55	58	**
Head clergyperson's race (%)						
White	97	71	***	93	81	**
Black or African American	0	2	***	2	2	**
Hispanic or Latino	2	17	***	4	9	**
Asian or Pacific Islander	1	9	***	1	7	**
Other	0	1	***	0	1	**
Demographics (%)						
Regular adult participants with BA education or more	32	37		36	42	*
Regular adult participants over 60 years old	32	43	*	31	41	***
Regular adult participants over $100K/year	10	14		13	17	†
Regular adult participants that are white	72	66		72	64	*
Regular adult participants that are Hispanic or Latino	14	25		16	25	**
Regular adult participants that are recent immigrants	4	5		5	7	*
Congregations that are ≥ 80% Hispanic or Latino	8	18		4	14	***
Congregations that are ≥ 80% white	65	58		64	51	*
Local culture (%)						
Theological orientation						
Theologically conservative	44	52		38	50	*
Theologically moderate	50	38		55	41	*
Theologically liberal	6	9		7	9	*
Worship Style						
Time for people, other than leaders, to testify	40	35		53	45	†
Congregants raised hands during main service	45	36		54	41	**
Community and political activities (%)						
Voter guides distributed in the last 12 months	14	41	***	26	40	**
Voter registration drive in the last 12 months	14	28	†	16	38	***
A group that marched in the last 12 months	26	56	***	42	58	**
A group that lobbied in the last 12 months	12	24	*	23	34	*

***p < .001, **p < .01, *p < .05, †p < .10

decades of resurgence in Hispanic religious activity. Yet, Hispanics' impact on traditionally non-Hispanic institutions and geographic areas is still relatively under-studied (Ospino 2014; Stevens-Arroyo 1998; Stevens-Arroyo et al. 2003).

As Table 2 shows, a quarter of regular attenders at the average parish are Hispanic. But this number belies the strong demographic growth of Hispanics in the US Catholic Church. Additional NCS data show that in 1998, 37 percent of parishes had *no* Hispanic members. By 2012, only 25 percent of parishes had no Hispanic members. In other words, by 2012, fully three-quarters of American parishes reported having at least one Hispanic member (and usually many more).[8] As others have reported (Ospino 2014), this has led to important changes on the ground in parish life. For example, by 2012, 32 percent of *all* parishes reported having at least one Spanish-language service. That was 6 percent higher than in 2006. Based on 17,000 total parishes, it means an additional 1,000 parishes were providing worship services in Spanish, in just six years' time.

The change in Hispanic presence in parishes is especially striking when we understand one way that it is happening. Sociologists who study the racial and ethnic integration of congregations say that a congregation with more than 80 percent of its members belonging to one racial group is a "uniracial" congregation (Emerson and Woo 2006).[9] By that measure, in 1998, 8 percent of Catholic parishes were uniracial Hispanic. By 2012, fully one-fifth (18 percent) of parishes were uniracial Hispanic. Thus, while the population of Catholic parishes overall shows a more widespread Hispanic presence, there has also been growth in uniracial Hispanic parishes. Both the *population of parishes* and the *population inside parishes* have diversified. These two trends could have different meanings over the long run. As scholars of Catholicism have long known, "ethnic" parishes can be crucial for sustaining religious identity and mediating the experience of mi-

---

8. NCS data on the national origin, descent, and ethnicity of Hispanics in parishes shows the large importance of Mexico. Among all parishes in the NCS that report any Hispanic adult participants (i.e., 75 percent of parishes in 2012), 75 percent of those reported Mexico as the largest "Hispanic ethnicity" group, followed by Puerto Rico at 8 percent.

9. For clarity and comparison purposes, we refer to Hispanic as a "racial" category, notwithstanding the problems and implications of such a statement.

norities in an often-hostile American racial context. But other scholars, including Hoover, Pratt, and Bane in this volume, show that unjust and unequal exclusion processes can sometimes keep nonwhite parishioners out of uniracial white parishes—and fail to include them fully when they do join. These issues are crucial to the future of American Catholicism and require more research.

Local Parish Culture: More Conservative, Less Charismatic

If you've visited more than one parish, you're aware of how much parishes differ. For example, one parish might overflow with statutes and icons while another may have just a few. The people in one parish might dress formally and talk quietly in the sanctuary, while casual dress and boisterous energy might be the norm elsewhere. These contrasts are examples of differences in local parish culture.

There are many ways to measure the local culture of parishes. Other essays in this book, for example, pay close attention to variation in worship style or ways that different age groups (like single young adults) get involved in parish life. Organizational surveys like the NCS rely on broader categories to measure local culture. One such measure is theological orientation, since differences in theology can greatly influence what religious life looks like at the local level (Ammerman 1997; Beyerlein and Chaves 2003; Konieczny 2009). Theological orientations differentiate how congregations interpret their religious tradition in relation to contemporary life. Conservative theology tends toward orthodox resistance of social change; liberal theology tends toward accommodation with social life. These are blunt, organizational measures that do not reference the beliefs of individuals or theologians but instead help locate parishes on a distinct spectrum that has defined American religious life since at least the 1980s (Adler 2012; Hunter 1991). Theological differences are not *prima facie* evidence of polarization. However, since theological leanings and political identities among Americans overlap more these days, shifts in theological leanings among parishes could point toward increased polarization.

Figure 2 shows changes in theological orientation among parishes over the period from the view of the average parish. Half of parishes were theologically moderate in 1998, dropping to 38 percent by 2012. Meanwhile, the percent of parishes reporting theological conservatism has risen

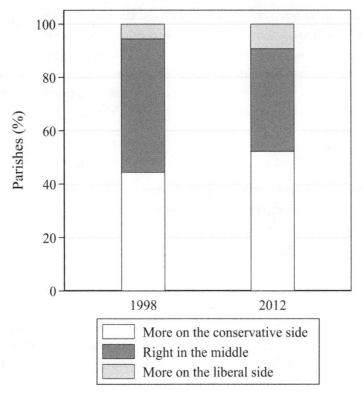

FIGURE 2. Theological orientation (by parish)

slightly. These changes were *not* statistically significant, but they do suggest a slow-moving trend.

We cannot be sure exactly what happened, but there are a few possible
reasons for this trend. American religion on the whole is increasingly understood as a conservative social institution (Putnam and Campbell
2010). This might color how religious activity is reported, with *any* religious activity more likely to be interpreted as conservative. Alternatively,
a more orthodox vision of Catholicism among some Catholic leaders and
within Catholic seminaries may have influenced how key informants responded to the question.

It may also be the case that the increasing presence of Hispanics in
American Catholicism has produced some theological change. Some evidence supports this. The NCS data indicate that uniracial Hispanic parishes are significantly more likely to report conservative theology. In 2012,

70 percent of uniracial Hispanic parishes reported conservative theology, while 49 percent of all other parishes did. *No* uniracial Hispanic parishes reported liberal theology, while 11 percent of all other parishes did. So there appears to be a contemporary correlation between conservative theology and uniracial Hispanic parishes. Since the number of uniracial Hispanic parishes more than doubled over the period, this could be shaping the trend toward conservatism among the Catholic parish population in general.

But is there actually a correlation between conservative theology and uniracial Hispanic identity over time? No—and this is where the trend gets complex. In 1998, the large majority of uniracial Hispanic parishes (86 percent) actually reported moderate theology. By 2012, it had decreased to 30 percent. That is a major decrease in less than twenty years. So not only has the proportion of uniracial Hispanic parishes grown in the US parish population, but uniracial Hispanic parishes have increasingly identified as theologically conservative. Together, these two trends have had a large impact on the trend toward conservatism among Catholic parishes more broadly.

Nonetheless, we should not be quick to equate Hispanic identity with conservative theology. The measure we are examining is blunt, revealing less than we would like to know. It is likely that the meaning of uniracial parishes within American Catholicism changed over the period, leading uniracial Hispanic parishes to present themselves in a more distinctive way vis-à-vis the rest of parishes. Notably, there is no such trend toward theological conservatism among parishes with small percentages of Hispanic members or even among parishes that are half Hispanic. This suggests a wide variety of theology among Hispanics and their parishes, just as among all Catholics. This nudges us away from concluding that a natural connection exists between one ethnic identity and its influence on parish life.

The change in parish theological orientation looks slightly different when seen from the view of the average attender. In short, the conservative shift appears even larger. As Figure 3 shows, in 1998, more than half (55 percent) of parish attenders were in a theologically moderate parish. Only 41 percent were in 2012. By 2012 half of parish attenders were in a parish that was theologically conservative, compared to 38 percent in 1998.

The change away from a moderate theological position to a conservative theological position from the view of attenders was significant across

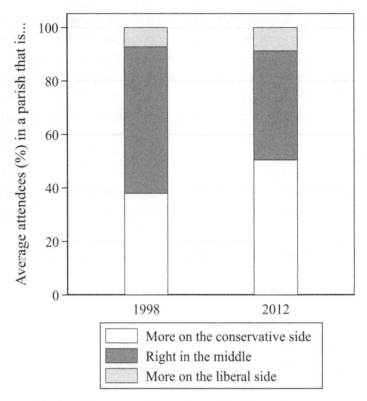

FIGURE 3. Theological orientation (by parish attendance)

the period, suggesting that larger parishes, in particular, were more conservative by 2012. Why? It could be that the pastors of larger congregations in 2012 perceived their parishes as more conservative, part of their own preference for parish life. Or more conservative priests might be assigned to larger parishes. Or larger parishes in 2012 may have drawn a more conservative type of parishioner.

Or, again, Hispanic ethnicity could matter. In this case, the story is a bit different, given the effect of parish size. Over the period, uniracial Hispanic parishes were increasingly likely to be very large. Thus, the effect of Hispanic presence—especially uniracial Hispanic parishes—was concentrated among bigger parishes, which is where attenders are concentrated. Parishes with *no* Hispanics tended to show up on theological poles over the period: fewer were moderate, more were liberal, and many more were conservative. The theological movement toward conservatism seems to have especially involved large parishes, with complex dynamics connected to ethnic composition.

One other aspect of local culture that the NCS survey measures relates to a parish's worship style. One of the most talked about changes in Catholicism during the 1970s and 1980s was an increase in charismatic Catholicism (Hunt, Walter, and Hamilton 2016; Martin 2002). To many Catholics, including Pope Francis until late in his life, this type of Catholicism is unfamiliar (Ivereigh 2014).

There are numerous ways of measuring charismatic worship. One marker of charismatic Catholicism is "speaking in tongues." There is no evidence that the average parish has more or less of this activity over the period. Other measures of charismatic worship have decreased. Table 2 shows that the percentage of parishes reporting two other markers of charismatic worship—testimonials by lay people and raised hands during the main worship service—have declined. The decline is not large enough to be statistically significant at the parish level. However, these changes *are* significant when considered from the view of the average parishioner. By 2012, the percent of attenders in a parish that had testimonials during the main worship service had declined eight points (to 45 percent). Figure 4 displays this trend from the view of attenders.

Those in a parish in which parishioners raised hands during the main service had declined fourteen points (to 41 percent). This suggests that larger parishes, in particular, were less likely over the period to have charismatic worship as part of their main service. The influence of charismatic Catholicism as a prominent aspect of parish worship seems to have weakened in recent decades.

This is an area in need of further research, for two reasons. First, scholars have tracked the global spread of spirit-centric worship (Christerson and Flory 2017; Coleman and Hackett 2015). Given that parishes in the United States are attached to a global religious institution, the increasing salience of Pentecostal practices and beliefs worldwide has implications for any uniqueness in American Catholicism or potential transnational parish partnerships (Adler and Offutt 2018). Second, these changes are likely filtered by demographic changes. Hispanics in the American Catholic Church frequently have closer connections to the worship styles and supportive religious structures of the Catholic charismatic renewal movement (Ospino 2014). The NCS data show significantly higher (and rising)

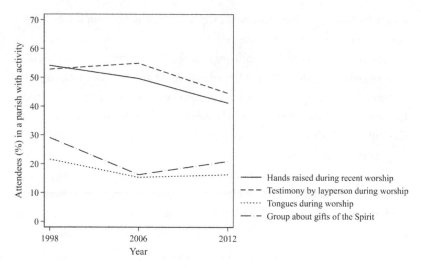

FIGURE 4. Charismatic liturgy indicators

levels of speaking in tongues at majority Hispanic parishes. But similar evidence does not exist for other measures of the charismatic movement, no matter the Hispanic makeup of a parish. And the parish of the average attender shows less speaking in tongues over time—no matter the Hispanic makeup. Since these results challenge the typical picture of Hispanic Catholicism as especially charismatic, more research is needed to sort out their meaning.

Overall, the local culture of Catholic parishes has become more conservative and less charismatic. It is too early to predict the effect these trends will have on individual Catholics, but clearly the demographic growth of Hispanic parishes and Hispanics in parishes will matter going forward.

Way More Politics

Parishes do lots of things for their members and nonmembers. People get to know each other over coffee and donuts or say hello at the back of the church before sitting in a pew. Most parishes provide extensive social services for their members and local communities. But parishes also produce and enable political activity. This topic is an especially important one for researchers, since it reveals how parishes influence parishioners and

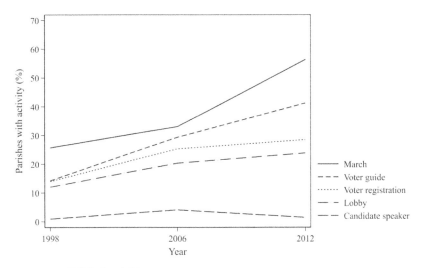

FIGURE 5. Political activities

communities in a way that engages with social life beyond the local context.

Simply put, parishes have become much more politically engaged. Since the late 1990s, Catholic parishes *increased* their rates of political activity, while all types of Protestant congregations *decreased* theirs. Parishes now have higher rates of almost every political activity, compared to congregations of all other religious groups (Fulton 2016). There is something going on with Catholic parishes in the realm of politics. In fact, the political dimension of parishes is one of the areas of parish life with the greatest change since the late 1990s. Across the fifteen-year period, just about every form of political activity increased among Catholic parishes. Figure 5 visualizes this trend.

The percentage of parishes using voter guides nearly tripled across the period. The percentage of parishes organizing a voter registration drive doubled. Parishes also increased their political activity not directly related to electoral politics—what social scientists refer to as high-cost political activism that requires more time, resources, and involvement. Twice as many parishes in 2012 reported participating in a march or lobbying an elected official. Among the parishes that lobbied and marched in 2012, 87 percent did so in relation to abortion, 44 percent in relation to poverty, 29 percent in relation to same-sex marriage, and 26 percent in relation to immigration.[10] These increases in political activity were also noticeable from the pews. Table 2 shows that, in 2012, the average attender was in a parish in which *all* these political activities had significantly increased.

These changes are big—bigger than any other trend in parish life. Clearly, parishes have been mobilized into politics, though it remains to be seen why this is the case. Priests may be responding to the urging of bishops or pressures from fellow parishioners (Calfano, Oldmixon, and Gray 2014; Geraty 2017). National social issues, like immigrant rights or same-sex marriage, and related special interest organizations may have drawn out parish political engagement (Coddou 2016). The NCS data provide no way to identify the partisan tilt in parishes' voter guides or voter registration drives. However, activist practices, like lobbying and marching, appear to be more frequently oriented toward "culture war" issues, especially abortion.

The findings about parish political activity do merit a couple of caveats. First, it is possible that these levels are inflated since the NCS survey occurred during the 2006 midterm election year and the 2012 presidential election year, both of which were especially focused on same-sex marriage (Green 2007; Jones 2016). While the trend in increasing politicization may be happening, the actual levels of activity might be higher here than in nonelection years. Second, it is not the case that parishes have become political machines, easily mobilizing hundreds of people. It is likely that most political activities of a parish are done by a small group within the parish, involving just a handful of people out of hundreds or even thousands of parishioners (Geraty 2017; Munson 2009; Starks 2009).

Membership Boundaries: Restricting Women, Gays, and Lesbians

The last trend to highlight concerns parishes' membership boundaries. Membership boundaries reveal the norms for membership and behavior

---

10. What factors differentiate which parishes engage in which political activities? NCS data show that theologically conservative parishes are significantly more likely to march or lobby related to same-sex marriage and abortion, but theological differences do not appear to influence involvement in other issues. Multivariate regression analysis of parishes—a rarity in parish-focused sociology—would help answer this question.

Table 3. Parish change from 2006 to 2012

	Mean				
	Parishes (org view)			Parishes (attender view)	
Membership boundaries	2006	2012		2006	2012	
Women's roles (%)						
Women can teach a class with adult men in it	98	88		98	97	
Women can be members of governing committee	96	92		96	98	
Women can preach at a main worship service	20	9	*	23	9	***
Homosexuality (%)						
An openly gay or lesbian couple in a committed relationship could be full-fledged members						
Yes	74	55	†	71	61	†
No	14	24	†	19	24	†
Don't know	12	21	†	10	15	†

***p < .001, *p < .05, †p < .10

in a religious organization (Iannaccone 1988; Johnson 1963). In short, membership boundaries tell us who belongs and whether belonging is equal for every person. A parish's restrictions on membership give a sense of how it relates to the surrounding social context—whether it is responding to social change regarding who is acceptable and who is not. Two central membership issues that Catholicism has struggled with since Vatican II are gender and sexuality (Adler 2012; Dillon 1999; Fuist, Stoll, and Kniss 2012).

The NCS survey has tracked identical membership questions only over two waves, from 2006 to 2012, as shown in Table 3. (With only two data points, we should be careful about concluding that a trend is happening.)

Catholic parishes appear to have become slightly less tolerant over the period regarding both women's roles and membership for gay and lesbian persons. In 2006, parishes had high levels of gender equality for women's roles in parish education and governance, as shown in Table 3. By 2012, though, the average parish was less likely to allow women to teach a class, to serve as members of a governing committee, and to preach at a main worship service. The change was only statistically significant for preaching, one of the most controversial activities for Catholic women. Catholic rules limit the most common form of preaching—a homily after the Gospel reading—to ordained persons, who are only men. From the survey, we do not know how or whether parishes enforced these rules. We do know that the Catholic Church has resisted fundamental changes in the permissible roles of women for some time (Chaves 1997; Katzenstein 1998). If this trend of excluding women broadens to non-ordained roles, like teaching or serving on a committee, it would signal a major shift in how parishes reject gender equity in practice.

Finally, the NCS asked congregations whether an openly gay or lesbian couple in a committed relationship could be full-fledged members. For parishes, this may have been a difficult question to answer. On the one hand, the question purposefully removed negative connotations of homosexual relationships outside a committed relationship (Adler 2012). This could make parishes more likely to acknowledge that they allow membership privileges. On the other hand, official Catholic moral teaching still expects that gay and lesbian persons will forgo sexual activity. The Roman Catholic Church rejects the moral legitimacy of civil same-sex marriage (which was legal only in a minority of states before 2016). So parishes might be less likely to acknowledge membership privileges for gay and lesbian persons.

Figure 6 displays a notable trend: parishes have become less officially tolerant of gay and lesbian persons. In 2006, about three-quarters of parishes allowed their membership, but by 2012 only about half did. (A similar shift happened in the "view from the pew.") This trend aligns with increased vocal concern about the legalization of same-sex marriage among many Catholic leaders. For example, even as I wrote this essay, the Catholic bishop of Springfield, Illinois, excluded those in same-sex unions from Communion and funerals—the exact sorts of membership privileges the NCS survey question implies (Pashman 2017). This institutional signaling from bishops and cardinals appears—over time—to have constrained what parishes say and do regarding gay and lesbian persons.

Despite this move toward exclusion, it's important to point out that more than half of Catholic parishes in 2012 reported being open to full

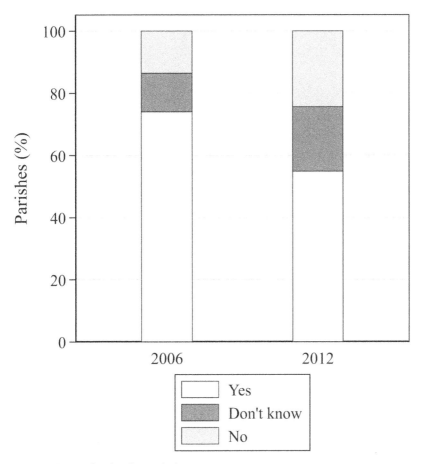

FIGURE 6. Membership for gay/lesbian persons

membership by gays and lesbians in committed relationships and fully 60 percent of average Catholic parishioners were in such a parish. One conclusion from this would be that the majority of Catholic parishes express the hospitable attitude associated with the current pope. A second conclusion is that local parishes navigate their own ways through social change without the strict enforcement of moral orthodoxy espoused by some Catholic leaders, as parishes were displaying openness to gay and lesbian persons *before* the current pope was elected in 2013.[11] This theme echoes throughout this book: the local-level practice of Catholicism is

11. American Catholics have long been ahead of the curve regarding acceptance of homosexuality. See Smith 2015.

often quite different from what official teachings would seem to suggest (Baggett 2009).

Conclusion

Any careful observer knows that Catholicism has changed in remarkable ways over two thousand years (Noonan 2005). American Catholics, too, have changed in their practice of Catholicism over the decades (Greeley 1989; Hout 2016). But what about parishes?

Our brief look at trends in parish life shows that important changes are taking place in and among parishes. First, parishes' organizational composition is becoming older and more Hispanic, both among priests and among people in the pews. Second, local parish cultures are becoming more theologically conservative, but also less charismatic in worship style. Changes in Hispanic demography appear to have played a role in these shifts. Third, there is a new politicization occurring in Catholic parishes, with large increases in political activity. Fourth, parishes have heightened membership and participation boundaries for women and gays and lesbians.

In discussing these trends, I have offered only brief suggestions for why any of these changes are taking place. The reasons why social change occurs are complex, rarely straightforward, and oftentimes obvious only after the fact. These are precisely the sorts of topics that social scientists are interested in, as other essays in this volume show. But to answer any "why" question, it is necessary to get some basic trends down first.

References

Adler, Gary. 2012. "An Opening in the Congregational Closet? Boundary-Bridging Culture and Membership Privileges for Gays and Lesbians in Christian Religious Congregations." *Social Problems* 59 (2): 177–206.

Adler, Gary, and Stephen Offutt. 2017. "The Gift Economy of Direct Transnational Civic Action: How Reciprocity and Inequality Are Managed in Religious 'Partnerships.'" *Journal for the Scientific Study of Religion* 56 (3): 600–19.

Ammerman, Nancy Tatom. 1997. *Congregation and Community.* New Brunswick, N.J.: Rutgers University Press.

Baggett, Jerome P. 2009. *Sense of the Faithful: How American Catholics Live Their Faith.* New York: Oxford University Press.

Bane, Mary Jo. 2005. "The Catholic Puzzle: Parishes and Civic Life." In *Taking Faith Seriously*, edited by M. J. Bane, B. Coffin, and R. Higgins, pp. 63–93. Cambridge, Mass.: Harvard University Press.

Beyerlein, Kraig, and Mark Chaves. 2003. "The Political Activities of Religious Congregations in the United States." *Journal for the Scientific Study of Religion* 42 (3): 17.

Calfano, Brian Robert, Elizabeth A. Oldmixon, and Mark Gray. 2014. "Strategically Prophetic Priests: An Analysis of Competing Principal Influence on Clergy Political Action." *Review of Religious Research* 56 (1): 1–21.

Cavendish, James C. 2000. "Church-Based Community Activism: A Comparison of Black and White Catholic Congregations." *Journal for the Scientific Study of Religion* 39 (1): 64–77.

Chaves, Mark. 1997. *Ordaining Women: Culture and Conflict in Religious Organizations*. Cambridge, Mass.: Harvard University Press.

———. 2011. *American Religion: Contemporary Trends*. Princeton, N.J.: Princeton University Press.

Chaves, Mark, and Shawna L. Anderson. 2014. "Changing American Congregations: Findings from the Third Wave of the National Congregations Study." *Journal for the Scientific Study of Religion* 53 (4): 676–86.

Chaves, Mark, M. E. Konieczy, Kraig Beyerlein, and Emily Barman. 1999. "The National Congregations Study: Background, Methods, and Selected Results." *Journal for the Scientific Study of Religion* 38 (4): 261–71.

Christerson, Brad, and Richard Flory. 2017. *The Rise of Network Christianity: How Independent Leaders Are Changing the Religious Landscape*. New York: Oxford University Press.

Coddou, Marion. 2016. "An Institutional Approach to Collective Action: Evidence from Faith-Based Latino Mobilization in the 2006 Immigrant Rights Protests." *Social Problems* 63 (1): 127–50.

Coleman, Simon, and Rosalind I. J. Hackett. 2015. *The Anthropology of Global Pentecostalism and Evangelicalism*. New York: New York University Press.

Davidson, James D., and Suzanne C Fournier. 2006. "Recent Research on Catholic Parishes: A Research Note." *Review of Religious Research* 48, no. 1 (September): 72–81.

Dillon, Michele. 1999. *Catholic Identity: Balancing Reason, Faith, and Power*. New York: Cambridge University Press.

Emerson, Michael O., and Rodney M. Woo. 2006. *People of the Dream: Multiracial Congregations in the United States*: Princeton, N.J.: Princeton University Press.

Frenk, Steven M., Shawna L. Anderson, Mark Chaves, and Nancy Martin. 2011. "Assessing the Validity of Key Informant Reports About Congregations' Social Composition." *Sociology of Religion* 72 (1): 78–90.

Fuist, Todd Nicholas, Laurie Cooper Stoll, and Fred Kniss. 2012. "Beyond the Liberal-Conservative Divide: Assessing the Relationship between Religious Denominations and Their Associated LGBT Organizations." *Qualitative Sociology* 35 (1): 65–87.

Fulton, Brad R. 2016. "Trends in Addressing Social Needs: A Longitudinal Study of Congregation-Based Service Provision and Political Participation." *Religions* 7 (5): 51.

———. 2018. "Organizations and Survey Research: Implementing Response Enhancing Strategies and Conducting Nonresponse Analyses." *Sociological Methods & Research* 47 (2): 240–76.

Geraty, Kristin. 2017. "Challenges and Opportunities of Community Organizing in Suburban Congregations." In *Religion and Progressive Activism: New Stories About Faith and Politics*, edited by Ruth Braunstein, Todd Nicholas Fuist, and Rhys H. Williams, p. 161–80. New York: New York University Press.

Greeley, Andrew M. 1989. *Religious Change in America*: Cambridge, Mass.: Harvard University Press.

Green, John Clifford. 2007. *The Faith Factor: How Religion Influences American Elections*. Westport, Conn.: Greenwood Publishing Group.

Hout, Michael. 2016. "Saint Peter's Leaky Boat: Falling Intergenerational Persistence among U.S.-Born Catholics since 1974." *Sociology of Religion* 77 (1): 1–17.

Hunt, Stephen J., Tony Walter, and Malcolm Hamilton. 1997. *Charismatic Christianity: Sociological Perspectives*. London: Macmillan.

Hunter, James Davison. 1991. *Culture Wars: The Struggle to Define America*. New York: Basic Books.

Iannaccone, Laurence R. 1988. "A Formal Model of Church and Sect." *The American Journal of Sociology* 94 (Supplement: Organizations and Institutions: Sociological and Economic Approaches to the Analysis of Social Structure): S241–S68.

Ivereigh, Austen. 2014. *The Great Reformer: Francis and the Making of a Radical Pope*. New York: Henry Holt.

Johnson, Benton. 1963. "On Church and Sect." *American Sociological Review* 28 (4): 539–49.

Jones, Robert P. 2016. *The End of White Christian America*. New York: Simon & Schuster.

Katzenstein, Mary. 1998. *Faithful and Fearless*. Princeton, N.J.: Princeton University Press.

Konieczny, Mary Ellen. 2009. "Sacred Places, Domestic Spaces: Material Culture, Church, and Home at Our Lady of the Assumption and St. Brigitta." *Journal for the Scientific Study of Religion* 48 (3): 419–42.

Lichter, Daniel T., and Kenneth M Johnson. 2009. "Immigrant Gateways and Hispanic Migration to New Destinations." *International Migration Review* 43 (3): 496–518.

Marsden, Peter V. 2012. *Social Trends in American Life: Findings from the General Social Survey since 1972*: Princeton, N.J.: Princeton University Press.

Martin, David. 2002. *Pentecostalism: The World Their Parish*. Malden, Mass.: Blackwell.

Matovina, Timothy. 2012. *Latino Catholicism: Transformation in American's Largest Church*. Princeton, N.J.: Princeton University Press.

Munson, Zaid W. 2009. *The Making of Pro-Life Activists: How Social Movement Mobilization Works*. Chicago: University of Chicago Press.

Noonan, John Thomas. 2005. *A Church That Can and Cannot Change: The Development of Catholic Moral Teaching*: Notre Dame, Ind.: University of Notre Dame Press.

Ospino, Hosffman. 2014. *Hispanic Ministry in Catholic Parishes: A Summary Report of Findings from the National Study of Catholic Parishes with Hispanic Ministry*. Boston: Boston College School of Theology and Ministry. http:// www.bc.edu/content/dam/files/schools/stm/pdf/2014/HispanicMinistryinC atholicParishes_2.pdf.

Palmer-Boyes, Ashley. 2010. "The Latino Catholic Parish as a Specialist Organization: Distinguishing Characteristics." *Review of Religious Research* 51 (3): 302–23.

Pashman, Manya Brachear. 2017. "Springfield Bishop: No Communion, Last Rites, Funerals for Same-Sex Couples." *Chicago Tribune*. June 27, 2017. http://www.chicagotribune.com/news/local/breaking/ct-springfield-bishop -same-sex-marriage-met-20170622-story.html.

Putnam, Robert, and David E. Campbell. 2010. *American Grace: How Religion Divides and Unites Us*. New York: Simon & Schuster.

Schwadel, Philip, and Kevin D. Dougherty. 2010. "Assessing Key Informant Methodology in Congregational Research." *Review of Religious Research* 51 (4): 366–79.

Smith, Mark A. 2015. *Secular Faith: How Culture Has Trumped Religion in American Politics*. Chicago: University of Chicago Press.

Starks, Brian. 2009. "Self-Identified Traditional, Moderate, and Liberal Catholics: Movement-Based Identities or Something Else?" *Qualitative Sociology* 32 (1): 1–32.

Stevens-Arroyo, Anthony M. 1998. "The Latino Religious Resurgence." *The Annals of the American Academy of Political and Social Science* 558 (1): 163–77.

Stevens-Arroyo, Anthony, Anneris Goris, Ariela Keysar, Irene Quiles, Andras Tapolcai, Dorothy Craig, and Christina Spinuso. 2003. *The National Survey of Leadership in Latino Parishes and Congregations*. Brooklyn, NY: Program for the Analysis of Religion among Latinas/os (PARAL).

Zech, Charles E., Mary L. Gautier, Mark M. Gray, Jonathon L. Wiggins, and Thomas P. Gaunt. 2017. *Catholic Parishes of the 21st Century*. New York: Oxford University Press.

4　Stable Transformation
Catholic Parishioners in the United States

MARK M. GRAY

Perhaps no trend line in American public opinion polling is more stable than the measurement of Catholic affiliation over the long term. In commercial and academic surveys (including Gallup, the American National Election Study, and the General Social Survey), about a quarter of US adults have self-identified as Catholic since the end of World War II. Yet beneath this apparent stability, enormous changes have taken place. Religions, like all social organizations and movements, have cores and peripheries and people moving in and out of orbit. At the center of each is an inner core of highly active individuals. American Catholicism has seen its core weaken and its periphery grow over the last seventy years. Changes wrought by immigration have also altered the demographic, cultural, and linguistic composition of the Church (see essays in this volume by Gary J. Adler Jr., Mary Jo Bane, and Brett Hoover).

In this essay, I explore the changing composition of the Catholic population and its core parishioners in the United States in the first fifteen years of the twenty-first century using surveys conducted by the Center for Applied Research in the Apostolate (CARA) at Georgetown University as well as the General Social Survey (GSS). I detail the relative sizes of the core and periphery and explore differences between these groups.

Describing Catholic Populations

It is unfair to compare Catholicism today to some mythical golden age. Historians and social scientists have noted that Catholic churches were far from full in the past. As Rodney Stark notes, using original source material, "As for the ordinary people, during the middle ages and during the Renaissance, the masses rarely attended church. . . . In further support of these reports, an extensive survey of surviving parish churches in various parts of Europe reveals them to be too small to have held even a tiny fraction of local inhabitants" (Stark 1999, 255–56).

In the United States, there is also a nostalgic lens to many recollections of Catholicism in the 1950s and early 1960s, which fail to match sociological studies of the Church from this period. In the 1954 volume *Social Relations in the Urban Parish*, Joseph H. Fichter, SJ, relied on an anthropological case study approach to understand parish life. Rather than using surveys, he would spend time in parishes, count heads, knock on doors, and have conversations. This methodology led him to define four Catholic subgroups based on their connection to a parish and their activity within this community. Dormant Catholics "have in practice 'given up' Catholicism but have not joined another religious denomination." Marginal Catholics "are conforming to a bare, arbitrary minimum of the patterns expected in the religious institution." Modal Catholics "are normal 'practicing' Catholics constituting the great mass of identifiable Catholic laymen." Nuclear Catholics "are the most active participants and the most faithful believers."

In this study from the mid-1950s, Fichter estimated that 46 percent of Catholics were in the modal category, 12 percent in the marginal category, and 39 percent were dormant. Only 3 percent fit within the nuclear subgroup of very active Catholics. According to Gallup's telephone surveys, weekly Catholic Mass attendance peaked in 1955 at 75 percent (Saad 2009). Yet as Robert Putnam and David Campbell note, "research on the accuracy of reporting church attendance . . . suggests that we should take these self-reports with a grain of salt" (2010, 571).[1] In his 1954 study, Fichter had estimated Mass attendance levels based on the number of individuals registered with the parish. Once one includes the number of dormant Catholics he had identified from his census within parish boundaries, typical weekly attendance could have been no more than 62 percent (Fichter 1954, 85).[2]

1. This notion has been confirmed in several recent studies on social desirability bias by Philip Brenner (2011, 2012).

2. The difference between Gallup's estimates for the period and other nonsurvey observations and estimates are consistent with more current research that indicates that telephone surveys exaggerate weekly Mass attendance by 7 to 13 percentage points (Cox, Jones, and Navarro-Rivera 2014, 6; Gray 2013).

In a 1951 study, Fichter examined affiliation retention within a parish. He began by counting the number of infant baptisms in the parish in the previous twenty years. He then compared this to the number of Catholics and the number of active parishioners under twenty within parish boundaries. From these data, we can estimate youth retention in the early 1950s was about 78 percent (Fichter 1951, 19).[3] In other words, approximately 22 percent of those baptized Catholic no longer self-identified as such. Only 56 percent of those baptized were active parishioners. The popular notions that most or nearly all Catholics stayed Catholic and went to Church regularly in the 1950s do not match observations on the ground from this period.

Fichter's observations also include considerable variations in what people were doing at Mass. He notes:

> A measure of the parishioners' devotion to the Mass and of their fulfillment of this obligation is seen in the numbers who arrive late and who leave early. By actual count it was noted that, at all Sunday Masses, 8.37 per cent of the congregation arrived after Mass had started and that 6.35 per cent left before it was completed. . . . Although we have no accurate count, we have noticed that many of these persons are duplicated in both categories. In other words, those who come late also tend to leave early. . . . By actual count, 35.08 per cent of the congregation read the missal all during Mass, while another 22.08 per cent read some sort of prayer-book while following the priest's reading of the Gospel. . . . The remaining persons simply stare off into space, although several men in the last pews sometimes read a copy of *Our Sunday Visitor* during Mass. (Fichter 1951, 138)

Fichter's classic studies provide some context to what is happening in the Catholic population today. Figure 1 shows participation in parish life, based on CARA's recent national surveys of adult self-identified Catholics (CARA Catholic Polls, or CCPs).[4] Extrapolating from these surveys, more

---

3. By comparison, the 2014 GSS estimates Catholic retention to be 66 percent today.

4. CARA surveys are self-administered by the respondents and thus lack an interviewer. This has been shown to reduce social desirability bias and produce Mass attendance estimates consistent with headcounts and time diary methods (Gray 2013).

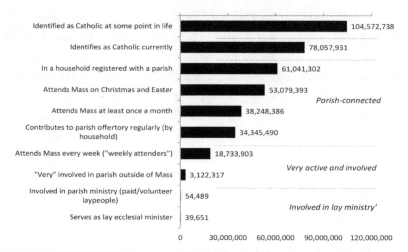

FIGURE 1. US Catholic populations and parish life, 2014. (*Source*: CARA Catholic Polls, multiple years. *Note*: Generally, each group is a subset of those above it.)

than 100 million Americans have been baptized Catholic.[5] Of those baptized, approximately 78.1 million self-identify as Catholic today. Some 61 million Catholics are registered with a parish. CARA surveys indicate this is becoming less common—especially among younger Catholics and immigrants. Registration is not required for parish activity. CARA's in-pew surveys with parishioners estimate that approximately two in ten of the people in the pews at Catholic Masses are not in a household registered with a parish (Gray, Gautier, and Cidade 2013, 12).

About 53.1 million Catholics attend Mass weekly, monthly, or at least a few times a year (most likely on Ash Wednesday, Easter, and Christmas). Some 38.3 million attend at least once a month. This population is similar in size to the 34.4 million who make regular financial contributions to their parish.

Moving closer to the core of the Catholic population, there are an estimated 18.7 million Catholics who attend Mass every week. Near the very

5. According to *The Official Catholic Directory* (*OCD*) there were 71.8 million infants baptized in the United States since 1943. This figure does not include child, teen, and adult baptisms or other previously baptized Christians received into full Communion. It also does not include those baptized in other countries who immigrate to the United States. No infant baptism data in the *OCD* is available before 1943.

center, there are 3.1 million Catholics who are very active in their faith beyond attending Mass. Within that population are more than 54,000 providing some aspect of parish ministry—including more than 39,000 lay ecclesial ministers (professional, paid, and trained staff providing pastoral ministry at least twenty hours a week).

Extrapolating these populations to a per parish point of view, there are an average of nearly 6,000 baptized Catholics within a typical parish's boundaries, of which about 4,500 self-identify as Catholic. From this population, there are nearly 2,000 Catholics who attend Mass at least once a month. About 180 are very active in their parish, including 3 who are involved in parish ministry.

Comparing the Core and Periphery

How different are the core and the periphery among the US Catholic population today? As Fichter showed, the defining feature for such a comparison is the person's relationship with their parish. Because the data used here are national surveys rather than observational case studies of single parishes, we must redefine terms with the aim of maintaining the character of what Fichter identified. Although frequency of Mass attendance is but one component of religious behavior, it is the most powerful proxy for other behaviors and beliefs that is available to us in surveys.[6] For example, in CARA's national surveys, more than nine in ten of those who attend Mass at least once a month are registered with their parish compared to just more than a third of those who attend Mass less often. More than half of those who attend Mass at least once a month go to confession at least once a year, compared to 6 percent of those who attend Mass less often. Nearly all Catholics (98 percent) who attend Mass less than once a month say they are only "involved a little" or "not involved at all" in their parish outside of attending Mass.[7]

6. It is also the case that the Catholic Church creates a "unique place" for receiving the Eucharist at Mass as a "Sacrament of sacraments" (USSC 1997, 341). This is a celebration that is at the "center of the Church's life" (374). Thus, the Church states, "the faithful are bound to participate in Mass" (583).

7. These results are based on CCP 2008, $N = 1,007$. This is one of the most comprehensive surveys CARA has conducted looking at different ways in which Catholics practice

Table 1. How important are each of the following aspects of Mass to you?

	Percentage responding "very"	
	Core (%)	Periphery (%)
Receiving the Eucharist	85	55
Feeling the presence of God	82	66
Prayer and reflection	78	62
Hearing the readings and the Gospel	74	47
Hearing the homily	64	31
Worshiping with other people	40	23
The music	31	22
The church environment and decorations	24	22

Source: CARA Catholic Poll (CCP) 2008, $N = 1,007$.

Using the Mass attendance proxy, we combine Fichter's notions of dormant and marginal groups as the *periphery*. These are those whom we can identify in a national survey as self-identifying as Catholic, but who are either not connected to parish life at all or attend Mass at Christmas and Easter and perhaps Ash Wednesday or Palm Sunday from time to time. We combine Fichter's notions of modal and nuclear groups as the *core*. These are the Catholics attending less than weekly but at least once a month; those attending every week; and those involved in activities, programs, and ministries in parish life beyond attending Mass.

As shown in Figure 2, the 2014 GSS estimated that there were as many core Catholics as there were people who had left the Catholic faith in the US adult population (12 percent each). Yet, larger than either group were Catholics in the periphery (14 percent). Due to limited sample sizes, the GSS is not suitable to look much further into these subgroups. Instead, I explore the data from CCP to further understand the differences between core and periphery Catholics in the twenty-first century.[8]

---

their faith. Overwhelmingly, these different aspects were found to be strongly related to frequency of Mass attendance.

8. GfK Custom Research (formerly Knowledge Networks) is a highly respected online polling firm that has assembled a national random probability sample of US households. Their surveys are regularly used in academic research that is published in peer-reviewed journals in a variety of fields. Contacted initially by phone or mail (ran-

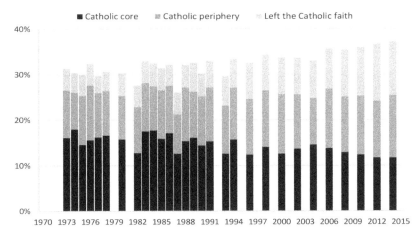

FIGURE 2. Catholic core, Catholic periphery, and formerly Catholic groups among US adults, 1973–2014. (*Source:* General Social Survey.)

The primary reasons that core and periphery Catholics give for being in their parishes differ somewhat. As shown in Table 1, core Catholics are most likely to cite receiving the Eucharist and feeling the presence of God as being the most important aspects of Mass to them. By comparison, peripheral Catholics cite feeling the presence of God and prayer and reflection as their two most important aspects. In all cases, core Catholics are more likely than peripheral Catholics to identify different aspects of Mass as very important. Perhaps most noteworthy is that peripheral Catholics are substantially less likely than core Catholics to view receiving the Eucharist (85 percent compared to 55 percent) or hearing the priest's homily (31 percent compared to 64 percent) as very important.

As shown in Table 2, there are also distinct differences for why core and peripheral Catholics say they are *not* in a parish on Sundays. Core Catholics are most likely to cite a busy schedule or lack of time, family

domly), each participating household in the GfK Custom Research panel agrees to be available for surveys. These surveys are completed by respondents on-screen using a computer, tablet, smartphone, or television. The panel is not restricted to existing computer or internet users. Those persons who are sampled and asked to join the GfK Custom Research panel are supplied with subsidized internet access or a MSN TV appliance to take the self-administered surveys. Others conduct internet panel surveys but do so using people who electively join their panels. This is a self-selected method of sampling and is not representative.

Table 2. If you missed Sunday Mass at least once in the last six months, how well
do each of the following explain, if at all, why you missed Mass?

	Percentage responding "very much"	
	Core (%)	Periphery (%)
Busy schedule or lack of time	23	17
Family responsibilities	22	12
Health problems or disability	22	9
I don't believe missing Mass is a sin	15	36
Conflict with work	14	9
Inconvenient Mass schedule	4	8
I am not a very religious person	4	25

Source: CARA Catholic Poll (CCP) 2008, $N = 1,007$.

responsibilities, or a health problem or disability. Peripheral Catholics are
most likely to say they don't believe missing Mass is a sin or that they are
not very religious.

As shown in Figure 3, one defining characteristic between core and
peripheral Catholics is simple religiosity. A majority of core Catholics
(66 percent) say their faith is the "most important part" or "among the
most important parts" of their daily life. Only 22 percent of peripheral
Catholics respond similarly.

Demographics of the Core and Periphery

In 2012, a CARA Catholic Poll related to interest in vocations included
an oversample of 503 self-identified Catholic teenagers ages fourteen to
seventeen. These data provide a glimpse at the near future of the faith. At
this age, young Catholics often express beliefs and behave in a manner
that is consistent with their parents' practice of the faith. Fifty-four percent
of the teens fit the definition of a core Catholic and 46 percent as a peripheral Catholic.

One of the biggest differences between core and peripheral Catholics
at this age is having been enrolled in some form of formal religious education. Among core Catholic teenagers, 32 percent attended a Catholic
primary school, and 21 percent attended a Catholic secondary school.
Additionally, 74 percent of core Catholic teens indicate that they have been

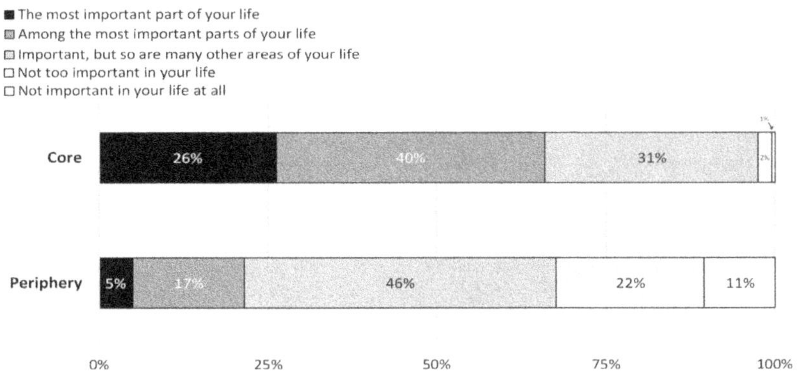

■ The most important part of your life
▣ Among the most important parts of your life
☐ Important, but so are many other areas of your life
☐ Not too important in your life
☐ Not important in your life at all

Core	26%	40%	31%	
Periphery	5% 17%	46%	22%	11%

0%   25%   50%   75%   100%

FIGURE 3. How important is your Catholic faith in your daily life? (*Source:* CARA Catholic Poll, 2008.)

enrolled in parish-based religious education at some point. As shown in Table 3, minorities of peripheral Catholic teens have been enrolled in these programs and institutions.

Core Catholic teens are much more likely than peripheral Catholic teens to have celebrated their First Communion (94 percent compared to 71 percent) and to have been confirmed (75 percent compared to 45 percent). Peripheral Catholic teens are generally less connected to parish life. Only 57 percent are in a household registered with a parish, compared to 84 percent of core Catholic teens. Only 19 percent of peripheral teens say it is somewhat or very important to their sense of being a Catholic to be involved in their parish, compared to 57 percent of core Catholic teens.

Peripheral teens may also be less likely to be involved in their broader communities. Sixty-seven percent of core Catholic teens indicated that they had ever volunteered to be a part of a service project to help people in need. By comparison, 52 percent of peripheral Catholic teens indicated this.

The roots of disengagement that lead Catholics out into the periphery appear to begin in Catholic youth. Children who are not in formal religious education and do not receive childhood sacraments are already patterning futures as peripheral Catholics—or perhaps even departures from the Church sometime in their later teens or twenties.

There are also notable findings in the demographics of adult Catholics in the periphery and core. Table 4 shows demographic breakdowns for

Table 3. Religious Education and Sacramental Practice of Catholic Teens (ages 14 to 17)

	Core (%)	Periphery (%)
Religious Education		
Has been enrolled in parish-based religious education (CCD)	74	49
Has attended a Catholic primary school	32	18
Has attended a Catholic secondary school	21	8
Sacramental Practice		
Has celebrated First Communion	94	71
Has been confirmed	75	45

Source: CARA Catholic Poll (CCP) 2012: Interest in Vocations, teen, $N = 503$.

periphery and core Catholics among adults in 2012 from a CCP related to religion and media use. As noted already in this volume, the racial and ethnic demography of Catholics in the United States has been shifting over the last forty years. Immigration from Latin America, Asia, and Africa have been important factors. In the GSS, the percentage of Catholics saying they were born outside the United States has increased from 13 percent in 1977 to 28 percent in 2014. And yet, in the 2012 CCP survey, there are not statistically significant differences by race and ethnicity in terms of likelihood of being in the core or periphery.[9]

Younger adult Catholics (under thirty) are more likely to be in the periphery than older Catholics. This finding is entirely consistent with the life cycle model of religiosity. About half of Catholics sixty or older are in the periphery, and half are in the core. Comparatively, nearly two-thirds of those under thirty are in the periphery, and more than a third are in the core.

Female adult Catholics are less likely than male adult Catholics to be in the periphery (52 percent compared to 61 percent), which is also consistent with existing models and research. Some of the biggest differences relate to marital status. Only about three in ten of those who are divorced, separated,

9. Due to limited sample size, respondents who identify as something other than non-Hispanic white or Hispanic/Latino must be collapsed into one "other" race and ethnicity category. Statistically significant differences between individuals in this subgroup may be evident in larger samples that would allow for comparisons.

Table 4. The Demography of the Catholic Periphery and Core in the
United States, 2012

	Periphery (%)	Core (%)
Race and Ethnicity		
Non-Hispanic white	57	43
Hispanic or Latino	57	43
Other	49	51
Age		
18 to 29	64	36
30 to 44	59	41
45 to 59	56	44
60 or older	51	49
Sex		
Male	61	39
Female	52	48
Marital Status		
Married or widowed	52	48
Divorced or separated	71	29
Single, never married	60	40
Unmarried, living with a partner	71	29
Region of Residence		
Northeast	65	35
South	58	42
West	53	47
Midwest	49	51

Source: CARA Catholic Poll 2012: Religion and Media Use, $N = 1{,}047$. Results for race and ethnicity are not statistically significant. All other comparisons are statistically significant ($p < .05$). There are fewer than 100 respondents among the following subgroups: other race and ethnicity ($n = 64$); divorced or separated ($n = 93$); unmarried, living with a partner ($n = 64$).

or unmarried and living with a partner are in the core. By comparison, 48 percent of those who are married or widowed are in the core, as are 40 percent of those who are single and have never married. These differences may be related to the welcome, or lack thereof, in the parish as perceived by parishioners who are experiencing divorce or cohabitation.

There are also regional differences; where Catholics reside matters. Sixty-five percent of those residing in the Northeast census region are in the periphery. There are many hypotheses that could be explored here. This could be a remnant of the clergy sex abuse crisis that began in 2002 in the New England area. It also could be a reflection of the more urban and coastal context, characterized by younger and more secular cultures.[10] At the other end of the spectrum, in the Midwest, about half of Catholics are in the core. Here again, plausible hypotheses come to mind. This is a region of smaller parishes and more rural communities. It also is home to more aging communities in the Rust Belt, and older Catholics may be a bigger factor here.

Conclusion

The future of the Catholic core and periphery is certainly not fixed on any distribution. One thing that has been consistent in CARA's national surveys and those conducted with parishioners in the pews is the proportions of adult Catholics who left the faith for a time and have now returned to self-identifying as Catholic. Across CARA surveys conducted since 2010, about 10 percent of respondents have said they are returned Catholics. Apparently, it is possible for the gravity of the core to pull some Catholics back out of the periphery.[11]

Yet, even with this empirical reality, the Church loses more Catholics to other faiths or to those adopting no religious affiliation at all. While the Catholic Church maintains its steady share of the population through immigration, reverts, and smaller numbers of adult converts, it maintains this stability with smaller shares of the Catholic population connected to parish life.[12]

10. Catholics residing in the Census Bureau's metropolitan statistical area (MSA) are more likely to be in the periphery than those not residing in one of these more high-population density areas, according to the 2012 CCP data (57 percent compared to 49 percent).

11. For some comparison, a 2015 poll conducted by the Pew Research Center estimates that 52 percent of those raised Catholic leave the Catholic faith at some point in their lives, with 11 percent of this population later returning to self-identify as Catholic at some point. Pew researchers refer to these respondents as "reverts."

12. Note, even as a share of a total population declines, if the overall population growth is sufficient, the total size of that population in absolute numbers may remain relatively unchanged.

References

Brenner, Phillip. 2011. "Identity Importance and the Overreporting of Religious Service Attendance: Multiple Imputation of Religious Attendance using American Time Use Study and the General Social Survey." *Journal for the Scientific Study of Religion*, 50 (1): 103–15.

———. 2012. "Investigating the Effect of Bias in Survey Measures of Church Attendance." *Sociology of Religion* 73 (4): 361–83.

Cox, Daniel, Robert P. Jones, and Juhem Navarro-Rivera. 2014. *I Know What You Did Last Sunday: Measuring Social Desirability Bias in Self-Reported Religious Behavior, Belief, and Identity*. Retrieved March 1, 2015. http://publicreligion.org/site/wp-content/uploads/2014/05/AAPOR-2014-Final.pdf

Fichter, Joseph H. 1951. *The Dynamics of a City Church*. Southern Parish, vol. 1. Chicago: University of Chicago Press.

———. 1954. *Social Relations in the Urban Parish*. Chicago: University of Chicago Press.

Gray, Mark. 2013. "When Surveys Lead to Sins: An Unholy Trinity." *1964* (blog), Center for Applied Research in the Apostolate. July 9, 2013. Retrieved March 1, 2015. http://nineteensixty-four.blogspot.com/2013/07/when-surveys-lead-to-sins-unholy-trinity.html.

Gray, M., M. Gautier, and M. Cidade. 2013. *Views from the Pews: Parishioner Evaluations of Parish Life in the United States*. Washington, DC: Center for Applied Research in the Apostolate and the Emerging Models of Pastoral Leadership.

Pew Research Center. 2015. *U.S. Catholics Open to Non-Traditional Families*. Washington, DC: Pew Research Center. http://www.pewresearch.org/wp-content/uploads/sites/7/2015/09/Catholics-and-Family-Life-09-01-2015.pdf.

The Official Catholic Directory. New Providence, N.J.: P. J. Kenedy & Sons.

Putnam, Robert, and David E. Campbell. 2010. *American Grace: How Religion Divides and Unites Us*. New York: Simon & Schuster.

Saad, Lydia. 2009. *Churchgoing Among U.S. Catholics Slides to Tie Protestants*. April 9, 2009. Washington, DC: Gallup. Retrieved March 1, 2015. http://www.gallup.com/poll/117382/church-going-among-catholics-slides-tie-protestants.aspx.

Stark, Rodney. 1999. "Secularization, R.I.P." *Sociology of Religion*, 60 (3): 249–73.

USSC (United States Catholic Conference). 1997. *Catechism of the Catholic Church: Revised in Accordance with the Official Latin Text Promulgated by Pope John Paul II*. 2nd ed. Washington, DC: United States Catholic Conference.

Part III: Race, Class, and Diversity in Parish Life

As we learned in Part I, for a long time, sociologists of religion attempted to build a theory of "THE" parish. This line of reasoning emphasizes similarity among Catholic parishes and the notion that one grand theory could explain behavior at any and all parishes. While we continue to look for patterns of similarity, the following essays advance the idea that we must also account for diversity within and across parishes. All too often, certain parishes and parish experiences get left out when we reference a "typical" Catholic parish. The reality of American Catholics and their communities today is that parishes differ in terms of who attends (e.g., variations by race, class, and region) as well as the style of Catholicism therein. This produces a multitude of parish cultures and lived interactions.

These next three essays (by Brett Hoover, Tia Noelle Pratt, and Mary Jo Bane) show us how different Catholics bring different backgrounds into parishes and how parishes themselves build diverse collective cultures (at times fraught with tension). It is for this reason that this book emphasizes a sociology of American parishes rather than of "THE" American parish.

Suggested Additional Readings

Bruce, Tricia. 2017. *Parish and Place: Making Room for Diversity in the American Catholic Church.* New York: Oxford University Press.

Cherry, Stephen M. 2014. *Faith, Family, and Filipino American Community Life.* New Brunswick, N.J.: Rutgers University Press.

Garces-Foley, Kathleen. 2007. *Crossing the Ethnic Divide: The Multiethnic Church on a Mission.* New York: Oxford University Press.

Hoover, Brett C. 2014. *The Shared Parish: Latinos, Anglos, and the Future of U.S. Catholicism.* New York: New York University Press.

Konieczny, Mary Ellen. 2013. *The Spirit's Tether: Family, Work, and Religion among American Catholics.* New York: Oxford University Press.

Matovina, Timothy. 2012. *Latino Catholicism: Transformation in America's Largest Church.* Princeton, N.J.: Princeton University Press.

Menjívar, Cecilia. 1999. "Religious Institutions and Transnationalism: A Case Study of Catholic and Evangelical Salvadoran Immigrants." *International Journal of Politics, Culture, and Society* 12 (4): 589–612.

Mooney, Margarita. 2009. *Faith Makes Us Live: Surviving and Thriving in the Haitian Diaspora.* Berkeley: University of California Press.

Nabhan-Warren, Kristy. 2005. *The Virgin of El Barrio: Marian Apparitions, Catholic Evangelizing, and Mexican American Activism.* New York: New York University Press.

Ospino, Hosffman. 2014. *Hispanic Ministry in Catholic Parishes: A Summary Report of Findings from the National Study of Catholic Parishes with Hispanic Ministry.* Boston: Boston College School of Theology and Ministry. http://www.bc.edu/content/dam/files/schools/stm/pdf/2014/HispanicMinistryinCatholicParishes_2.pdf.

5   Power in the Parish

BRETT C. HOOVER

Early on a Sunday afternoon in July, between the Spanish and Filipino Masses at Queen of Heaven parish, parishioners pass alongside a string of tables assembled on the long cement pathway toward the parking lot.[1] The tables sprawl out under tents in the summer sun. Some offer books and pamphlets—such as one table from the *Movimiento Cristiano Familiar*, or Christian Family Movement. Others sell food—parish school parents proffer donuts and candy. The tables are handled by representatives—nearly all either Latino or Filipino—from countless groups and ministries of the parish. Most conversations occur in English or Spanish, or some combination thereof. Beyond the tables are restrooms along the north wall of the church. Opposite the church is one of several other parish buildings, this one containing multiple meeting rooms used by the different groups and ministries. The building also contains a gift shop where people can buy candles to light inside the church, devotional manuals in English (aimed at Filipinos) and in Spanish, small images of saints and the Virgin Mary, and gifts for baptisms and other religious occasions.

Inside the church, several hundred immigrants from Mexico and Central America crowd the pews with their families. One of the parish's five weekend Spanish Masses—there are also six in English—is coming to a close. At this eleven-thirty Mass, some of the men are wearing palm-leaf straw cowboy hats characteristic of those worn in rural Mexico. So many people are in attendance that some people stand in the vestibule (foyer), and others spill into a side chapel dedicated to the Virgin of Guadalupe, an image of the Virgin Mary crucial to Mexican culture and nationhood. At other times during the day, women kneel here in private prayer. The priest at the Mass, an associate pastor around forty and a native of the Philippines, is speaking in clear Spanish to the congregation. He finishes

---

1. The names of all faith communities and people in this essay are pseudonyms.

the announcements and calls out for "un aplauso para Jesucristo," a round of applause for Jesus Christ. The people oblige enthusiastically. After the final song has ended and the priest has departed, the choir suddenly breaks out into "Las Mañanitas," the traditional Latin American birthday serenade.

As the Latino congregation exits, however, others are already entering the church for the next Mass, this one at one o'clock and in English with music in Tagalog. Those entering the narrow but capacious church are mostly Filipinos. There is little to no conversation between them and the Mexican and Central American people exiting. Some of the Filipino parishioners coming for the Mass enter through another side chapel next to the one devoted to Our Lady of Guadalupe. This one is formally known as the Chapel of All Saints, though some refer to it as the Filipino Room. As some enter the chapel, they kneel and pray for a few minutes before a large image of Divine Mercy, a Christ with multicolored beams of light coming from his heart. Near the front of the church, in the sacristy (a kind of "green room" for Mass), two Nigerian priests are donning green vestments—the color of Ordinary Time, the current liturgical season—in preparation for the Filipino Mass. One of the priests is older and well known to the Filipino community at Queen of Heaven. In another corner of the sacristy, two young Filipino men prepare slides of music lyrics in Tagalog on a laptop; they will project them on the back wall of the church during Mass. The Mass will draw a good crowd, but it will unfold with fewer people and much less ebullience than the previous Mass in Spanish.

Power Dynamics in Shared Space

The juncture between the eleven-thirty and one o'clock Masses at Queen of Heaven presents us with a sprawling, multifaceted, multicultural tableau. Many different religious practices as well as distinct ministries and parish organizations appear. Yet almost all—with the possible exception of the parish school—belong clearly to one or the other of the parish's chief ethnic communities. Latinos and Filipinos literally pass one another by as they make parallel use of common ecclesial space in the cultural work of constructing distinct experiences of Catholic worship—different in language, music, and even emotional expressiveness.

But this "passing one another by" is also metaphorical, emblematic of a broader Catholic experience of different ethnic and racial groups sharing parishes like Queen of Heaven. Much of the time, they do pass one another by, conducting a dance of avoidance in order to focus attention on modes of participation in parish life specific to their distinctive languages and cultures. Yet, when they have to negotiate their sharing of the ecclesial space, tensions and even conflict often appear. But more than simply the internal structure of the parish shapes these processes of avoidance, participation, and tension. They occur within the context of larger social environments and histories embedding unequal power between racial and ethnic groups. Parishes shared by different racial or ethnic groups operate as organizational spaces of contested power.

To demonstrate this phenomenon of the shared parish and the power dynamics that arise as a result, I present three case studies of shared parishes from different contexts across Southern California. Information about them was collected during a 2012–2014 research project.[2] One of the three parishes is Queen of Heaven, a megaparish with a reported weekend attendance of seven thousand that serves a largely Latino suburb of Los Angeles. The parish hosts English-speaking Mexican Americans, Spanish-speaking immigrants from Mexico and Central America, and a smaller community of Filipino immigrants and their families. The second parish, Holy Nativity, lies in a working-class neighborhood in south Los Angeles that is now majority Latino. Self-identifying as an African American parish for decades, Holy Nativity has also uneasily hosted a small community of Mexican, Central American, and South American immigrants since the late 1980s. Finally, the small parish of St. Martin de Porres, once a mission church for Mexican immigrants, is located in a tiny Southern California suburb. The largely Americanized descendants of those immigrants now form a single cultural-linguistic community with affluent whites and Asians in contradistinction to a small Spanish-speaking community made up of Mexican and some Central American immigrants who live in working class suburbs not far away.[3]

2. The research was supported by a grant and mentoring from the Congregational Studies Team.

3. The Shared Parish Research Project on which these accounts are based used familiar qualitative procedures such as participant observation, open-ended individual interviews,

Table 1. Parish characteristics

Parish	Location	Distinct cultural groups
Queen of Heaven	Working/middle-class Latino suburb	English-speaking Mexican Americans, Spanish-speaking Mexicans and Central Americans, Filipinos
Holy Nativity	Poor, urban neighborhood	African Americans, Spanish-speaking Latinos
St. Martin de Porres	Affluent suburb	English-speaking, Spanish-speaking

The term *shared parish* describes any Catholic parish that includes two or more distinct cultural groups (usually ethnic or racial groups), each possessing its own Masses and ministries yet sharing the same parish leadership and facilities. Shared parishes provide, on the one hand, safe space for relatively marginalized racial and ethnic groups to enact their distinct Catholic identities and for more powerful groups to retain theirs in the midst of demographic change. But they also compel all these groups to negotiate with one another over the details of sharing the facilities (Hoover 2014). This dynamic of safe space and negotiation translates to a social environment where the asymmetrical racial and ethnic power relationships of the larger society create distinct patterns of parallel participation, tension over resources, and episodic overt power struggles. This is now occurring in a significant proportion (though not the majority) of Catholic parishes across the United States. For example, in 2014, researchers found that a quarter of all US parishes intentionally served Hispanics, but 51 percent of the parishioners at such parishes

_____

and open-ended group interviews. The project relied on parish tours conducted by one or two representatives from each cultural community at each parish; participant observation at multiple Sunday Masses (in English and Spanish); individual interviews with staff members and other intermediaries between cultural groups (14 total, 3–6 at each parish); and group interviews with small numbers of parishioners from each distinct cultural group (8 total interviews, 2–3 at each parish). The work was done entirely by me and two graduate research assistants.

were not Hispanic (43 percent of them non-Hispanic whites) (Ospino 2014, 14).

In shared parishes, the broader power dynamics of racial and ethnic identity in society strongly influence relationships between groups. But the internal complexity of parishes themselves introduces yet another layer of intergroup power dynamics. As Nancy Ammerman points out in this volume, Catholic parishes tend to be much larger than other kinds of faith communities. Even a parish comprised entirely of one racial or ethnic group requires space for multiple ministries and organizations: religious education programs for children, liturgical ministers' groups, youth ministry groups, men's and women's organizations, devotional societies, and the like. Each intraparish ministry creates its own distinct organizational culture, some ministries larger in size than the average Protestant congregation.

Moreover, as Mark Gray writes in this volume, Catholic parishes serve both core and periphery Catholics with variations in belief and practices. Most parishes have several different Masses favoring distinct styles of worship, often catering to different musical tastes and age demographics. Indeed, with the potential exception of very small rural parishes, Catholic parishes in the United States exhibit such organizational complexity that they cannot properly be thought of as having a *single* congregational culture. All this suggests that the issues of parallel participation and power struggles evident in shared parishes are just as likely to be found in other parishes, even if the modes of participation and power struggles are shaped by different factors.

Here, I focus on two areas where the dynamics of power become readily evident inside shared parishes: language and leadership. I describe how each play out in Holy Nativity, St. Martin de Porres, and Queen of Heaven.

Scenes from the Language Barrier

The most visible manifestation of difference in shared parishes is undoubtedly the language barrier, and increasingly so. Nationally, some 29 percent of parishes in 2010 had Mass at least once a month in a language other than English, up from 22 percent in 2000 (Gray, Gautier, and Cidade 2011, 31). In the Archdiocese of Los Angeles, where the case study parishes are located, 76 percent of parishes have Mass in more than one language.[4] Ebaugh and Chafetz note how language segregates and evinces tensions in faith communities with multiple language groups (2000, 110–13).

Parishioners in all three parishes considered the language barrier a self-evident practical problem. At St. Martin de Porres, English-speaking parishioners admitted to not attending Spanish events on account of the language barrier. A young Latina working in the parish office at Queen of Heaven noted, "The language is a really big thing," mentioning that her mother does not speak English. Language differences encapsulate the monolingual communities within the parishes. What happens on the other side of the "barrier" remains hidden and obscure. Such a barrier creates and maintains distinct spaces where different practices of liturgy and ministry flourish and where different cultural standards for those practices are sustained. At Holy Nativity, Eulalia, an older, Spanish-speaking, long-time parishioner, said simply, "The language separates us," and other parishioners in the same group interview agreed. But she also elaborated, "We don't have the same culture; we don't celebrate the same feast days, and therefore in this aspect there has always been something that has separated us." Language is not just a practical dilemma, then, but also carries considerable symbolic value, both as a gateway to distinct cultural expressions of Catholicism and a conscious marker of identity associated with those distinct expressions (Isasi-Díaz 2004, 66–68; Ebaugh and Chafetz 2000, 109). Nowhere among the three case studies was this more apparent than at Holy Nativity, the African American and Latino parish. Only some adults in the Latino community and almost none in the African American community could speak both languages. As a result, very few people knew much about what happened in the other's Masses and ministries. Parishioners lived in a tense, bifurcated social world, and that world was shaped by the racial and ethnic history of both church and society.

4. By way of regional comparison, 70 percent of the parishes in the Brooklyn Diocese (New York), 51 percent of the parishes in the Chicago Archdiocese (Illinois), 41 percent of parishes in the Diocese of Charleston (South Carolina), and 12 percent of the parishes in the Archdiocese of Omaha (Nebraska) have Mass in more than one language.

Holy Nativity was a historically self-identifying African American parish that developed at a time when African American Catholicism as an identity was fragile and contested in Los Angeles. One middle-aged parishioner recalled the coming and going of gospel Masses in the 1960s and 1970s, depending on the pastor. This sense of fragile identity was exacerbated by declines in the number of African American parishes in Los Angeles, something the pastor and several parishioners mentioned repeatedly. Further complicating matters, the local neighborhood suffered from crime and violence—on Good Friday a couple of years back, for example, a local burger place was robbed at gunpoint. When longtime African American parishioners had the economic means and opportunity to move out, they generally did; their houses and apartments were then purchased or rented by immigrants from Latin America. Yet African Americans retained ownership in many local businesses and had a greater presence in civic leadership. The Los Angeles City Council representative for the district was African American. At the parish, few younger members of the African American community still lived in the neighborhood—most drove to church from a distance. Yet nearly all the Latino parishioners lived locally, many of them recent immigrants with fewer economic options.

The language barrier exposed the way these complex neighborhood power dynamics shaped life within the parish. Nearly all the parish employees (including ministry staff) were African American, and none of them spoke Spanish. African Americans also dominated the major parish committees at Holy Nativity, especially the parish pastoral council and the liturgy committee. These committees conducted business in English, with some translation. The white pastor, Fr. Mark, seemed universally appreciated for his energy and commitment, but he spoke a halting Spanish. The lack of Spanish competency among the pastoral leadership at Holy Nativity looked to some Latino parishioners like a sign that their community was barely valued or welcome. Thus, they found it expedient to "shelter in place," to withdraw into their own community and events and minimize their contact with the other community, a pattern observed in other shared parishes (Hoover 2014). This retreat is a strategic response to power differences. When asked why Latino leaders did not attend joint liturgy committee meetings, at least one Latino leader replied that they were at a distinct disadvantage in doing so, since the translation (usually by Fr. Mark) was never adequate to enable genuine participation.

While the lack of Spanish signaled to Latinos their inferior power position, its use proved a negative symbol for other members of the parish. Passionate commitment to the African American identity of the parish made any other identity assertion a source of contention (an issue illustrated by the mission statement controversy described in the next section). Indeed, in his study of liturgical music at Protestant multiracial churches, Gerardo Marti argues that "aggressive, unreflective commitment to enculturation may so veer in the trajectory of a particular non-Anglo culture that the church becomes unable to accommodate the cultural specifics of still other cultures as they move into the region" (2012, 107). At Holy Nativity, as in Marti's accounts, leaders assumed the normativity of English language dominance. Both Fr. Mark and several African American parishioners described the inability or unwillingness of parishioners to speak English at Holy Nativity as an obstinate refusal to adapt. The religious education director complained about a previous staff member who insisted that Latino parishioners could not speak any English. It infuriated some African American parishioners when Latinos refused to participate in parish liturgy committee meetings in English, even with translation available.

But more than simple English language dominance is at work here. As Tia Noelle Pratt observes in this volume, liturgy functions as one of the primary ecclesial spaces where African American Catholics conduct the cultural work of producing *their* distinct Catholic identity; liturgy meetings were where negotiations over common liturgical practices and joint liturgies took place. Of course, the *English* language was the linguistic gateway to this cultural experience. Ironically, even Spanish Masses at Holy Nativity incorporated characteristics of African American liturgical style, such as the use of choir robes and the announcement of birthdays and anniversaries at the end of Mass.

Language: From Barrier to Boundary

At Holy Nativity, language functioned not only as a practical barrier encapsulating two parish communities in their distinct cultural forms of Catholicism, but also as a fault line separating two different, embattled senses of identity. Language in shared parishes need not act as an impassible barrier, though. The dynamics at St. Martin de Porres and Queen of Heaven illustrate this.

At St. Martin de Porres, language functioned as an identity marker on its own, more salient at this parish than ethnicity or race. This was an outcome of the parish's unique history. St. Martin de Porres Church was built as a mission for Mexican Catholics in 1927, initially staffed by priests fleeing the *Cristiada*, that is, the 1920s war between the secularist Mexican government and Catholic peasants (Moreno Arayan 2007). By mid-century, the hilly area around the parish was a poor Latino barrio (Nicolaides 2002, 41). The St. Vincent de Paul Society, a Catholic charitable organization that assists the poor, purchased the land and built a "Mexican chapel" (History of Parish #6). Mexican American Catholics flourished there, and many current parishioners are their descendants. After World War II, the area grew whiter, and by the 1990s, the area around St. Martin de Porres had begun to gentrify and gain affluence (City Council 2000). By the 2010 census, the city was 80.9 percent non-Hispanic white and only 8.4 percent Hispanic.

At the time of the research project, the leadership of the English-speaking community at the parish consisted of mostly Anglos, a small number of Asians, and a larger group of third- or fourth-generation Mexican Americans who no longer speak Spanish. The Spanish community, in contrast, consisted almost entirely of Latin American immigrants and their families, a large number from Mexico. The members of this community did not live in the neighborhood; they drove or took the bus from nearby working-class suburbs. Some were relative newcomers; others had been in the parish for decades. I witnessed a sixty-fifth wedding anniversary celebration for a couple from one of the "original" families. Many longtime members of the Spanish community also spoke English and interacted regularly with people from the English-speaking community. The effect was a certain permeability between the English- and Spanish-speaking communities. I spoke in English to an usher at the Spanish Mass, and the Anglo music director led the Spanish choir (without any friction, according to members of the choir). The parish director of religious education, Virginia, the granddaughter and great-granddaughter of Mexican immigrants, coordinated the religious education programs in both languages, though she does not speak Spanish. She noted that even some of the parents who want their children to learn about the Catholic faith in Spanish can read and write only in English. The director of the Rite of Christian Initiation for Adults in English, Adriana, is a Mexican immigrant who coordinated Hispanic ministry for the parish in the years when there was no Spanish-speaking priest.

Still, the two language communities remained distinct and were never fully integrated with one another—language still functioned as a barrier, though a weaker one than at Holy Nativity. There was still incomprehension and minor tension regarding the "other" on each side. But the permeability demonstrates what Tomás Jiménez (2010) observes about "replenished ethnicity" among US Latinos, where even highly assimilated third- or fourth-generation Mexican Americans have access to the symbols and practices of ethnic identity as immigration continues. Jiménez points out that this replenishment can have ambiguous effects, depending on the conditions of reception. It can "draw down" the social status of Mexican Americans as they are associated in the mainstream with (undocumented) labor migrants. It can also firm up the status of Mexican Americans, making them into "good Mexicans" in contrast to recent immigrants. Jiménez found that these outcomes were more likely in places with a substantial time gap between waves of immigrants from Mexico. St. Martin de Porres, however, had seen continuous waves of immigrants, and not just from Mexico. More than a few parishioners went back and forth between the language communities, and longer-assimilated Mexican Americans explicitly identified in some way with more recent immigrants. Large numbers of Latinos in the parish spoke English and interacted comfortably with Anglo parishioners. Anglo parishioners, in turn, appeared more tolerant and even solicitous of parishioners in the Spanish-speaking community than the English-speaking parishioners at Holy Nativity.

At the third case study parish, Queen of Heaven, language rarely emerged as a significant topic of conversation at all. The eastern suburb where Queen of Heaven lies is majority Latino (80.1 percent Latino, according to the 2010 census) and has been since 1980 (when Latinos comprised 58 percent). The suburb also contains a small but significant Asian population (14.2 percent in 2010) and virtually no whites (US Census Bureau 1980, 2010). Nearly half of the population is foreign born; 83.6 percent speak a language other than English at home. Latinos occupy all the elected city government positions. More than half of city businesses are owned by Latinos, according to the 2007 Economic Census.

Language divides the Latino community at Queen of Heaven in the same way it does in the other parishes. As noted at the beginning of the essay, Latino parishioners gravitated toward particular Masses and ministries depending on their preference for English or Spanish. The pastor, Fr. Joe, described the concerns of the two linguistic groups as distinct. At the same time, in an overwhelmingly Latino suburb, the experience of replenished ethnicity among the US-born Latinos of the parish was more pronounced than it was even at St. Martin de Porres. Most English-speaking Latino parishioners were much closer to the immigration experience, and more spoke Spanish.

At Queen of Heaven, it was Filipino parishioners that stood out as different from the Latino mainstream, though not for reasons of language. Like the US-born Latinos in the parish, the vast majority of Filipino immigrants speak English very well. Filipinos did not need Spanish as a gateway to very different cultural expressions of Catholicism: parishioners pointed to the fact that Filipino and Latino Catholicism displayed a similar cultural style, with its focus on popular religion. "The way the Filipinos did the Divine Mercy celebration," one Central American woman said, "it was something beautiful." Despite these similarities, Filipinos, whose one o'clock Mass began in the late 1980s, remained a racial and ethnic minority at Queen of Heaven. Filipino parishioners' minority status at the predominantly Latino parish contrasted with their more affluent, higher social status both locally and nationally (Migration Policy Institute 2014; Ong and Azores 1994, 116). This combination of minority parish status and higher social status led to interesting exchanges in the parish, such as when Filipino parishioners donated items for use in youth ministry but required the help of Spanish-speaking Eucharistic ministers at Mass. Yet, even with this higher social status, many Filipinos felt out of sorts in the parish—that is, until a Filipino parochial vicar was assigned to Queen of Heaven. Leadership emerged as one of the major ways in which the cultural work of distinguishing Filipino Catholic identity was accomplished at Queen of Heaven, a topic we turn to next.

Priests, Polity, and Shared Parishes

As Nancy Ammerman points out in this volume, congregational leadership works largely through the production of congregational culture. "As producers of congregational culture," Jackson Carroll argues, "clergy give shape to a congregation's particular way of being a congregation—that is, to the beliefs and practices characteristic of a particular community's life and ministry" (2006, 25). Ammerman raises needed questions about how cultural production works in the larger, internally diverse contexts of Catholic parishes. This may prove particularly vexing to understand in shared parishes. Research on multiracial congregations suggests that those that persist usually possess a pastoral leadership who shapes congregational culture according to a vision of diversity (Garces-Foley 2007; Emerson 2006; and Marti 2005). But in a large Catholic parish, what ought leaders do to shape *multiple* congregational cultures operating in a parallel but interconnected fashion?

In the three case study parishes, we encountered a significant class of lay leaders who did much of the cultural work of reproducing practices and beliefs in Sunday liturgy as well as a host of ministries, movements, and organizations. Almost all tended to focus their attention in one community or another (many in one ministry or another), and they were anything but passive. Yet lay leaders—professional or volunteer—did this work with a great deal of deference for the pastor and other priests, an attitude that many implicitly connected with Catholic identity. One elderly Latino parishioner at St. Martin de Porres hesitated even to lead my research assistant on a parish tour until his priest showed strong support for the idea. At Holy Nativity, tales of conflict between the two cultural communities never included an indictment of Fr. Mark, and the harshest words were saved for those who spread rumors about the previous pastor.

This kind of deference demonstrates respect for the "symbolic presence" of the priest. This is not to say that such deference was universal. At Queen of Heaven, an elderly Filipina parishioner, Fe, spoke frankly about damage she saw as having been inflicted by her former pastor: "The priest comes and goes, but it's just sad, but it's just sad that [he] ruined and scattered a lot [of parishioners]. When you've lost trust, it's hard, and people are already at other parishes. It's hard to get out to start all over. Six years so long." On the other hand, the pastor who succeeded him, Fr. Joe, very quickly surprised and energized parishioners with his hands-on approach, vision for the parish, ability to listen, and support for a great variety of organizations and ministry groups across the multiple cultural communities of the parish.

It is clear that polity and church governance affects the process of leadership as cultural production in Catholic parishes. Takayama and Cannon found that among Protestant denominations, episcopal polity led to a greater power differential within the denomination (1979). At the parish level in Catholicism, canon law invests nearly all deliberative power at the parish in the pastor, assigned by the bishop (Coriden, Green, and Heintschel 1985, 515–32). Scott Appleby has shown how, in the mid-twentieth century, this led to the "ombudsman" priest, the priest who acted by himself but on behalf of his parishioners in nearly every sphere of parish life. Appleby sees this as the outcome of the priest's symbolic and functional presence in the parish (1989). Priests represent the sacred in a way almost extrinsic to their personal qualities, and that symbolic representation is embedded in Catholic beliefs—sometimes contested—about divinely appointed structures of Church governance. As Richard Schoenherr put it, "In providing authoritative and legitimate access to creed, code, and cult, the parish priest serves as the hierarchical link necessary for preserving the Church's authentic hierophanic traditions" (2002, 64).

Priests also serve in a number of practical leadership roles whose success depends on their personal skills. Following Vatican II reforms, Appleby argues, this combination of symbol and function created an image of the priest as "orchestra leader": "He is no longer the only one who knows the score, but he interprets it for the musicians and *by his presence during the performance* signifies the group as a whole" (1989, 91; italics mine).

This accurately describes, to a greater or lesser degree, the pastors of the three shared parishes examined here, with some important caveats. While none of the three pastors saw themselves as the "ombudsman priest" acting on their own, they made different kinds of efforts to persuade parishioners in different constituencies of their vision for the parish. The most successful of the three focused particular attention on ensuring that he and his priests served each of the ethnic communities within the parish without favoritism (Hoover 2017). He demonstrated through their symbolic and functional roles that the power dynamics embedded in the larger society would not fully determine power relationships within the parish.

The Orchestra Leaders

Perhaps the most ombudsman-like was Fr. Pat, the pastor at St. Martin de Porres. By his own and others' accounts, he had concentrated much of his attention during his tenure on fundraising and the renovation of the church and other parish buildings. Appleby notes that the ombudsman model worked well with the "brick and mortar" pastors of the early to mid-twentieth century (1989). Though space renovation often evokes conflict in churches, tellingly, little commentary emerged in interviews. This was true even as a leader described the church renovation as "led by the English-speaking part of the community." In reality, Fr. Pat seems to have made most of the decisions about the renovation himself, and he did move the large image of the Virgin of Guadalupe, a potential point of controversy for a largely Mexican Latino community. But she remains in a prominent place within the church, and Fr. Pat's renovation uncovered evidence of her connection to the original image in Mexico City (writing in Spanish indicated that the image had been touched to the original). By all accounts, the condition of the entire worship space improved markedly. Fr. Pat functioned more like the orchestra leader in recruiting a young Mexican-born priest, Fr. Santiago, to work with the Spanish-speaking community, which he saw as long neglected.

Holy Nativity was perhaps the most challenging orchestra to lead, especially for a white priest in a majority African American parish. Fr. Mark often chose to lead from behind the scenes, surrendering leadership roles in preaching to his deacons and deferring to lay commentators at the beginning and end of Mass. But Fr. Mark's biggest challenge as an orchestra leader was leading the parish through a conflict centered on the revision of the parish's mission statement. The conflict began at a parish pastoral council meeting. Fr. Mark recalled to me what happened:

> The first paragraph just said who we are. "A Roman Catholic community rooted in a rich tradition of African-American spirituality. We hear the call which Pope Paul VI spoke to all the sons and daughters of Africa: 'You must give your gift of blackness to the whole church.'" That's where it stopped. But that's not a mission statement. That's just a statement of who we are. So we put in the second paragraph, and as soon as the word "Hispanic" was put in, it blew up.

The main argument over the inclusion of the word "Hispanic" occurred between different African American factions within the parish. Some African Americans saw the parish's black Catholic identity as solid enough to withstand a more inclusive mission statement. Others worried this was a "watering down" of the parish's identity. They saw this as part of a larger (and dramatic) pattern of African American parishes in Los Angeles losing their identity over demographic change. (The director of religious education said, "We saw ourselves falling into oblivion.") African American friends of a Latino parishioner told him that the Hispanic community would displace blacks at Holy Nativity just as they had been displaced from other churches. Meanwhile, Latino parishioners, working from a relative position of powerlessness, tried not to stoke the fires, some arguing that the mission statement should say only that this was a Roman Catholic community of faith.

The mission statement incident demonstrates how, even in a bifurcated context where power favors one of the two groups, the broader social context shapes the dynamics of power within parishes. At Holy Nativity, Latinos tried to avoid embroiling themselves in the mission statement controversy, feeling their lack of power. They were successful in this, given that the controversy reanimated longstanding differences. And though African Americans were the dominant group at the parish, they carried a long history of discrimination (several parishioners grew up in the segregated South). Many felt that they remained disadvantaged vis-à-vis the larger society and especially in Catholic Los Angeles, where Latinos had become the majority group, numerically. This motivated opposition to the explicit mention of a less powerful group in the parish identity statement.

True to his commitment as orchestra leader empowering the faithful, Fr. Mark did not attempt to resolve the crisis by fiat, despite clear deference in the parish to the role of the pastor. He was, no doubt, sensitive to the implications of a white pastor imposing a solution on a parish full of people of color. Dialogue and arguments went on for months. Ultimately unable to coordinate a solution acceptable to all parties, Fr. Mark turned to the centralized power structure of Catholic Church governance. He contacted the bishop. The bishop invited the parish council to come to his office, where he would "help them resolve" the conflict. He instructed them that the mission statement had to describe the parish's real makeup today, not any long-term ambitions to remain a black Catholic parish. Accordingly, "Hispanic" stayed in the mission statement and everyone accepted it, albeit with resentment. At the end, a Latino leader in the parish noted to me in Spanish, "The important thing is that it was resolved.

But in order that it could say, 'African [Americans] and Hispanics,' it cost us that the word 'Hispanics' appeared here. It cost a lot."

The most successful orchestra leader among the three pastors was Fr. Joe at Queen of Heaven. Everyone interviewed there agreed that, since the beginning of Fr. Joe's tenure, there had been positive rapport between the cultural communities at Queen of Heaven. The Filipino community, in particular, was operating more confidently. Fr. Joe told me that his explicit strategy there was to engender trust in his leadership as inclusive, that is, without favoritism (Hoover 2017). He strategically deployed his own value as a symbolic person in service of the cultural production of a shared vision of a harmonious, ethnically inclusive parish. He put it in characteristically blunt fashion, saying, "The Filipinos, you know, still cry when I spend too much time with the Spanish-speaking, and the Spanish-speaking will cry if I spend too much time with the Filipinos, (chuckle) but that's okay. . . . I like it that way."

Both leaders and parishioners confirmed that they saw Fr. Joe in this inclusive way. "Father's really good at inviting everyone . . . he doesn't like separation at all," said a parish secretary. The youth minister noted, "I think Father is really good at integrating himself into all cultures. . . . I've always heard that before . . . well, one priest favors this community better, or one priest favors *this* community better." A Filipina parishioner pointed out, "The energy that he puts into the activities in the church that he wants, you can feel how much he wants to unify both cultures." Fr. Joe proved successful not only at articulating this inclusive vision for the parish, but in drawing others into it.

Upon arriving at Queen of Heaven, Fr. Joe called a town hall meeting with Filipino parishioners and listened to their concerns. He heard their strong desire for a Filipino parochial vicar, and he managed to recruit one to the parish within a few months. At the time of my interviews, he was forming a Filipino leadership group to replace one that had petered out some years before. A high-energy man by nature (many people commented on his speedy manner of speaking), he would visit ministries and groups from all the cultural communities. He blessed and supported the initiatives of parishioners, whether it be Filipino parishioners seeking to erect a new statue of the Virgin Mary or the Spanish-speaking going out to the neighborhoods to tell people about the parish. All this remained crucial to his campaign of persuading all the different groups and ministries of the various cultural communities that they mattered and had influence in the parish.

Of course, it was difficult to persuade people that power in a parish did not function as a zero-sum game. Whenever a lay leader began to operate out of that assumption, either Fr. Joe or one of the other staff members would quickly intervene (Hoover 2017). Fr. Joe noted this, and his secretary confirmed it: "People's pride get[s] in the way of . . . them being on, you know, board with unity. It's like, no, I want to do it my way. And they'll start to try to get people in with them. . . . Fr. Joe's been doing pretty good at . . . nipping those right away. . . . When something is happening or whatever, he just calls them in. And once you get confronted face to face, it's hard to be like, 'I'm not talking about you; we're not doing this.' So, he'll be like, 'What's the issue? What's happening?'"

Though this sounds like a self-evident victory of persuasion, the interventions worked because through them, the pastor (or delegates) brought both his symbolic presence and the authority church governance afforded him to bear on the situations. Even more difficult interventions apparently succeeded, as when Fr. Joe insisted that his assistant priests (both now Filipinos) intervene with elders in that community, a duty both priests found difficult but nevertheless performed (Hoover 2017). The priests that assisted Fr. Joe cooperated so consistently with him in promoting the message of a parish without favoritism that he remarked, "I think . . . that our priest house is very united right now. . . . It's not one of these houses where they try to play us off on each other. Everybody knows what's going on. And I think that's what's caught everybody by surprise."

Conclusion: Power in the Parish

Even though they remain a minority among American Catholic parishes, shared parishes serve as ambiguous sites where much of the ongoing demographic transformation of American Catholicism occurs in practice. We measure demographic change in statistics at the macro-level and experience it interpersonally at the micro-level. But as the editors of this volume write, the parish constitutes one of the organizational forms at the *meso*-level. In shared parishes, we can see the power dynamics of race and ethnicity working themselves out in American life. In my previous work, I described the power dynamics involved in the intercultural avoidance and negotiations of Mexican immigrant and Euro-American communities in a shared parish in the Midwest (Hoover 2014). Here, I have described how the power dynamics of race and ethnicity in larger society play out in distinct ways within parishes.

Language and leadership stir these power dynamics, in different forms, in parishes. Among the three case study parishes, we found one, Holy Nativity, whose language conflicts brought into relief the contentious fault lines that divided African Americans from Latinos Americans. Both held loosely united cultural expressions of Catholicism, each with an embattled sense of identity produced by historical and contemporary expressions of discrimination in church and society. The pastor, a white priest with imperfect Spanish, strove to coordinate harmonious power relationships within the parish but found himself thwarted by the complexity of the situation. In one of the bigger tests of his leadership, he had to rely on the hierarchical intervention of the bishop.

St. Martin de Porres demonstrated that, under conditions of replenished and permeable ethnicity, language can serve as a more salient boundary marker than race or ethnicity, even in a nation riven by both. Even so, the Spanish-speaking Latino community continued to live in the shadow of the English-speaking community, and the "ombudsman" style of the priest-pastor may have perpetuated that.

Finally, the megaparish of Queen of Heaven demonstrated even more permeability between English- and Spanish-speaking Latinos, such that the relatively affluent community of Filipino Catholics emerged as the minority ethno-cultural group. There, however, the endless energy of the pastor and his razor-sharp focus on the cultural production of an inclusive vison for the whole parish resulted in a more equitable distribution of power. Table 2 summarizes these patterns of similarity and divergence across all three parishes.

My hope is that this case study analysis sheds light on the power dynamics of Catholic parishes. After all, shared or not, Catholic parishes in the United States are complex organizations where multiple communities coexist and interact. Those interactions produce, perpetuate, and challenge power dynamics. In shared parishes, the cultural work of constructing Catholic identity necessarily involves deploying distinct cultural

Table 2. Parish similarities and differences

Parish	Distinct cultural groups	Place of language	Leadership issues
Holy Nativity	African Americans, Spanish-speaking Latinos	Contentious fault line between racial/ethnic communities	Unsuccessful "orchestra leader" pastor forced to hierarchical intervention
St. Martin de Porres	English-speaking, Spanish-speaking	Boundary line between groups of unequal power	"Ombudsman-like" pastor
Queen of Heaven	English-speaking Latinos, Spanish-speaking Latinos, Filipinos	Second language common among most parishioners, language minor issue	Successful "orchestra leader" pastor

expressions of Catholicism shaped by broader power dynamics of race, ethnicity, and language. My conclusions here raise new questions about, for example, perceptions of decline among black Catholics and the power positioning of Filipino and other Asian Catholics in diverse parishes.

Once we allow that all Catholic parishes (even monolingual and monocultural ones) possess considerable internal complexity, other internal divisions come into view. What shapes the power dynamics in these parishes? Do parochial school parents battle with retirees in Anglo parishes? Do the parachurch apostolic movements so ubiquitous in Latino parishes—the Catholic charismatic renewal, Cursillo, *Jovenes para Cristo*—compete for resources and priestly attention? Structures of Church governance—especially the bishop and the diocese—also matter if we wish to understand how parishes work and who has influence within them. Church governance positions the pastor and priests in a dual role: priests operate from day-to-day within the myriad internal social networks of the parish and must shape multiple organizational cultures to be effective "cultural producers." Yet they also arrive with a hierarchical mandate from the bishop, with the symbolic authority of the priesthood, and with nearly limitless canonical authority. We need to better understand how this shapes the experience of different groups of parishioners—core and periphery, ethnic and racial, from different ministries and movements—and how it affects power dynamics in the complex organization we call the Catholic parish.

References

Appleby, R. Scott. 1989. "Present to the People of God: The Transformation of the Roman Catholic Parish Priesthood." In *Transforming Parish Ministry: The Changing Roles of Catholic Clergy, Laity, and Women Religious,* edited by J. P. Dolan, R. S. Appleby, P. Byrne, and D. Campbell, pp. 1–107. New York: Crossroad.

Carroll, Jackson. 2006. *God's Potters: Pastoral Leadership and the Shaping of Congregations.* Grand Rapids, Mich.: William B. Eerdmans.

Coriden, James A., Thomas J. Green, and Donald Heintschel, eds. 1985. *The Code of Canon Law: Text and Commentary.* New York: Paulist Press.

Ebaugh, Helen Rose, and Janet Saltzman Chafetz. 2000. *Religion and the New Immigrants: Continuities and Adaptations in Immigrant Congregations.* Walnut Creek, Calif: Altamira Press.

Emerson, Michael O. 2006. *People of the Dream: Multiracial Congregations in the United States.* Princeton, N.J.: Princeton University Press.

Garces-Foley, Kathleen. 2007. *Crossing the Ethnic Divide: The Multiethnic Church on a Mission.* New York: Oxford University Press.

Gray, Mark M., Mary L. Gautier, and Melissa A. Cidade. 2011. *The Changing Face of U.S. Catholic Parishes.* Emerging Models of Parish Leadership Project, Center for Applied Research in the Apostolate (CARA), Georgetown University. Washington, DC: National Association for Lay Ministry. Retrieved April 2015. http://cara.georgetown.edu/CARAServices/Parishes%20Phase%20One.pdf.

Hoover, Brett C. 2014. *The Shared Parish: Latinos, Anglos, and the Future of U.S. Catholicism.* New York: New York University Press.

———. 2017. "No Favoritism: Effective Collaborative Leadership Practices in Multicultural Parishes." In *Collaborative Parish Leadership: Contexts, Models, Theology,* edited by William A. Clark and Daniel Gast, pp. 103–23. New York: Lexington.

Isasi-Díaz, Ada María. 2004. *En la Lucha/In the Struggle: Elaborating a Mujerista Theology.* Minneapolis, Minn.: Fortress Press.

Jiménez, Tomás R. 2010. *Replenished Ethnicity: Mexican Americans, Immigration, and Identity.* Berkeley: University of California Press.

Marti, Gerardo. 2005. *A Mosaic of Believers: Diversity and Innovation in a Multiethnic Church.* Bloomington: Indiana University Press.

———. 2012. *Worship Across the Racial Divide: Religious Music and the Multira-cial Congregation.* New York: Oxford University Press.

Migration Policy Institute. 2014. *The Filipino Diaspora in the United States.* Prepared for the Rockefeller-Aspen Institute Diaspora Program. July 2014. Washington, DC: Migration Policy Institute. Retrieved April 2015. http://www.migrationpolicy.org/research/select-diaspora-populations-united-states.

Moreno Arayan, Alex. 2007. *Mexican Americans in Hermosa and Redondo Beach.* Images of America. San Francisco: Arcadia Publishing.

Nicolaides, Becky M. 2002. *My Blue Heaven: Life and Politics in the Working-Class Suburbs of Los Angeles, 1920–1965.* Chicago: University of Chicago Press.

Ong, Paul M. and Tania Azores. 1994. "Asian Immigrants in Los Angeles: Diversity and Divisions." In *The New Asian Immigration in Los Angeles and Global Restructuring,* edited by P. M. Ong, E. Bonacich, L. Cheng, pp. 100–130. Philadelphia: Temple University Press.

Ospino, Hosffman. 2014. *Hispanic Ministry in Catholic Parishes: A Summary Report of Findings from the National Study of Catholic Parishes with Hispanic Ministry.* Boston: Boston College School of Theology and Ministry.

Schoenherr, Richard A. 2002. *Goodbye Father: The Celibate Male Priesthood and the Future of the Catholic Church,* edited by D. Yamane. New York: Oxford University Press.

Takayama, K. Peter, and Lynn Weber Cannon. 1979. "Formal Polity and Power Distribution in American Protestant Denominations. *Sociological Quarterly* 20 (3): 321–32.

United States Census Bureau. 1980. *Decennial Census of Population and Housing.* https://www.census.gov/programs-surveys/decennial-census/decade.1980.html

United States Census Bureau. 2010. *Decennial Census of Population and Housing.* https://www.census.gov/programs-surveys/decennial-census/decade.2010.html.

Archival Sources

"History of Parish #6." N.d. History file, St. James parish collection, Archives of the Archdiocese of Los Angeles. San Fernando, Calif.

City Council of Hermosa Beach. 2000. Minutes of the Study Session of the Housing Element of the City's General Plan, September 19, 2000, City Hall Council Chambers.

6 Liturgy as Identity Work in Predominantly African American Parishes

TIA NOELLE PRATT

> The Black presence within the American Catholic Church is a precious witness to the universal character of Catholicism.
>
> —"What We Have Seen and Heard": A Pastoral Letter on Evangelization from the Black Bishops of the United States

American Catholicism and the African American religious experience are both well documented across a number of disciplines. Black Catholics, in particular, occupy a unique social space at the intersection of religious practice and the black American experience. But black Catholics' experiences—and their parishes—have received far too little attention from sociologists.

One of the main reasons for black Catholics' limited place in research is the prevailing notion that being black *and* Catholic is so disparate that there must not be enough black Catholics to merit inclusion in the discussion (Du Bois [1903] 1994; Gilkes 2001). The perceived incompatibility between Catholicism's emphasis on ritual and symbols and the exuberance that typifies the African American religious experience results in a mischaracterization of black and Catholic as fundamentally incompatible (Black Bishops of the United States 1984; Braxton 1988; Braxton 2014; McGreevy 1996; Ochs 1990). This misperception is partially a result of the Catholic Church's overtly racist past, typified by segregated communion lines and the outright denial of access to the priesthood for black men (Ochs 1990; Magnoni 2015). These overt acts of an earlier era have given way to more subtle but equally systemic instances of racism today, including tacit disregard from episcopal leadership and disproportionate impact of church closings and mergers (Otterman 2014; Schenk 2015; Schlossberg 2015; Hahn 2018).

Despite these obstacles, black Catholics continue to pursue full incorporation into the Church's fold. This essay—part of a larger, ongoing work—asserts that while the approximately three million black Catholics in the United States are indeed a minority, their historically rich past and dynamic present make them an integral part of both American Catholicism and the African American religious experience. This essay explores how black Catholics in predominantly African American parishes use liturgy—the principal form of religious expression for Roman Catholics—to actively combine their dual heritages in forming identity (Hellwig 2002).

Because the black Catholic community is rich and diverse, any attempt to incorporate all experiences under one umbrella would not give any one group the attention that each rightly deserves. For that reason, this study concentrates on the group often referred to as "black American" Catholics. This group has the longest history in the United States. Its cultural ties are linked to the United States more so than to the Caribbean or African continent, as is the case for many recent black Catholic immigrants. Furthermore, this is the group that directly experienced segregated communion lines and other overt acts of racism within the Roman Catholic Church. It is important for scholars and pastoral leaders to know how black American Catholics have used the survival skills passed down through generations in an effort to overcome obstacles that have thwarted their efforts to obtain full inclusion in the Church. Predominantly African American parishes have a history that is complex and often deeply painful. There is no one, specific way that these parishes came into existence. Some were founded specifically by black Catholics to affirm their culture and presence within the Church, while others, such as those described in this essay, developed over time as the racial demographics of the surrounding neighborhood changed (Cressler 2017; Hahn 2018; McGreevy 1996). A third group developed out of the nineteenth-century national parish model not as means of cultural affirmation but as a way to keep blacks out of already established white churches (Davis and Phelps 2003; Ochs 1990).

Black Catholics—whether they belong to predominantly black, mixed race, or predominantly white parishes—are stakeholders in the broader discussion of the African American religious experience, but they should not be conflated with "the black Church." Scholars of the African American religious experience from Du Bois ([1903] 1994) to Lincoln and Mamiya

(1990) to Gilkes (2001) have dismissed black Catholics when discussing the black Church. Catholics may appear in a conceptual definition of the black Church but not in an operational one. Lincoln and Mamiya make this point concretely in their definition of the black Church:

> In general usage any black Christian person is included in "the Black Church" if he or she is a member of a black congregation. In this study, however, while we recognized that there are predominantly black local churches in white denominations such as the United Methodist Church, the Episcopal Church, and the Roman Catholic Church, among others, we chose to limit our operational definition of "the Black Church" to those independent, historic, and totally black controlled denominations which were founded after the Free African Society of 1787 and which constituted the core of black Christians. Today the seven major black denominations with a scattering of smaller communions make up the body of the Black Church. (Lincoln and Mamiya 1990, 1)

By this rubric, black Catholics are excluded from the black Church entirely. Moreover, while musical and aesthetical similarities exist between black Catholics and their Protestant brethren, these do not overcome theological and doctrinal differences. For these reasons, it would be inappropriate and even disrespectful to force a discussion of black Catholics into the realm of the black Church.

Studying Identity Work at Black Catholic Parishes

Music, the homily, social programs, and church aesthetics give shape to black Catholics' identity as black Catholics. Their identity is distinct from those of Catholics from other racial and ethnic groups, as well as from blacks who are not Catholic. The ongoing identity work of black Catholics may be interpreted as "owning" (Dillon 1999), whereby individuals holding seemingly disparate identities "own" their multiple identities and build a community where those identities can be expressed freely. Owning happens when community building occurs through participation in rituals. The use of symbols brings multiple, seemingly disparate identities together cohesively through liturgy. This is important, because "not to maintain the Mass's distinctive characteristics could be taken as indicating tacit acknowledgment that what they are doing is 'not really' Catholic and never could be authentically Catholic" (Dillon 1999, 142).

Another means of interpreting the identity work observed at predominantly African American parishes is "sifting," or "the process of constructing a fairly stable, biographical identity that incorporates aspects of two or more potentially conflicted identities" (Dufour 2000, 94). The process of sifting involves individuals taking on only parts of an identity and sifting out those that are unsuitable (94–95). This happens when "the practices and attitudes which are sifted into the mix of . . . identity define what that identity means" (97).

In black parishes, these different routes of identity work (both owning and sifting) are aspects of congregational culture that is produced and maintained through a congregation's "activities, artifacts, and accounts" (Ammerman 1998, 84). Black Catholics' seemingly disparate identities come together through ritual. Understanding these elements of congregational life (or, in the case of Catholics, parish life) allows us to see how congregations build a sense of community, document their identity, and immortalize institutional memory. In this way, a congregation's culture consists of what members do together, the things they make, and the stories they tell, with ritual as a primary focal element. Black Catholics engage in "parish culture production."

Both owning and sifting can happen through ritual, a process in which "our sense of who we are is shaped by what we do, what we make, and how we talk about ourselves" (Ammerman 1998, 84). While owning is important for conceptualizing how identity work can occur, sifting and parish culture production are the theoretical constructs best suited for the current study. These constructs provide a means for understanding and articulating *what* happens at black parishes (vis-à-vis sifting) and *how* it happens (vis-à-vis parish culture production).

Understanding Liturgical Styles in Black Catholic Parishes

Black Catholics' identity work through liturgy is a dynamic process that uses sifting to bring together elements of Roman Catholic tradition and the African American religious experience in the parish setting. Scholars have asserted the centrality of liturgy as well as cultural expression through liturgy in the black Catholic community (Davis 1988; Eugene 1998; Rivers 1998; Rowe 1994; Whitt 1998). For black Catholics who have both the freedom and desire to bring cultural tools into liturgy, Mass is more than just a weekly ritual required of all Roman Catholics. It is a means of forming and expressing a specific, parish-based identity. Different parishes and even different Masses within each parish have their own tenor and flavor based on the atmosphere of the parish and the constituency of each Mass.

Here, I identify three liturgical styles (traditionalist, spirited, and gospel) to articulate how sifting occurs in parishes and how it results in parish culture production. All three styles incorporate music, homilies, and church aesthetics to achieve a level of sifting appropriate for the respective communities and a cultural expression that leaves parishioners satisfied in their worship experience.

The traditionalist liturgy style is so named because it is the most dominant liturgical form in the United States and is closely associated with Catholics of European descent. Because of the traditionalist liturgy style's dominance in the United States, it has transcended its European origins and can be found in parishes whose members are not of European descent. Hallmarks of this style include rather short homilies and songs from the missalette—a book commonly found in Catholic churches that contains scripture readings for the liturgical year and a selection of well-known hymns.

The traditionalist style is most likely to appeal to Catholics with conservative liturgical preferences. In predominantly black parishes, this style is more likely to be found at Saturday vigil Masses or Masses very early on Sunday morning. Attendance at these Masses is often dominated by senior citizens—a group less likely to want a worship experience that is noticeably different from what they have known throughout their lives.

Masses in the spirited liturgy style bear similarity to the traditionalist liturgy style but incorporate a livelier means of expression. This livelier expression manifests itself most concretely in the type of music used during liturgy and a more animated style of preaching. Masses in this style frequently incorporate songs from the *Lead Me, Guide Me* hymnal (GIA Publications 1987), which has played a pivotal role in incorporating black culture into liturgy since it was first introduced more than thirty years ago. The spirited liturgy style seeks a deeper and more palpable engagement with parishioners than is found in the traditionalist liturgy style.

Finally, the gospel liturgy style invokes the style of worship most often associated with congregations in the black Church. It specifically targets the African American experience by using preaching, music, and church aesthetics to invoke African American history and a clear African American heritage while connecting that history and heritage to Catholicism. Masses in the gospel liturgy style are more likely to use gospel hymns not found in the missalette or any hymnal. The homilies at these Masses use a lengthier and more animated preaching style that engages the parishioners through the call-and-response technique. Priests deliver their homily from the center aisle rather than from a podium. This liturgy style offers the most overt example of how sifting and parish culture production occurs within the realm of black Catholics.

No one liturgical style is more authentically black or truly Catholic than another. Each meets the mandate from the Black Catholic Bishops of the United States (1984) to be "authentically Black" and "truly Catholic." Each works for those who attend these liturgies and belong to these parishes. These descriptions are not intended to be rigid boxes, either, with every Mass fitting into one box or another. Rather, these descriptions of liturgy styles are best understood as a continuum: the categories of traditionalist, spirited, and gospel serve as benchmarks along a spectrum. Music and homilies differ across categories. Aesthetics, on the other hand, remain constant in parishes offering more than one style. It would be impractical to alter aesthetic features between Masses.

The synopsis provided in Table 1 shows the three liturgical styles and their key features not as a means of compartmentalizing liturgical expression but as a way of succinctly summarizing each category.

In the following section, I describe the liturgical styles observed in two parishes: St. John Vianney in the Archdiocese of New York and St. Bernadette Soubirous in the Archdiocese of Philadelphia.[1] A concluding section discusses these ideal types, showing how each provides a different way of sifting black Catholic identity that is appropriate to a parish's history and internal diversity, as reflected by the demographic profiles linked to different Mass times.

---

1. The names of all parishes, priests, and parishioners are pseudonyms.

Table 1. Liturgical styles and their key features

	Music	Homily	Aesthetics
Traditionalist	Standard hymns usually found in missalette More likely a Saturday vigil or early Sunday morning Mass	Generally short—less than 10 minutes Delivered from podium	Emphasis on African American events such as Kwanzaa and Black History Month Images of Jesus and Mary depicted as black Emphasis on black saints Depictions of Jesus, Mary, and black saints are present side by side with white depictions
Spirited	Standard hymns in a more upbeat style Songs from *Lead Me, Guide Me* hymnal	Not as short as a traditionalist homily Up to 15 minutes More engagement Delivered from center aisle or podium	
Gospel	Gospel songs not in a hymn book or missalette	Can last as long as 25 minutes Animated presence Uses call-and-response technique Delivered from center aisle	

Black Catholic Identity in Two Parishes

St. John Vianney

St. John Vianney sits in the Central Harlem section of Manhattan. The parish is well known throughout the Archdiocese of New York, most notably for Msgr. Jones, the charismatic pastor during the time of my data collection in 2005 and 2006. Because of the parish's notoriety, it draws parishioners not only from within parish boundaries, but also from outside the immediate area, including northern New Jersey. During my visits to St. John Vianney, I observed clear distinctions between the styles of liturgy at the 9:30 a.m. and 11:30 a.m. Masses.

The general tone of St. John Vianney's 9:30 a.m. Mass foregoes the notion that exuberant expression is either incompatible with Catholicism or must be limited to the black Church. The 9:30 a.m. Mass is conducted in gospel liturgy style, its tone set primarily by the music and the homily. The parish's gospel choir provides the music. The members of the gospel choir wear robes like those typically found in Protestant congregations. They are floor-length red and white robes with large bell-style sleeves. The gospel choir's songs do not come from the *Lead Me, Guide Me* hymnal; instead, the selections invoke an expressiveness and level of emotion that is not readily identified with Catholicism. That expressiveness was indicated by the choir swaying in time to the music and the parishioners clapping and joining in song with the choir. A number of parishioners stood. The use of Protestant-style choir robes and gospel songs exemplify sifting: traditional songs and choir attire are sifted out of the liturgy to make room to sift in emotive music and elements that are more culturally relevant and in line with the Protestant style. This is a distinct means of parish culture production. Through music ministry, the choir engages the parish community and helps create a specific parish identity.

Some of the rituals performed during the 9:30 a.m. Mass would be recognizable to Catholics accustomed to attending another style of Mass. For example, the Baptismal Rite begins with a renewal of baptismal vows by those present and concludes with the officiating priest gently sprinkling holy water on the parishioners to remind those present of their baptism. To those familiar with the Roman Catholic Mass, a Baptismal Rite would not be viewed as foreign or in any way unusual. What makes it unusual at St. John Vianney is having it *every* Sunday. The parish replaces the Penitential Rite with a Baptismal Rite. During the Penitential Rite, parishioners communally acknowledge their sins and sinfulness in preparation for receiving the Body of Christ in the form of Holy Communion. Generally, the Penitential Rite is performed by having those present recite one of two commonly used prayers. On special occasions, such as Easter Sunday, the Penitential Rite is replaced by a Baptismal Rite. But at St. John Vianney, it is replaced weekly. In this way, the 9:30 a.m. Mass takes a ritual that is unabashedly Catholic and reimagines it. The parish makes this ritual its own, thus distinguishing St. John Vianney from nonblack parishes.

Because this ritual lies within the structure of Mass, the parish community does not run the risk of incurring episcopal admonition by performing it every Sunday. The ritual would be easily recognizable to any Roman Catholic; however, its conventional use is sifted out in order to sift in a use that fits the parish's needs. This Mass clearly borrows from the black Church's cultural playbook. The choir robes, gospel songs, and ritual adaptation are symbols of the African American religious experience that are used to incorporate black culture into the Roman Catholic Mass. By doing so, the parish produces a specific black Catholic cultural identity.

The celebration of the 9:30 a.m. Mass at St. John Vianney takes almost two hours to complete. The extra time (compared to the one hour more typical of Masses in the traditionalist liturgy style) can be accounted for in a number of components. For example, in addition to the aforementioned Baptismal Rite, the homily can last anywhere from twenty minutes to a half hour. The recitation of the Nicene Creed, also known as the Profession of Faith, is sung. This lengthens Mass considerably. Furthermore, parishioners recite the Hail Mary after the General Intercessions. While the Hail Mary is a prayer that is well known to Roman Catholics, it is uncommon to recite it during Mass. This is another distinctly Catholic practice that is reimagined by St. John Vianney's parishioners as a means of distinguishing this Mass from a more traditional one.

Yet another component that can account for the length of the 9:30 a.m. Mass is the Offertory. During the Offertory, the gifts of bread and wine that will be used for Holy Communion are presented to the priest. The Offertory also includes parishioners making monetary offerings to support the parish. In most Catholic parishes in the United States, ushers collect the money donated by parishioners. However, at St. John Vianney, each person present walks up the center aisle to leave his or her envelope in a common basket.

All these practices are not contradictory to practices commonly found at other Roman Catholic Masses. While the recitation of the Hail Mary may give some staunch traditionalists pause, reciting it during Mass is not tantamount to a disavowal of Roman Catholic doctrine. In each of these instances, the parish is sifting out standard uses of practices to make room to sift in reimagined practices that both distinguish this Mass and produce unique cultural elements.

Another illustration of sifting and cultural production in the gospel liturgy style occurs during the homily (sermon). During the Gospel reading and homily at St. John Vianney's 9:30 a.m. Mass, the priest typically uses techniques that are closely identified with the black Church. The priest proclaims the Gospel from the center aisle and remains there to offer the homily. Msgr. Jones uses the call-and-response technique that is generally associated with black Protestant congregations.

During one of my visits to St. John Vianney's 9:30 a.m. Mass, for example, Msgr. Jones used the call-and-response technique effectively as a means of connecting with parishioners and connecting scripture readings to parishioners' lived experience. He used his homily to ask parishioners, "Who does God's will?" After asking those in attendance if the tax collectors and prostitutes mentioned in the Gospel reading were doing God's will, he heard a resounding "NO!" from parishioners. He connected this point to his parishioners' lived experience by emphasizing that doing the will of God involves not blaming others for one's own failings, including issues related to work, family life, and other personal relationships. Msgr. Jones then deftly managed to connect this message to the parish's mandatory capital campaign, in conjunction with the Archdiocese of New York's bicentennial. Msgr. Jones connected these two seemingly unrelated topics by articulating the parish's needs—such as an elevator to accommodate disabled and elderly parishioners—then emphasizing parishioners' duty to contribute to the campaign so that the parish's needs could be met. The implication was that otherwise, members of the parish were not doing God's will and would have no one else to blame for their failings.

Through his homilies, Msgr. Jones instills in parishioners an appreciation for black history and Catholic history alike. This was especially evident during a Mass celebrating the feast of the parish's patron. Msgr. Jones went to great lengths to provide those in attendance with an understanding of St. John Vianney's life and how he used his ministry to serve God. The pastor described how St. John Vianney used his personal wealth to minister to the community and refused to abandon those he served when a plague began to overtake the community. In doing this, Msgr. Jones carves space for his parishioners within larger Catholic history and makes the life of a sixteenth-century Italian saint resonate for twenty-first-century

African Americans in Harlem. Establishing a connection between the parishioners and the parish's patron saint generates a concrete identity for members of the parish. Parishioners can see themselves in relation to a long-dead saint and, thus, can develop a broader sense of what it means to be a Roman Catholic.

These techniques associated with the homily demonstrate combining elements identified with Catholicism with elements firmly ensconced in the black Church. All examples above show how elements from both the African American and American Catholic traditions are sifted into liturgy to create a worship experience that meets the needs of parishioners and creates a uniquely black Catholic culture.

The 11:30 a.m. Mass in the spirited liturgy style contrasts with the 9:30 a.m. Mass in gospel liturgy style in a number of ways. The most notable difference is in the music. The music at the later Mass is provided by the men's chorus instead of the gospel choir (which consisted entirely of women). During my visits, the 11:30 a.m. chorus had approximately eight members, while the 9:30 a.m. choir had nearly twenty participants. The songs selected for the 11:30 a.m. liturgy came from the *Lead Me, Guide Me* hymnal and consisted of both traditional Catholic hymns such as "Let There Be Peace on Earth" and more African American oriented songs such as "We've Come This Far by Faith." The style of the men's chorus is much more reserved than that of the gospel choir. They do not wear robes, nor do they sway in time with the music or clap in the same way as the gospel choir. This could be because of the chorus' smaller number; however, it is more likely a result of the muted tenor and flavor of the 11:30 a.m. liturgy.

The duration of the 11:30 a.m. Mass is noticeably shorter than the 9:30 a.m. liturgy. The service does not regularly replace the more traditional Penitential Rite with the longer Baptismal Rite. Music selections and homily length are also among the aspects that account for Mass lasting approximately thirty minutes less than the 9:30 a.m. Mass. There is some measure of sifting, as the music sifts out an abundance of traditional Catholic hymns to make room for more African American oriented songs from the *Lead Me, Guide Me* hymnal. The muted tone of the 11:30 a.m. spirited Mass is no more or less indicative of the production of a unique black Catholic cultural identity than the gospel Mass. Rather, it reflects the depth and breadth of the identity and diversity of the community that produces it.

The only exception to the general tone of the 11:30 a.m. Mass that I observed was during one celebrating the feast of the parish's patron saint. On this occasion, the 9:30 a.m. gospel choir stayed to lead the processional for the 11:30 a.m. Mass. The processional included multiple verses of a hymn that was not found in any hymnal present the church. The parishioners stood while clapping and singing along with the gospel choir, who stood along the altar railing instead of in their usual place on the altar. The men's chorus occupied that area, since the 11:30 a.m. Mass is their usual venue. The processional turned toward the theatrical as altar servers carrying crosses began dancing up the main aisle. The dance was in a style that is best described as a combination of hopping and marching in time to the music that is often found in the African American tradition. Initially, the altar servers made their way approximately halfway up the aisle, then returned to the back of the church. The Eucharistic ministers, then the lectors, and finally the priests followed in a procession—more a march in time to the music and less a dance—to the altar. The entire procession lasted twenty minutes.

This display set a palpable tone for the occasion, which celebrated the parish, its members, and its patron saint. Having attended Roman Catholic Masses regularly for my entire life, I had never seen the feast of a parish's patron—or any other feast for that matter—celebrated with such fervor and gusto. It conjured the character of the music and frenzy that Du Bois offered more than one hundred years ago when he invoked "the Preacher, the Music, and the Frenzy" when describing the black worship experience (Du Bois [1903] 1994, 116).

Unequivocally, this 11:30 a.m. Mass celebration included a sifting in of practices borrowed from the black Church—such as the dancing and long processional to begin the liturgy—and a sifting out of a more straightforward and, frankly, bland opening to the liturgy. Once Mass began, there was no ambiguity regarding what type of service was taking place. During the homily, Msgr. Jones spoke at length about St. John Vianney's personal narrative and how his life experience influenced his actions. He spoke extensively about how St. John Vianney used his personal wealth to the benefit of the impoverished people he served and remained with them when illness devastated the community and threatened his own life.

At both the 9:30 a.m. and 11:30 a.m. Masses at St. John Vianney, the music chosen and the homily emphasize Jesus as "Lord and Savior."

Parishioners are compelled to follow the high example set by Jesus's life on earth and to ask for Jesus's help in facing the problems and concerns of everyday life. There is much less emphasis placed on God as Creator and the Holy Spirit as Sanctifier. This emphasis on Jesus as Savior, rather than God as Creator or the Holy Spirit as Sanctifier, is more commonly found in the black Protestant Church than in the Roman Catholic Church (Grant 1989; Lincoln and Mamiya 1990). There are certain characteristics of Jesus—his humanity, poverty, and earthly suffering—that could make this aspect (or person) of the Trinity more tangible and palatable to an African American audience. This worldview is an example of how liturgy can be adapted to serve the needs of a constituency by sifting out one commonly used image, God the Creator, to create room to sift in another, Jesus the Savior.

St. Bernadette Soubirous

St. Bernadette Soubirous is located in an overwhelmingly African American and economically depressed section of Philadelphia. Having been raised in the Archdiocese of Philadelphia, I have known about the parish for some time. St. Bernadette Soubirous is a parish known for its numerous social programs, including a prison reentry program and outreach to the homeless. Because of its social programs and openness to gay and lesbian Catholics, it carries a reputation as a "last stop" for disaffected Catholics who would otherwise cease to practice Catholicism. For this reason, the parish has for many years drawn parishioners from within traditional parish boundaries and from neighborhoods outside the immediate area.

In 2013, the year before my field observation at the parish, St. Bernadette Soubirous merged with two other parishes, each located approximately one mile away. Mergers of this sort have occurred throughout the Archdiocese of Philadelphia in recent years. This type of parish reorganization has especially impacted parishes within the city of Philadelphia. Many affected parishes within city limits are the remnants of the national parish model, which dominated a number of urban dioceses from the middle of the nineteenth century to the middle of the twentieth century (Rzeznik 2009). Over the last fifteen years, similar reorganizations of parishes and Catholic schools have also occurred in the Archdioceses of Boston, New York, and Chicago (Belluck 2004; Otterman 2014; Pashman

2014; West 2015). These (often painful) reorganizations have occurred frequently of late and disproportionately affect already marginalized Catholics, including African American Catholics. This context shapes any consideration of parish life therein.

St. Bernadette Soubirous currently operates a prison reentry program among its social ministries. It also partners with local organizations, renting space in its former school building to a local nonprofit with a soup kitchen and other services for the homeless. These outreach efforts are of particular relevance to both the neighborhood where the parish is and the African American community more broadly. These are ways in which the parish works as a parish to connect the social justice teachings of the Roman Catholic Church and the social issues of specific concern to the African American community.

For the current discussion, the emphasis is on liturgy as a form of identity work and parish cultural production. Here again, the homily, music, and church aesthetics combine the Roman Catholic tradition and the African American religious experience. St. Bernadette Soubirous has three regularly scheduled weekend liturgies: a 4:00 p.m. vigil Mass on Saturday evening and 9:00 and 11:00 a.m. Sunday Masses. While the parish is now predominantly African American due to the recent merger, African Americans form a majority of attendees only at the 11:00 a.m. Mass. I draw from my field observations of this 11:00 a.m. Mass.

Like the 9:30 a.m. Mass at St. John Vianney, the 11:00 a.m. Mass at St. Bernadette Soubirous is in the gospel liturgy style. Music is facilitated by the gospel choir, which is led by two of the parish's three ministers of music. One leads the choir; the other provides musical accompaniment on the piano. Both of them have come over to St. Bernadette as a result of the merger. While the group is called a gospel choir, they do not reach the depths and breadths of exuberance of the choir at St. John Vianney. St. Bernadette's choir uses songs that are not found in either the missalette or the *Lead Me, Guide Me* hymnal. The repetition of the lyrics makes the songs easy for the parishioners to follow and join in the singing. St. Bernadette's choir does not present a unified appearance by wearing choir robes. On only one occasion did I see the choir members dressed in a coordinated color scheme. That occurred when the choir was leaving directly from Mass to sing at a concert event at another church. Thus, while the choir is sifting in music akin to the black Church tradition, it is not sifting in more visual aesthetics. Nevertheless, the parishioners' engagement with the music is apparent not only in the abundant singing, but also in parishioners' clapping and occasionally standing in the pews. It appeared that the choir leader, in particular, desired even more exuberance from the parishioners. However, the parishioners may not find a full-on gospel style palatable. As such, the choir leader may be trying to force something the parishioners are not ready to accept.

St. Bernadette has two priests on staff—the pastor, Fr. Peters, and the parochial vicar, Fr. Wolfe. The two priests have noticeably different but related styles pertaining to preaching and connecting with the parishioners during Mass. Fr. Wolfe delivers his homily from the podium, while Fr. Peters uses a handheld microphone to deliver his homily from the center aisle. Both priests tap into the lived experience of the parishioners to connect them to the teachings of the Roman Catholic Church.

On my first visit to the parish, Fr. Wolfe used his homily to deliver a fairly standard message of moving from darkness into light. He invoked the well-known image of Jesus as the Light of the World and, therefore, the path out of darkness. Fr. Wolfe discussed how, in order for the light of the world to enter our lives, we must first be in darkness. He went on to relate several contemporary forms of darkness, including the deaths of Michael Brown in Ferguson, Missouri, and Eric Garner in New York City at the hands of police officers, and the societal disaffection these incidents have caused, particularly in the African American community. He described the "darkness of prison and addiction." Fr. Wolfe connected the struggle of having a loved one in prison or in the throes of addiction to darkness, saying, "It is a special grace to see the light of Jesus" come into one's life.

He went on to discuss an incident from his work in prison ministry. He said that when he arrived at the prison, he was instructed to put his belongings in a locker. The locker could be accessed only by first paying a quarter, but he didn't have one. He feared that his entire trip would be wasted for want of a quarter until a woman standing behind him offered him one. Fr. Wolfe described the appearance of this woman and the aid she offered him at the exact moment he needed it as "Jesus's light in the darkness." Fr. Wolfe spoke heavily about addiction and prison as a darkness that envelopes not only those directly affected, but also their loved ones. In this example, Fr. Wolfe was sifting in relatable events from the parishioners' lived experience with a standard teaching about Jesus. By doing so, his homily worked to make the parish a space where African American Catholics feel comfortable and the experience of liturgy relatable.

The following week, Fr. Peters's homily focused on the importance of prayer. Whereas Fr. Wolfe's homily had been animated, Fr. Peters's was downright zealous. At the beginning of his homily, Fr. Peters called on the parishioners to rejoice and told them that "the family that prays together, stays together." He used a variation of the call-and-response technique by asking parishioners to repeat the aforementioned statement after him. Fr. Peters also called on parishioners to turn to the person nearest them and say, "This homily is about you." He then moved on to several statements that began with the phrase "We REJOICE," such as "We REJOICE in the love of God!" and "We REJOICE in the gift of another day!" He implored the parishioners to be in relationship with God through prayer. Parishioners applauded at key moments in the homily, such as when he said, "Our brothers and sisters in the Muslim community put us to shame by stopping to pray five times a day!"

As Fr. Peters delivered this message, he did so with vocal inflections more reminiscent of a black Protestant preacher than a white Catholic priest. He began at the podium with the rhythmic cadence of the "We REJOICE" statements. He eventually picked up a wireless handheld microphone and moved into the center aisle to deliver the second half of the homily. His style includes boisterous, even flamboyant, arm gestures. At times, the music minister plays the piano softly while Fr. Peters speaks. On occasion, Fr. Peters will call on the choir to sing as a means of reiterating his message. All of this is meant to energize and excite the parishioners while (consciously or unconsciously) invoking the preacher, music, and frenzy made famous by Du Bois. The liturgy exemplifies the process of sifting in practices commonly associated with the black Church experience.

In addition to the homily, St. Bernadette uses aesthetics to sift in elements of African American and Roman Catholic culture. A stunning, but likely unintended, example is the use of a cross carried by an altar server during the entrance and recessional processions. The cross depicts a black crucified Jesus. During Mass, the cross rests in a stand in the front of the church. This results in the black Jesus being positioned directly in front of a painting on the wall behind the altar of a white Jesus being crucified.

The juxtaposition of these two images of the crucifixion is a powerful, unequivocal example of how a parish can use artifacts to sift African American aesthetics into liturgical practice.

During the holiday season, the church decorations included an Advent wreath with one pink candle and three purple candles, which is typical of churches in the Roman Catholic tradition and other Christian denominations. However, within inches of the Advent wreath was a kinara holding seven candles, representing the principles of the African American celebration of Kwanzaa. Posters adorned the walls of the church, explaining the principles that are the hallmarks of Kwanzaa. The two sets of candles are powerful, tangible examples of an identity that exists as the outcome of sifting. One is readily identified with the Roman Catholic tradition, while the other is uniquely associated with African Americans. Putting them side by side shows how black American Catholics use artifacts to produce a distinct African American Catholic cultural identity. It also identifies the parish as a space where this identity is celebrated and perpetuated.

I observed another notable use of aesthetics in identity work when I visited St. Bernadette Soubirous on the first Sunday in February. I immediately noticed that the church was decorated for Black History Month. The posters used to decorate the church were those commonly found in elementary schools. The posters depicted key people and moments in African American history, such as Rosa Parks, Barack Obama, Jackie Robinson, and the Harlem Renaissance. Other posters depicted values such as courage, creativity, hope, and citizenship. None of the people depicted are Catholic, and none of the depicted values are uniquely identified with Catholicism. Yet having them in church as part of the celebration of Black History Month indicates that the parish is a place where the sifting of cultural, racial, and civic identities with religious identity occurs. Interestingly, at St. Bernadette I did not observe a specific sifting out of God the Creator in favor of concentrating on Jesus the Savior. St. Bernadette Soubirous made room for both.

Conclusion

St. John Vianney and St. Bernadette Soubirous are two of the 516 predominantly African American parishes in the United States (Gray, Cidade,

Gautier, and Gaunt 2014). These parishes, each in their own way, exemplify the pronouncement by the Black Bishops of the United States in their only pastoral letter to date, *What We Have Seen and Heard* (1984). The Black Bishops declared that black Catholics' liturgy was both authentically black and truly Catholic. Mass at these two parishes exemplifies liturgy as a rich, dynamic process. There is more than one way to be authentically black and truly Catholic, as seen in the descriptions of liturgies at St. John Vianney and St. Bernadette Soubirous as well as the summary in Table 1. More recently, Pope Francis expressed a complementary point to the one in *What We Have Seen and Heard*, saying, "Unity . . . does not mean uniformity of . . . cultural life, or ways of thinking" (Pope Francis 2014, 4). To this end, we have seen how both of these two parishes produce a unique black Catholic cultural identity.

At St. John Vianney, standard Mass rituals have been reimagined to incorporate song and communal activity, thus creating specific black Catholic rituals. St. John Vianney's focus on Jesus the Savior over the other two persons of the Trinity draws on the black Church's emphasis on Jesus, without sacrificing Catholicism's depiction of God. St. Bernadette Soubirous's side-by-side placement of the Kwanzaa kinara and the Advent wreath create a tangible symbol of how black Catholics' dual heritages are not disparate at all. Rather, they exist as parts of a larger cultural tradition. In addition, the parish's use of secular Black History Month posters offers a way to integrate civic, racial, and religious identity. This integrated identity is further advanced by the parish's emphasis on social justice, borrowed from both Catholic social teaching and the long tradition of civic engagement by leaders in the black Church. Both parishes use music and the homily—in content and delivery—to sift in elements of Roman Catholic tradition and the African American religious experience. Doing so produces a distinct black Catholic cultural identity. Black Catholics actively produce black Catholic parish culture.

Black Catholics must face the lingering ramifications of an often-painful history with the Church in the United States, including implicit and explicit support of slavery, segregated communion lines, and systematic exclusion from the priesthood. They must negotiate their own membership in the Roman Catholic Church with this painful history. Black Catholics do so, in part, by sifting in elements of the African American religious experience and Roman Catholic tradition to produce a unique black Catholic cultural identity. Black Catholics' sifting through liturgy challenges the idea that all Catholics must either acquiesce to or vocally reject conventional Roman Catholic practices. While sifting was more prominent in the liturgies described here, both sifting and owning can have a deep emotional resonance for the social actors engaged in it. Understanding black Catholic identity work in parishes is essential if African American Catholics are to claim—and not just find—a place at the table of American Catholicism.

References

Ammerman, Nancy T. 1998. "Culture and Identity in the Congregation." In *Studying Congregations: A New Handbook*, edited by N. T. Ammerman, J. Carroll, C. Dudley, and W. McKinney, pp. 78–104. Nashville, Tenn.: Abingdon Press.

Belluck, Pam. 2004. "Archdiocese in Boston Plans to Close 65 Catholic Parishes by the End of the Year." *New York Times*, May 26, 2004. Retrieved April 4, 2015. http://www.nytimes.com/2004/05/26/us/archdiocese-in -boston-plans-to-close-65-catholic-parishes-by-the-end-of-the-year.html.

Black Bishops of the United States. 1984. *"What We Have Seen and Heard": A Pastoral Letter on Evangelization from the Black Bishops of the United States.* Cincinnati, Ohio: St. Anthony Messenger Press.

Braxton, Edward K. 1988. "Black Catholics in America: A Challenge to the Church's Catholicity." In *One Lord, One Faith, One Baptism: The Hopes and Experiences of the Black Community in the Archdiocese of New York*, pp. 63–82. Vol. 2, *Appendices*. New York: Archdiocese of New York, Office of Pastoral Research.

———. 2014. "The Racial Divide in the United States: A Reflection for the World Day of Peace 2015." *The Messenger*, December 31, 2014. Retrieved March 8, 2015. http://bellevillemessenger.org/2014/12/bishop-braxton-writes-a-letter -on-racial-divide-in-the-united-states/.

Cressler, Matthew J. 2017. *Authentically Black and Truly Catholic: The Rise of Black Catholicism in the Great Migration.* New York: New York University Press.

Davis, Cyprian. 1988. "Black Spirituality: A Catholic Perspective." In *One Lord, One Faith, One Baptism: The Hopes and Experiences of the Black Community in the Archdiocese of New York*, pp. 37–62. Vol. 2, *Appendices*. New York: Archdiocese of New York, Office of Pastoral Research.

Davis, Cyprian and Jamie Phelps, eds. 2003. *"Stamped with the Image of God": African Americans as God's Image in Black.* Maryknoll, N.Y.: Orbis Books.

Dillon, Michele. 1999. *Catholic Identity: Balancing Reason, Faith, and Power.* New York: Cambridge University Press.

Du Bois, W. E. B. (1903) 1994. *The Souls of Black Folk*. New York: Dover Publications.

Dufour, Lynn Resnick. 2000. "Sifting Through Tradition: The Creation of Jewish Feminist Identities." *Journal for the Scientific Study of Religion* 39: 90–106.

Eugene, Toinette M. 1998. "Between 'Lord Have Mercy!' and 'Thank You, Jesus!': Liturgical Renewal and African American Catholic Assemblies." In *Taking Down Our Harps: Black Catholics in the United States*, pp. 163–175. Maryknoll, N.Y.: Orbis Books.

GIA Publications. 1987. *Lead Me, Guide Me: The African American Catholic Hymnal*. Chicago: GIA Publications.

Gilkes, Cheryl Townsend. 2001. *If It Wasn't for the Women*. Maryknoll, N.Y.: Orbis Books.

Grant, Jacquelyn. 1989. *White Women's Christ and Black Women's Jesus: Feminist Christology and Womanist Response*. Atlanta, Ga.: Scholars Press.

Gray, Mark, Melissa Cidade, Mary Gautier, and Thomas Gaunt. 2014. *Cultural Diversity in the Catholic Church in the United States*. Washington, DC: Center for Applied Research in the Apostolate at Georgetown University.

Hahn, Ashley. 2018. "Saying Goodbye to Philadelphia's First Black Catholic Church." Eyes on the Street, March 28, 2018. Retrieved April 1, 2018. http://planphilly.com/eyesonthestreet/2018/03/28/goodbye-philadelphia-first -black-catholic-church-st-peter-claver.

Hellwig, Monika. 2002. *Understanding Catholicism*. 2nd ed. New York: Paulist Press.

Lincoln, C. Eric, and Lawrence H. Mamiya. 1990. *The Black Church in the African American Experience*. Durham, N.C.: Duke University Press.

Magnoni, Greg. 2015. "Black and Catholic in the U.S." *Northwest Catholic*, October 28, 2015. Retrieved November 6, 2015. http://www.nwcatholic.org /features/nw-stories/black-and-catholic-in-archdiocese-of-seattle.

McGreevy, John T. 1996. *Parish Boundaries: The Catholic Encounter with Race in the Twentieth-Century Urban North*. Chicago: University of Chicago Press.

Ochs, Stephen J. 1990. *Desegregating the Altar: The Josephites and the Struggle for Black Priests, 1871–1960*. Baton Rouge: Louisiana University Press.

Otterman, Sharon. 2014. "Heartache for New York's Catholics as Church Closings Are Announced." *New York Times*, November 2, 2014. Retrieved April 4, 2015. http://www.nytimes.com/2014/11/03/nyregion/new-york -catholics-are-set-to-learn-fate-of-their-parishes.html?_r=o.

Pashman, Manya Brachear. 2014. "Cardinal: Closing 7 Schools Unavoidable in Cash-Strapped District." *Chicago Tribune*, October 29, 2014. Retrieved April 4, 2015. http://www.chicagotribune.com/news/local/breaking/chi -cardinal-george-says-school-closings-coming-20141029-story.html#page=1.

Pope Francis. 2014. "Address of Pope Francis to European Parliament." *Vatican Radio*, October 31, 2014. Retrieved November 1, 2015. http://en .radiovaticana.va/news/2014/11/25/pope_francis_address_to_european _parliament/1112318.

Rivers, Clarence Rufus J. 1998. "The Oral African Tradition Versus the Ocular Western Tradition: The Spirit in Worship." In *Taking Down Our Harps: Black Catholics in the United States*, pp. 232–46. Maryknoll, N.Y.: Orbis Books.

Rowe, Cyprian Lamar. 1994. "A Tale of War, A Tale of Woe." *Plenty Good Room* September/October: 10–13.

Rzeznik, Thomas. 2009. "The Church in the Changing City: Parochial Restructuring in the Archdiocese of Philadelphia in Historical Perspective." *U.S. Catholic Historian* 27: 73–90.

Schenk, Christine. 2015. "Should We Care about What Happens to Displaced Parish Communities?" *National Catholic Reporter*, July 16, 2015. http:// ncronline.org/blogs/simply-spirit/should-we-care-about-what-happens -displaced-parish-communities.

Schlossberg, Tatiana. 2015. "Catholic Church Closings in New York Bring Sadness and Anger." *New York Times*, July 31, 2015. Retrieved December 7, 2015. http://www.nytimes.com/2015/08/01/nyregion/catholic-church -closings-in-new-york-bring-sadness-and-anger.html.

West, Melanie Grayce. 2015. "New York City Catholics Brace for Fresh Wave of Parish Mergers." *Wall Street Journal*, February 10, 2015. Retrieved April 4, 2015. http://www.wsj.com/articles/new-york-city-catholics-brace-for-fresh -wave-of-parish-mergers-1423594957.

Whitt, D. Reginald. 1998. "*Varietates Legitimae* and an African American Liturgical Tradition." In *Taking Down Our Harps: Black Catholics in the United States*, pp. 247–80. Maryknoll, N.Y.: Orbis Books.

7 A House Divided

Catholic parishes are shaped by and shape larger demographic and economic trends. Two significant trends—ethnic diversity and economic inequality—are shaping a new future for the United States, with both positive and negative potential for the country's people and social and civic institutions. This essay explores how these trends are manifesting themselves in Catholic parishes and examines the issues parishes face in the future as a result of these two trends.

Two Important Trends

Demographic Diversity

The United States is in the midst of a dramatic and rapid change in its demographic structure, shaped largely by the magnitude and character of immigration since the mid-1960s. The country is becoming more ethnically diverse, and in a few decades non-Hispanic whites will be a minority. Already, the majority of births in 2011 were to minorities. Public school enrollment in 2011 was only 52 percent non-Hispanic white. The Latino population now outnumbers that of the African American population. A 2015 analysis of immigration trends documents how immigration has driven population growth in the US since 1965, noting that by 2015 foreign-born residents made up 14 percent of the population, projected to grow to 18 percent by 2065 (Frey 2015; Pew Research Center 2015b).

Latinos from Latin America have made up the largest share of immigration since 1965. Americans who identify themselves as Latino or Hispanic now constitute 18 percent of the population. Asians now make up about a quarter of annual immigration flows and constitute 6 percent of the 2015 population. The Pew Research Center projects that by 2055 the nation will be 13 percent black, 24 percent Hispanic and 14 percent Asian (Pew Research Center 2015b).

Economic Inequality

The facts about economic inequality are well known but still quite startling. One set of measures looks at how well the bottom fifth of the household income distribution has been doing economically. In 2013, according to Census Bureau data, the bottom fifth of households—those with income below $20,900—received 3.2 percent of total household income. (If income were evenly distributed, they would have received 20 percent.) In 1976, the *best* year for the poor in terms of income share between 1967 and the present, their share of total household income was 4.3 percent.[1] Over the ensuing four decades, the share of income earned by the bottom 20 percent of households has declined by about a quarter.

Using a different data source, Emmanuel Saez finds that the top *10 percent* of households, those with incomes over $116,000 in 2013, took home almost 50 percent of total household income, up from a still shocking 35 percent in the 1960s and 1970s (Saez 2015; Piketty 2014). Meanwhile, the top *1 percent* received 20 percent of total household income in 2013. The average income of the top 1 percent grew 62 percent between 1993 and 2013. This high-earning group, representing just 1 percent of households, has captured over 90 percent of the gains in income since the Great Recession of 2008.

These trends may have positive or negative impacts on other aspects of social life, depending in part on the degree of separation or integration of the various ethnic and economic communities. It seems clear, however, that both racial/ethnic segregation and economic segregation threaten to limit opportunities for disadvantaged groups. The evidence on the adverse effects of racial segregation on schooling and of geographic concentration on overall opportunity is compelling (Owens, Rearden, and Jencks 2014; Jargowsky 2015; Orfield and Frankenberg 2014).

At the neighborhood level, racial segregation has historically been high, with blacks and whites living in neighborhoods that are separate

1. These data are from the US Census Bureau report *Income and Poverty in the United States: 2013* (DeNavas-Walt and Proctor 2014). This data source is considered to be high quality for measuring household income in the bottom 99 percent of the distribution. It is considered to be less accurate for the top of the income distribution, since the number of top income recipients in the Census Bureau sample is quite low and they tend to underreport their income on surveys.

and unequal and new immigrants concentrated in ethnic neighborhoods (Massey 2007; Logan and Stults 2011). Black/white segregation
remains high, but there are some indications that it is decreasing, especially in the South and West. The segregation of Hispanics and Asians
into ethnic neighborhoods is less than that of blacks, and some cities, like
Los Angeles, actually have a large proportion of multiracial neighborhoods (Frey 2015).

Economic segregation, both the concentration of the poor and the isolation of the affluent, appears to be increasing (Reardon and Bischoff 2011;
Jargowsky 2014). Because of the huge income gaps between the rich and
the poor and of growing economic as well as racial/ethnic segregation, it
seems to be increasingly difficult for the polity to engage in civil conversations, to come together to address its collective problems, to provide opportunities for its children, and to care for its vulnerable members (Putnam
2015). The farther apart the rich are from the poor, in lifestyle and geography, the harder it is for the rich to be understanding and empathetic toward
the poor and for different economic groups to see themselves as members
of a single community with shared needs and responsibilities.

Catholics and Their Parishes

What do these trends mean for life within the United States' single largest religious tradition? The Catholic population, when looked at in the aggregate, looks remarkably heterogeneous economically and ethnically.
The 2014 Pew Religious Landscape Survey found that the Catholic population is 34 percent Latino, significantly higher than the overall national
population. The income and educational distribution of Catholics mirrors
that of the population as a whole (Pew Research Center 2014). But looking more closely, we see that there are essentially two populations within
US Catholicism: non-Hispanic whites and Latinos, with small proportions
of African Americans, Asians, and others. The two major population
groups—white Catholics and Latino Catholics—are very different in their
age structures, incomes, levels of education, and geography (Table 1).
White Catholics have higher education and income levels and are much
older and more concentrated in the Northeast and Midwest.

To what extent do these two populations come together in local parish
communities? As Table 1 shows, the distribution of the two groups

Table 1. Income, education, region, and age of adult Catholics, 2014

	Latino Catholics (%)	White Catholics (%)	All Catholics (%)	Full sample (all religions) (%)
Income				
< $30K	60	23	36	35
$30–50K	19	19	19	20
$50–100K	14	32	26	26
> $100K	7	26	19	19
Education				
HS or less	67	36	46	41
Some college	21	30	27	32
College grad	9	20	16	17
Post grad	3	14	10	11
Region				
Northeast	14	33	26	18
Midwest	9	30	21	21
South	33	23	27	37
West	44	14	26	23
Age of adults				
18–29	22	13	17	22
30–49	44	27	33	34
50–64	23	33	29	26
65+	11	27	20	18
Percent of sample	34*	59*	21**	

Note: Tabulations using Pew Research Center 2014.

* Percent of self-identified Catholics in the Pew Religious Landscape Survey who identify as Latino and as white.
** Percent of total Pew Research Center sample who identify as Catholic.

across regions of the country is quite different. Nonetheless, there is enough overlap that integrated parishes would be possible in many places. Nancy Ammerman reminds us in this volume that Catholic parishes are much larger, on average, than congregations of other religions (with the exception of megachurches). The combination of large parishes and diversity in the Catholic population suggests the possibility of genuinely diverse parish communities. While it is true that belonging to the same parish does not guarantee a shared community, a basic question is whether diverse ethnic and economic groups worship together in the same parishes.

The National Congregations Study (NCS) hints at answers to this question (see the essay by Gary Adler in this volume for a detailed introduction to the NCS).[2] The NCS is unquestionably the best methodology for constructing a sample of congregations, since it does not rely on denominational or phone book lists and inherently weights by representation in the population. Key informants provided information on the demographic and economic composition of their congregations as well as on the life of the congregation. Nonetheless, it is worth keeping in mind that informants' descriptions of congregants may contain considerable error, since in most cases they are estimates based on the perceptions of the informants rather than systematic surveys of congregants. The NCS provides suggestive data on many aspects of parish life, including ethnic and economic diversity (Chaves and Anderson 2014).

My analysis of the Catholic sample of parishes in the NCS yields three suggestive findings on the issue of diversity within American parishes.[3]

1. *Latinos appear to be underrepresented and the affluent overrepresented in parish composition, compared to the overall self-identified Catholic population. (Table 2)*

I first looked for evidence on the issue of whether parish demographic composition looks like self-reported Catholics' demographic composition more generally or whether parish composition is disproportionately well-off and well educated. This question is prompted by findings from other research that suggests greater religious and civic engagement among affluent people and increasing isolation of the poor from social and civic institutions (Putnam and Campbell 2011; Murray 2012). Table 2 compares responses from NCS Catholic parishes with data from the Census Bureau's

2. The NCS is well described on its website (http://www.soc.duke.edu/natcong/index.html, accessed April 20, 2015). The website also provides access to the data itself, which were used in the analyses reported here.

3. Data analysis of the NCS was done for this project by Dr. Catherine Hoegeman, assistant professor of sociology at Missouri State University, using the data set provided by the NCS. I am very grateful to her for the analyses and for her helpful suggestions.

Table 2. Rich and poor in Catholic parishes overall compared with the total population and with self-identified Catholics

	Adults reported to be in Catholic parishes* (%)	All households** (%)	Self-identified Catholics*** (%)
Household income < $35K	33	35	35
Household income > $140K	16	11	9
Education BA or higher	40	30	28
In traditional family	49	32	
Latino	29	15	32

* These numbers come from the information provided by parish informants in the NCS (http://www.soc.duke.edu/natcong/wave_3.html). Informants in 2012 were asked about the proportions of regular adult participants in the congregation who were Latino, who had four-year degrees or more, who lived in households with income less than $35,000 a year, who lived in households with income higher than $140,000, and who lived in households in which there were two married adults with children living at home. Percentages given are the means of all Catholic congregations, weighted by attendees.

** These numbers come from the American Community Survey of the US Bureau of the Census, Table HINC01, household income in 2012 (https://www.census.gov/data/tables/time-series/demo/income-poverty/cps-hinc/hinc-01.2012.html). The income, education, and family numbers are for households, not adults in households, so they are likely to overestimate the number of adults in low-income households (which tend to have fewer adults) and underestimate the number in high-income households (which tend to have more adults). The percent Latino is for all persons over 18.

*** The numbers come from the appendix in D'Antonio, Dillon, and Gautier 2013. They report the data from a survey of 1,442 self-identified Catholics in spring 2011. Respondents were asked about their education and their income. Income data are reported categorically in the appendix. I estimate the percent greater than $140,000 by adding the percent greater than $150,000 to one-fifth of the percent between $100,000 and $150,000. Respondents were asked if they were married but not, apparently, if they had children. Fifty-four percent reported being married.

Current Population Survey on the US population as a whole, as well as data from William D'Antonio, Michele Dillon, and Mary Gautier's survey of Catholics as reported in *American Catholics in Transition* (2013).

Table 2 suggests that US parishes report lower proportions of Latino parishioners and higher proportions of affluent, well-educated, and traditionally married parishioners than there are in the overall population and in the self-reported Catholic population. There are many reasons to believe that parish leaders might innocently misestimate the demographic characteristics of their parishioners. Future research on parishes would ideally match parish surveys with surveys of individual parishioners, from whom more accurate demographic information could be collected. But it is interesting to consider the possibility, as a hypothesis, that parishes are in fact differentially serving whites, the better off, the better educated, and those in traditional families.

We know from some other surveys that college-educated adults are more likely to identify with a religious tradition and are more likely to be regular religious participants than those with less education.[4] We do not know why this is, except that it seems to be part of a general pattern of the better off and better educated being more likely to be involved in a variety of social and civic institutions. They marry more, vote more, and participate more in civic life. To the extent that this phenomenon characterizes Catholic parishes, it suggests that parish leaders would do well to think more about who might and might not feel welcomed in the parish. This is especially the case in areas where new immigrants must join pre-existing, majority-white parishes.

2. *Catholic parishes are quite segregated economically and ethnically. Rich and Latino populations are considerably more segregated in Catholic parishes than they are in neighborhoods. (Tables 3 and 4)*

I next looked at the NCS data to ask whether different ethnic and economic groups are distributed across parishes evenly or unevenly. This is based on parish informants' answers to questions asking them to estimate the proportions of their congregations that are Latino, that have annual

4. This is documented in Putnam 2011 and is an important point made by Murray 2012. See also, however, the Pew Research Center Religious Landscape Study, a survey conducted by the Pew Forum on Religion and Public Life in 2005 and 2014, and other Pew Research Center surveys available through their website (http://religions.pewforum.org). The Religious Landscape Study shows higher proportions of college-educated and high-income respondents among the unaffiliated than among Christians. Those identifying with non-Christian religions have more education and higher incomes than the other groups.

Table 3. Parish composition for the median parishioner

	As reported* (%)	If evenly distributed** (%)
Poor in parish for median poor parishioner	50	33
Rich in parish for median rich parishioner	30	16
Latino in parish for median Latino parishioner	80***	28

* Percentages calculated from parish informants' reports in the 2012 NCS.
** If parishioners were evenly distributed, the percent for the median parishioner would be the same as the overall percent.
*** The neighborhood in which the median Latino lives is about 40 percent Latino, per Reardon, Fox, and Townsend (2015).

household incomes less than $35,000, and that have annual household incomes greater than $140,000.[5]

An important question in this is, Compared to what? One comparison is to an even distribution: a distribution within parishes that would mirror the distribution in the Catholic population as a whole. Table 3 makes this comparison. It takes the perspectives of a typical low-income parishioner, rich parishioner, and Latino parishioner and asks what proportion of his or her parish is similar along that dimension. It shows that the typical parish for a low-income parishioner has a larger proportion of low income co-parishioners than would be expected if the distribution were even. The typical rich parishioner is in a parish that has about twice the percentage of rich parishioners than would be expected. And the typical Latino parishioner worships in a parish which is almost three times more Latino than would be expected with an even distribution.

Table 4 makes a different comparison, showing the proportion of the population that lives and worships in neighborhoods and parishes that are rich, low income, or majority Latino. To do this, I use the definitions of

5. A $35,000 household income is well above the 2012 poverty line for a family of four, which was $23,492. So this group should not be considered "poor" but instead "lower income." For a summary of the issues around defining poverty and for trends in poverty, see Fox et al. 2014 and Jencks 2015.

the categories that have been used in other social science research on segregation (see, for example, Reardon and Bischoff 2011; Reardon, Fox, and Townsend 2015). Most of this research has examined residential neighborhoods, typically defined as census tracts. These are geographical units defined by the Census Bureau for purposes of describing the population. Tracts are similar in average population size to hypothetical parishes but considerably smaller in their geographic areas.[6] Because of their larger geographic areas, parishes should be more demographically diverse than census tracts. A recent review of multiracial (e.g., racially diverse) congregations shows that a key factor to achieving this diversity is the geographic area they draw from (Edwards, Christerson, and Emerson 2013). Comparing parish diversity to census tract diversity should, therefore, be an interesting and useful exercise.

Table 4 defines a "poor" parish and a "rich" parish using definitions that are comparable to those used by sociologists Reardon and Bischoff in the best-known study of the economic segregation of neighborhoods. The table defines a majority Latino parish as one that is 50 percent or more Latino, a definition that was used in an analysis of the 2000 census by researchers at the Pew Hispanic Center (Suro and Tafoya 2004).

In their research on the segregation of families by income level, Reardon and Bischoff report that 31 percent of American families in 2009 lived in neighborhoods that can be considered either rich or poor according to their definitions, making the point that the proportion of American families in mixed-income neighborhoods is disturbingly lower than it was in 1970.

Table 4 shows that the percentage of Catholics who are in poor parishes (more than 60 percent of parishioners with incomes less than $35,000) is about the same as the percentage of families who live in low-income neighborhoods. But the percentage of Catholics in rich parishes (more than

6. There are about 73,000 census tracts; the average population of a census tract is about 4,400. There are about 17,500 Catholic parishes in the United States. If every self-identified Catholic was part of a parish, the average parish size would also be about 4,400. So the population sizes of census tracts and theoretical parishes are roughly comparable, though parishes typically cover a much larger geographic area than census tracts.

Table 4. Rich, poor, and Latino Catholic parishes and neighborhoods

	Catholic parishes* (%)	Census tracts** (%)
Catholics or families in "poor" parishes or neighborhoods	18	17
Catholics or families in "rich" parishes or neighborhoods	31	14
Catholics or population in majority Latino parishes or neighborhoods	28	4

* These percentages were calculated from the estimates reported by parish informants to the NCS. A "poor" parish is defined as one in which 60 percent or more of the parishioners are estimated have household incomes below $35,000, which I estimated to be analogous to the definition of a poor neighborhood used by Reardon and Bischoff (2011). Median household income in 2012 was about $51,000; 67 percent of that is $31,000. I used the Census Bureau household income distribution table to estimate that for distributions where the median household income is $31,000 or less, then about 60 percent of the households would have incomes below $35,000, which is the definition of low income available in the NCS. A "rich" parish is defined as one in which 20 percent or more of the parishioners are estimated to have household incomes greater than $140,000. Also using the census household distribution tables, I estimated that in those neighborhoods with a median income 1.5 times the overall median, 20 percent of the households would have incomes above $140,000. For Latinos, I looked at the percentage in parishes that were reported to be more than 50 percent Latino.
** The percentages for rich and poor neighborhoods come from Reardon and Bischoff (2011). They divided neighborhoods into five categories and defined poor neighborhoods as those in which the median income for families in the neighborhood was 67 percent of the metropolitan median income. Reardon and Bischoff defined rich neighborhoods as those with family median incomes 1.5 times the area median. Middle-class neighborhoods are defined as those with median incomes between 80 and 125 percent of area median income. Note that in this analysis Reardon and Bischoff analyzed families, whereas the census and parish data are for households. Families on average tend to be larger and richer than households, so if the Reardon and Bischoff analyses had been done for households, the cutoffs would be lower for both rich and poor but the percentages presumably not much different. The percentage for Latino neighborhoods is from an analysis done for the Pew Hispanic Center using the 2000 Census by Suro and Tafoya (2004).

20 percent of parishioners with incomes greater than $140,000) is more than twice the proportion of families who live in rich neighborhoods. Forty-nine percent of Catholics worship in parishes that are either rich or poor.

The proportion of Catholics in majority (more than 50 percent) Latino parishes is seven times the proportion of the total population that lived in majority Latino neighborhoods in 2000. This evidence of segregation, both in terms of income and racial/ethnic identity, reaffirms other research

Table 5. Rich and poor in Catholic parishes heavily Latino and not heavily Latino

	Not heavily Latino (%)	Heavily Latino* (%)
In "poor" parishes	4	63
In "rich" parishes	39	9

* A heavily Latino parish is one that is reported to be at least 60 percent Latino; these parishes account for about 25 percent of all parishioners. The definitions of rich and poor parishes are the same as in Table 2.

that shows that congregations are often much more segregated than their neighborhoods (Emerson and Woo 2006).

3. *Ethnic and economic segregation are closely tied. The Catholic parish landscape is essentially made up of rich white parishes and poor Latino parishes. (Table 5)*

Table 5 looks at the relationship between a heavily Latino parish and a rich parish. It shows that heavily Latino parishes (here defined as more than 60 percent Latino) are highly likely to also be poor and that white parishes (not heavily Latino) are highly unlikely to also be poor. In contrast, white parishes are more than four times as likely to be rich as heavily Latino parishes.

This should not be surprising, given the substantial differences in income and geographic concentration between the Latino and non-Latino Catholic populations and the concentration of Latino Catholics in Latino parishes shown in earlier tables.

The differences in geographic distribution of ethnic groups are very important to generate the link between ethnic and economic separation. Table 1 shows that Latino Catholics are concentrated in the South and West, while white Catholics are much less prevalent in the West. Geographical differences are even more pronounced among metropolitan areas. Some heavily Catholic metropolitan areas are predominantly Latino in their Catholic population; some are more mixed. For example, Table 6 shows that Latinos make up 73 percent of the Catholic population in Los Angeles but 30 percent of the Catholic population in New York. Thus, dioceses will vary a lot in their opportunities for creating diverse parishes that mix ethnic and economic groups, assuming they want to.

Table 6. The Catholic population in selected metropolitan areas

	Catholic in metro area (%)	Of Catholics	
		White (%)	Latino (%)
Boston	29	82	15
Chicago	34	66	30
DC	19	50	23
Los Angeles	32	22	67
Miami	27	32	57
New York	33	57	35
Philadelphia	26	85	6

Tabulations using the Pew Survey online interactive tool (http://www.pewforum.org/religious-landscape-study/). These seven metropolitan areas are the only ones for which the Pew Survey permitted tabulations of the characteristics of the Catholic population, presumably because only in these seven metropolitan areas were sample sizes of Catholics large enough to allow for reliable estimates and to protect confidentiality. Not reported in this table are percentages of Asian Catholics (which make up most of the difference in LA) or African American Catholics (which make up most of the difference in DC).

Implications

The growth of Latinos as a proportion of Catholics has long been noted, as has the settlement of Latinos throughout the country, including in rural areas (Lichter, Parisi, and Taquino 2016). What has perhaps not been noted as much is how different the white and Latino populations are demographically and economically and how separate they are geographically and in parishes. Despite this separation, and because of dispersed immigration patterns, many Church leaders may have opportunities to nudge parishes toward more ethnic and economic mixing. This raises two questions: To what extent is more mixing possible? To what extent is it desirable?

A recent report on parishes with Hispanic ministries suggests that 25 percent of Catholic parishes report having Hispanic ministries and 6 percent of all Masses are said in Spanish (Ospino 2014). This same report includes the results of a survey question to parish informants in parishes with Hispanic ministries, asking how integrated four Hispanic groups (immigrants and children of immigrants and US-born Hispanics and their children) are to the life of the parish. The results are discouraging: between 54 and 66 percent of these parishes report that the groups are minimally or not at all integrated. Research on what sociologists call "multiracial congregations" shows that they are rare and often unstable but that a set of internal and external factors can prompt their formation (Edwards et al. 2013). In the case of Catholic parishes, as Brett Hoover has described in this volume, there may be more diocesan pressure to attempt this mixing. The data presented in this essay suggest that the extent to which more mixing is possible within parishes depends on the ethnic and economic composition of dioceses, patterns of ethnic and economic segregation within dioceses, parish boundaries within dioceses, and parishioner choice.

The demographic composition of dioceses, which are more or less analogous to metropolitan areas, is largely outside the control of the diocese. The patterns of growth and change in the Catholic population are largely driven by history and by past settlement patterns of immigrants. Catholic populations are growing especially in the metropolitan areas that attract new immigrants, such as the traditional melting pots of Miami, Los Angeles, Chicago, and New York. There are some indications that immigrant populations are beginning to spread out to other metropolitan areas in the Sun Belt and the South (Frey 2015). For both practical reasons and mission reasons, dioceses may want to present themselves as welcoming and attractive to new immigrants. The basic ethnic and economic demographic realities of dioceses, however, are largely externally driven. As Table 6 illustrates, for example, there is real potential for ethic mixing in the Catholic dioceses of Chicago and New York but much less potential in Boston and Philadelphia.

Within dioceses, parish boundaries are geographical (with the exception of personal parishes) (Bruce 2017). As such, they are constrained by the composition and degree of ethnic and economic segregation of residential neighborhoods. Some metropolitan areas are more heavily segregated than others. For example, analyses of 2010 census data show that Latinos are heavily concentrated in Latino neighborhoods in most of the large metropolitan areas that have historically attracted immigrants (Logan and Stults 2011). But if, as the data presented above suggest, parishes are actually less economically diverse then neighborhoods, which are smaller in geographic area than most parishes, then even geography-anchored parishes could potentially be more diverse than they are.

Those who draw diocesan boundaries are constrained by history and the physical location of church buildings. But these boundary drawers—especially when they are closing or merging parishes, as is happening in many dioceses, or establishing new ones, as in different dioceses—could make themselves aware enough of the demographic facts so as to avoid exacerbating ethnic and economic segregation, that is, so they do not gerrymander to make parishes *less* rather than *more* diverse. Especially when parish boundaries are being enlarged, as happens with mergers, parish boundary drawers have some ability to encompass more ethnic and economic diversity within parishes, to make them at least as diverse as the broader neighborhoods that they encompass.

But parish composition is also determined by parishioner choice. Rules about geographical parish membership notwithstanding, many Catholics (including me, I must admit) worship in parishes other than the one to which they are assigned. Congregants responding to surveys explain their choices to change worship locations as based on liturgical preferences, location, and friends. There is some evidence that worshippers look for congregations that are similar to themselves in education, life style, and both theological and political liberalism or conservatism. People, even believers, also choose not to belong to parishes or simply not to attend. It is quite possible, perhaps even likely, that the economic and educational segregation suggested by the analyses in this essay result from conscious choices among parishioners and would-be parishioners.

Leaders who would adjust the composition of parishes to achieve more diversity thus risk the loss of members through personal choice. This could be due to white parishioners fleeing or, alternatively, to nonwhite parishioners not wanting to merge with—and potentially get lost within—white parishes. Nonetheless, there are probably ways to help a greater diversity of people feel welcome in parishes. All of these ways have to do with diminishing the powerful—often unconscious—markers of class, status, and race. Parish leaders can do their best to welcome all and to not favor the well-off and the educated in explicit and implicit ways. They can do their best to make sure that parish members or potential members do not feel shunned or disapproved of because of their appearance, manner of speaking, or family structure. They can do their best to have a diversity of faces as lectors, acolytes, Eucharistic ministers, choir members, religious education teachers, and parish council members. They can plan after-Mass coffee hours and other social occasions to which all are invited and all feel welcome. They might even preach about how the example of Jesus and the early church in reaching out to and including all should guide their parish lives.

Dioceses might also think about ways to encourage cross-parish activities toward the end of enlarging communities. Dioceses are larger and therefore more diverse than parishes. Setting up parish clusters that are constructed to include a wide range of neighborhoods might make it more likely that parishioners interact as equals, perhaps engaging in service projects, educational activities, or special liturgies together.

Church leaders need to weigh the potential advantages of Latino parish communities as welcoming havens and services loci for Latinos, serving some of the same functions that national parishes served for earlier immigrants in the nineteenth and early-twentieth centuries. Dioceses and parishes that are predominantly white and rich (and probably also old) might want to pay special attention to their responsibilities in an unequal world. These parishes, especially those in heartland states, may also want to prepare themselves for declining numbers.

Dioceses, like parishes, are constrained by history, geography, and demographics. Some dioceses are richer and better educated than others; some are more heavily Latino than others. The point here is not that every parish should reflect the overall demographics of Catholics in America. But if parishes and dioceses were more attentive to the possibilities for diversity and inclusion, they might well be able to do better than it appears they are now doing.

The main reason for doing so, to the extent possible, is to be faithful to the mission and vision of Jesus for his community of disciples, a community that loves one another, that welcomes the stranger, and that "brings good news to the poor." The vision of the Christian communities of the Acts of the Apostles, which strove to welcome ethnic Jew and gentile, rich and poor, as full and equal participants in the body of Christ is a vision that today's Church, prodded by Pope Francis, ought also to aspire to.

A secondary reason is to contribute to bridging some of the chasms in American society that separate rich from poor, Latinos from whites, the well educated from the poorly educated, and political liberals from political conservatives. These chasms make it increasingly difficult for the polity to function civilly, to come together around common goals, and to cherish and care for the vulnerable among us. At the very least, I would argue that parish and diocesan leaders ought to do everything they can to avoid making things worse through explicit actions or implicit biases.

References

Bruce, Tricia. 2017. *Parish and Place: Making Room for Diversity in the American Catholic Church*. New York: Oxford University Press.

Chaves, Mark, and Shawna L. Anderson. 2014. "Changing American Congregations: Results from the Third Wave of the National Congregations Study," *Journal for the Scientific Study of Religion* 53: 676–86.

D'Antonio, William V., Michelle Dillon, and Mary L. Gautier. 2013. *American Catholics in Transition*. Lanham, Md.: Rowman & Littlefield Publishers.

DeNavas-Walt, Carmen, and Bernadette D. Proctor. 2014. *Income and Poverty in the United States: 2013*. US Census Bureau, Current Population Reports, P60–249. Washington, DC: US Government Printing Office.

Edwards, Korie L., Brad Christerson, and Michael O. Emerson. 2013. "Race, Religious Organizations, and Integration." *Annual Review of Sociology* 39: 211–28.

Emerson, Michael O., and Rodney M. Woo. 2006. *People of the Dream: Multiracial Congregations in the United States*. Princeton, N.J.: Princeton University Press.

Fox, Liana, Irwin Garfinkle, Neeraj Kaushal, Jane Waldfogel, and Christopher Winer. 2014. "Waging War on Poverty: Historical Trends in Poverty Using the Supplemental Poverty Measure," Working Paper 19789, National Bureau of Economic Research, January.

Frey, William H. 2015. *Diversity Explosion: How New Racial Demographics Are Remaking America*. Washington, DC: Brookings Institution Press.

Jargowsky, Paul. 2015. *Architecture of Segregation: Civil Unrest, the Concentration of Poverty, and Public Policy*. New York: The Century Foundation.

Jencks, Christopher. 2015. "The War on Poverty: Was It Lost?" *New York Review of Books*, April 2, 2015.

Lichter, Daniel T., Domenico Parisi, and Michael C. Taquino. 2016. "Emerging Patterns of Hispanic Residential Segregation: Lessons from Rural and Small-Town America." *Rural Sociology* 81 (4): 483–518.

Logan, John R., and Brian Stults. 2011. *The Persistence of Segregation in the Metropolis: New Findings from the 2010 Census*. Census Brief Prepared for Project US. http://www.s4.brown.edu/us2010.

Massey, Douglas S. 2007. *Categorically Unequal: The American Stratification System*. New York: Russell Sage Foundation.

Massey, Douglas S., Jonathan Rothwell, and Thurston Domina. 2009. "The Changing Bases of Segregation in the United States." *The Annals of the American Academy of Political and Social Science* 626 (November): 74–90.

Murray, Charles. 2012. *Coming Apart*. New York: Crown Forum.

Orfield, Gary, and Erica Frankenberg. 2014. *Brown at 60: Great Progress, a Long Retreat and an Uncertain Future*. Los Angeles: The Civil Rights Project.

Ospino, Hosffman. 2014. *Hispanic Ministry in Catholic Parishes: A Summary Report of Findings from the National Study of Catholic Parishes with Hispanic Ministry*. Boston Mass.: Boston College School of Theology and Ministry. http://www.bc.edu/content/dam/files/schools/stm/pdf/2014/Hispanic MinistryinCatholicParishes_2.pdf.

Owens, Ann, Sean F. Reardon, and Christopher Jencks. 2014. *Trends in School Economic Segregation 1970 to 2010*. CEPA Working Paper. Stanford, Calif: Center for Education Policy Analysis. https://cepa.stanford.edu/sites/default /files/owens%20reardon%20jencks%20school%20income%20segrega-tion%20july2014.pdf.

Pew Research Center. 2014. Religious Landscape Study. Washington, DC: Pew Research Center. http://www.pewforum.org/religious-landscape-study/.

Pew Research Center. 2015a. *America's Changing Religious Landscape*. Washington, DC: Pew Research Center. http://www.pewforum.org/2015/05/12 /americas-changing-religious-landscape/.

Pew Research Center. 2015b. *Modern Immigration Wave Brings 59 Million to US, Driving Population Growth and Change through 2065: Views of Immigration on US Society Mixed*. Washington, DC: Pew Research Center. http://www .pewhispanic.org/2015/09/28/modern-immigration-wave-brings-59-million -to-u-s-driving-population-growth-and-change-through-2065/.

Piketty, Thomas. 2014. *Capital in the Twenty-first Century*. Cambridge, Mass.: Harvard University Press.

Putnam, Robert D. 2015. *Our Kids: The American Dream in Crisis*. New York: Simon & Schuster.

Putnam, Robert D., and David E. Campbell. 2011. *American Grace: How Religion Divides and Unites Us*. New York: Simon & Schuster.

Reardon, Sean F., and Kendra Bischoff. 2011. *More Unequal and More Separate: Growth in the Residential Segregation of Families by Income, 1970–2009*. Report prepared for the Russell Sage US2010 Project. New York: Russell Sage Foundation.

Reardon, Sean F., Lindsay Fox, and Joseph Townsend. 2015. "Neighborhood Income Composition by Household Race and Income, 1990–2009." *The Annals of the American Academy of Political and Social Science* 660 (1): 78–97.

Saez, Emmanuel. 2015. *Striking It Richer: The Evolution of Top Incomes in the United States.* https://eml.berkeley.edu/~saez/saez-UStopincomes-2013.pdf.

Suro, Roberto, and Sonya Tafoya. 2004. *Dispersal and Concentration: Patterns of Latino Residential Settlement.* Report done for the Pew Hispanic Center. Washington, DC: Pew Research Center.

Part IV: Young Catholics
In (and Out) of Parishes

What do we know about how Catholic youth, young adults, and those transitioning into early adulthood interact with parishes? Sociologists analyze both age and generation as meaningful markers of social identity, social context, and social change. "Generation" refers to a cohort of people born during a certain set of years, who go on to experience life events around the same time. One longstanding, repeated survey of Catholic behavior split American Catholics into four generations: pre–Vatican II Catholics (born in 1940 or earlier), Vatican II Catholics (born between 1941 and 1960), post–Vatican II Catholics (born between 1961 and 1978), and millennial Catholics (born between 1979 and 1993). What this tells us is that your age—and when you experience things in the course of history—matters.[1]

The coming two essays use this lens to better understand Catholic parishes. Both Kathleen Garces-Foley and Courtney Ann Irby show how younger Catholics interact differently with their parishes. Rather than belonging to a single home parish, many Catholics participate in programming that is coordinated jointly across multiple parishes or the diocese. This means that American parishes are increasingly interconnected. Catholics respond accordingly, viewing parishes as hubs for ministry, worship, marriage preparation, and more. We'll also learn how parish offerings change alongside broader social change. Exploring this helps us see parishes as actively responding to structural and cultural shifts.

1. See D'Antonio, Dillon, and Gautier 2013. The years included in generations are not consistent across all studies: others, for example, group millennials as those born between 1982 and 2004. Catholics born after millennials don't even have an agreed-upon generational name as of yet. One Catholic research blog invites suggestions (http://nineteensixty-four.blogspot.com/2017/06/catholicism-next-generation.html)!

Suggested Additional Readings

Clydesdale, Tim, and Kathleen Garces-Foley. 2019. *The Twentysomething Soul: Understanding the Religious and Secular Lives of American Young Adults.* New York: Oxford University Press.

D'Antonio, William V., Michele Dillon, and Mary L. Gautier. 2013. *American Catholics in Transition.* Lanham, Md.: Rowman & Littlefield Publishers.

Dillon, Michele. 1999. *Catholic Identity: Balancing Reason, Faith, and Power.* New York: Cambridge University Press.

Hout, Michael. 2016. "Saint Peter's Leaky Boat: Falling Intergenerational Persistence among U.S.-Born Catholics since 1974." *Sociology of Religion* 77 (1) :1–17.

Smith, Christian, Kyle Lonest, Jonathan Hill, and Kari Christoffersen. 2014. *Young Catholic America: Emerging Adults In, Out of, and Gone from the Church.* New York: Oxford University Press.

Starks, Brian. 2009. "Self-Identified Traditional, Moderate, and Liberal Catholics: Movement-Based Identities or Something Else?" *Qualitative Sociology* 32 (1): 1–32.

Yamane, David. 2014. *Becoming Catholic: Finding Rome in the American Religious Landscape:* New York: Oxford University Press.

8   Parishes as Homes and Hubs

KATHLEEN GARCES-FOLEY

Though most national religion surveys indicate that the percentage of Americans affiliating with the Catholic Church has remained fairly stable over the last few decades, they also reveal two trends that are particularly strong among young adult Catholics: declining church attendance and declining importance of Catholic identity. These trends—highlighted already in an essay by Mark Gray—are confirmed in the work of sociologists Dean Hoge, Bill D'Antonio, and colleagues who began to survey US Catholics in 1987 at six-year intervals, paying particular attention to differences between generational cohorts. Their 2011 survey shows that millennial Catholics (then in the 18–31 age group), are less religiously active than earlier generations, less knowledgeable about their faith, and more individualistic in their approach to religious authority and beliefs (D'Antonio, Dillon, and Gautier 2013).

Underlying changes in religiosity are major cultural shifts that have made the transition from adolescence to adulthood more complex than in the past. For example, more young adults are pursuing college education and delaying marriage and parenthood until their late twenties. Some scholars argue that this lengthy period of exploration is a new life stage of "emerging adulthood," characterized by high levels of instability (Arnett 2014). Given these cultural shifts, it is reasonable to expect that today's young adults relate to parishes differently than previous generations.

This essay explores how educated, mostly single, English-speaking, racially diverse young adult Catholics relate to parishes through an ethnographic study in the Washington, DC, region. Using interviews, observations, and social media analysis, I found that many young adults were not tied to a specific parish but moved among a cluster of parishes as they engaged in young adult Catholic activities, including religious services, socializing, and volunteer work. Unlike survey research, which samples young adults to ensure representativeness, the strength of ethnographic research is the ability to explore group processes of interaction in action—as these processes temporally unfold. As we shall see, the parish remains the core of Catholic life for some young adults who seek out a parish home, but many others live out their faith through transparish young adult networks that are supported by parishes functioning as hubs of young adult Catholic activity. Understanding the novel ways these particular young adults are engaging with parishes requires a reevaluation of the role of parishes in the United States.

Existing survey research using various measures of beliefs and practices paints an overall picture of declining young adult engagement in the Church (see Mark Gray's essay in this volume). For example, *Young Adult Catholics: Religion in the Culture of Choice* (Hoge et al. 2001) presents findings from a study of 848 young adults (ages 20–39) who were confirmed as adolescents. Though they found a high level of religious affiliation and Mass attendance, respondents lacked knowledge of basic Church teachings and had difficulty articulating a coherent sense of Catholic identity. To identify the most active young adult Catholics among the confirmands, Hoge et al. used questions about involvement in parish groups or parish committees rather than Mass attendance or adherence to Catholic teaching. "We first identified the *most* active Catholics and named them 'Parish-Involved Catholics.' They represent the core of the laity in parish life" (Hoge et al. 2001, 69). In contrast, the National Study of Youth and Religion, led by sociologist Christian Smith, relied on questions about adherence to orthodox Catholic beliefs, Mass attendance, and private religious practices to determine levels of engagement. In the third wave of this longitudinal study, the researchers were able to resurvey more than seven hundred subjects ages 18–23 who identified as Catholic in the first wave in 2003. Smith et al. find decline in all measures except for a small group of "devout" Catholics, none of whom meet the highest threshold of "Super Catholics," who say their faith is very or extremely important to them and pray at least a few times a week (Smith et al. 2014, 201). For the purpose of this volume, it's important to note that while Hoge et al. (2001) use parish involvement to identify the most active Catholics, parish involvement is invisible—apart from Mass attendance—in Smith et al. (2014).

In response to declining young adult engagement with the Church, scholars like Smith and Hoge, along with Church leaders, offer varying solutions. These range from more orthodoxy; to less orthodoxy, especially on matters of sexual morality; to more focus on social justice, better catechism, and better Catholic parenting. One point of agreement is that parishes, as the center of Catholic life in the United States, need to do a better job welcoming and integrating young adults. The last major study of parish life in the United States, the Notre Dame Study of Catholic Parish Life, was conducted between 1981 and 1989. At that time, Catholic young adult ministry in the United States was in its infancy, and the study does not recognize young adults as a distinct demographic group. The Notre Dame study report does note the lack of organized programs or activities for single Catholics and their lower reported rates of participation in parish life, which may "attest that many parishes have made the intact family unit the primary focus of their attention and have ignored the needs of singles" (Legge and Trozzolo 1983). In the 1990s, young adult ministry was developed through the work of the National Catholic Young Adult Ministry Association (NCYAMA) and the United States Conference of Catholic Bishops (USCCB), which organized listening sessions with young adults to assess their needs and identify best practices (USCCB 2010). The USCCB issued a national pastoral plan for young adult ministry, *Sons and Daughters of the Light* (1996), noting an urgent need for the Church, and parishes in particular, to be more welcoming of young adults. *Sons and Daughters of the Light* identifies four goals for young adult ministry in parishes, dioceses, and campus ministry: connect young adults with Jesus Christ, the Church, the Church's mission in the world, and a peer community.

Many dioceses and parishes have since developed young adult ministry programs with the help of volunteers and some professional staff. Available resources include those from the USCCB; the NCYAMA, which was formed in 1982 to support the work of young adult ministers; and Busted Halo Ministries, launched in 2000 by the Paulist Fathers to help young adults explore their spirituality and to support parish outreach to young adults. More recently, the Busted Halo and NCYAMA created an online resource, Young Adult Ministry in a Box, which provides "effective strategies for becoming a young adult friendly parish" without adding staff (Young Adult Ministry in a Box, n.d.). The growing array of toolkits, guidebooks, videos, websites, consultants, and conferences indicate a robust response to the USCCB's call to create more welcoming parishes for those in their twenties and thirties. Nonetheless, recent parish survey data from the Center for Applied Research in the Apostolate (CARA) reveal that young adult ministry is the program that parishes are *least* likely to have.

This essay explores how active young adult Catholics relate to parishes: What do young adults look for in a parish, and conversely, what drives them away? How do parishes attract young adults and get them involved? To answer these questions, I conducted an ethnographic study in the Washington, DC, metropolitan region in 2010.[1] Washington, DC, has a vibrant young adult Catholic scene created through the efforts of individual leaders, groups, networks, parishes, and the two local dioceses that serve this region. Though I expected to focus exclusively on parish-based young adult groups, I quickly found that the two dioceses that serve this region—the Diocese of Arlington and the Archdiocese of Washington— have young adult ministry staff that play an integral role in creating a transparish Catholic young adult network. Moreover, I discovered that young adult ministry in this region does not belong exclusively to parishes or to the diocesan young adult offices. Also bringing young adult Catholics together are the Catholic Information Center's Young Professional Program, Catholic Singles Club/Catholic Alumni Club, and Contemplative Leaders in Action Program, along with alumni groups from FOCUS and Jesuit Volunteer Corps. Far from being the organizational center of Catholic life, parishes in this region operate alongside diocesan offices and other Catholic organizations that facilitate young adult Catholic engagement.

The research began with extensive document analysis of the official websites and Facebook pages of the Diocese of Arlington and the Archdiocese of Washington. I then attended several large events sponsored by the two dioceses, at which I spoke informally with young adults, asking them which parishes are best for young adults. Based on their recommendations, I selected four parishes to study in more depth.

Over a twelve-month period, I observed twenty-three young adult events sponsored by the two dioceses, four parishes, and the Catholic Information Center, or a combination of these organizations. I sought out

1. This research was part of a national study of young adults active in churches funded by the Lilly Endowment. Additional results from this study can be found in Clydesdale and Garces-Foley 2019.

young adult Catholics to interview through postings on parish and diocesan email lists and Facebook pages, seeking young adults willing to share their experience of being Catholic either in private or focus group settings. I also sought referrals from individuals I interviewed and met informally at events. In total, I interviewed twenty-eight young adults between the ages of 23 and 38, with a median age of 29. This included eighteen women and ten men, three of whom identify as Asian and Pacific Islander, one as Hispanic, one as black, and twenty-three as Caucasian. At 82 percent Caucasian, this is a racially diverse group, but it is less diverse than the young adult Catholics I observed attending events and less diverse than the young adult population of the Washington, DC, region, which is discussed in the next section. All the interviewees were college graduates, and some have graduate degrees. Their class backgrounds varied considerably, along with their countries of origin, but all are highly educated aspiring professionals, as were the young adult Catholics I observed attending events. Twenty-two of the twenty-eight interviewees are single, six are married, and one has young children.

In interviews lasting one to two hours, young adults answered questions about their religious upbringing, Catholic affiliation, process of finding a parish home, involvement in parish life and young adult ministry, and attitudes toward Church teaching on sexual morality and gender roles. Interviews were transcribed and analyzed using ATLAS.ti qualitative software to identify patterns in their responses to open-ended interview questions. While all twenty-eight interviewees attend Mass regularly and all are active in Catholic communities of young adults, they are not all "parish involved" in the traditional American Catholic mode of being registered and involved in the closest parish. Instead, some are active in young adult groups at multiple parishes, while others visit parishes primarily to receive sacraments and are involved in various diocesan and parachurch ministries. In addition to interviews and observations, I studied over the one-year period the online communication of the two dioceses responsible for the DC region and the four selected "young-adult friendly" parishes, reading everything pertaining to young adults on their websites, Facebook, and Twitter.

Together, the interviews, observations, and social media exchanges offer a window into the lives of college-educated, highly committed young adult Catholics in the Washington, DC, region who are tied to parishes but not limited to them. As you read about their experiences, keep in mind that these young adults and their chosen parishes are far from typical or representative of young adult Catholics—most of whom are neither college educated nor involved in young adult ministry. However, given their educational level and professional aspirations, we can expect young adult Catholics like these to have a disproportionate impact on the future of parish life in America (Smith et al. 2014, 272).

Young and Catholic in DC

The Washington, DC, metropolitan area encompasses the federal district and parts of Maryland, Virginia, and West Virginia. It has one of the highest per capita personal income and education levels in the country, but there are pockets of severe poverty, and 25 percent of the population is foreign born. In 2010, non-Hispanic whites dropped to 49 percent of the population (Center for Regional Analysis 2011). In this essay, "DC region" refers to the inner core of this area—the District of Columbia, Arlington, and Alexandria—surrounded by Interstate 495 and known to locals as "inside the Beltway." Adults 25 to 44 years old are the largest cohort in the region, and Arlington, Alexandria, and the District have disproportionate percentages of these age groups (42.7, 41.8 and 33.4 percent, respectively; Howell 2014). The DC region has one of the fastest-growing populations of educated millennials in the country and a booming creative class, drawn to the region for professional and educational opportunities.

The DC region is served by the Archdiocese of Washington and the Diocese of Arlington, and both have offices of young adult ministry (YAM, for short). Following the 1996 USCCB pastoral plan, the diocesan YAM supports Catholics in their twenties and thirties, single and married, recognizing that Catholic campus ministry focuses on undergraduate students. The Arlington and DC YAM offices organize events for all young adults in the region and communicate frequently to avoid scheduling competing events. They also support parish-based YAM by promoting parish events and helping young adults find a parish home, in accordance with the USCCB pastoral plan. Though the DC region has a large Hispanic population, diocesan YAM is advertised and conducted in English. There is a separate Programa De Jóvenes Adultos through the Diocese of Arlington's

Hispanic Apostolate for those ages 18–35, and some parishes in the District and Arlington offer Spanish-language programing for *jóvenes adultos*. It is important to keep in mind that the English-speaking Catholic population is very diverse in terms of racial and ethnic identity, including bilingual Hispanic Catholics, as it reflects the high levels of diversity in the region and the high levels of diversity within the Catholic Church. Based on event observations and Facebook analysis, I found that diocesan YAM in the DC region attracts racially diverse, college-educated, mostly single professionals between the ages of 25 and 35 with a two-to-one female majority.

Several young adults told me DC is a great city for Catholics. For example, Stephen, a 25-year old Caucasian man, shared: "There are pockets of young adult activity in this country. It's DC, Atlanta, Denver, Kansas City. Those are like the hubs of Catholic young adult activity."[2] Because the diocesan YAM offices readily use social media, English-speaking young adult Catholics can easily find opportunities for prayer, socializing, and volunteering. The monthly online calendars, which combine diocesan and parish-based activities, list events almost every day. The sheer volume of activities is impressive, but so is the range of activities. The dioceses organize annual events like the Bishop's Mass, March for Life, and retreats, as well as monthly opportunities for adoration, confession, praise singing, and fellowship—called Christ in the City in DC and Holy Hour in Arlington. Both dioceses host discussion series, and Arlington began a Catholic sports club through which young adults can "grow in your faith and your game" as my research was ending (Catholic Diocese of Arlington, n.d.). In 2010, the Diocese of Arlington had a more organized and better marketed YAM than the Archdiocese of Washington, but since then the DC office has revamped its website, rebranded itself "DCCatholic," and created regional hubs to host events for those outside the District.

By far the most popular diocesan-wide program is Theology on Tap, which began in 1981 in a Chicago parish and spread nationally. In the Diocese of Arlington, Theology on Tap is held on a Monday evening at an Irish pub that fills with 150–250 young adults in professional attire who drink beer, socialize, and listen to a talk on living the Catholic faith.

---

2. All personal and parish names are pseudonyms, and some details have been changed to obscure identity.

Theology on Tap is the most common "entry point" for those checking out the Catholic scene in DC. Young adults new to the area, converts, and reverts can enjoy a combination of inspiration, catechesis, practical tips, and Catholic jokes in the comfortable, noisy setting of a bar happy hour. Those looking for a parish can find a table reserved by parish young adult groups who will, ideally, invite any attending solo to join them. These parish table hosts—organized by the diocesan staff—are crucial to getting young adults connected with a home parish. Though the USCCB pastoral plan identifies the parish as the "pre-eminent" place through which young adults connect with Jesus Christ, the Church, the world, and peers, many young adults take a long time finding a parish home that fits, and some don't see a need to have a parish home when there are other ways to be engaged with the Church.

Active Young Adult Catholics

Sociologists try to identify and understand the variations among young adult Catholics by grouping them by common characteristics, like frequency of Mass attendance, parish involvement, and adherence to Church teaching. The twenty-eight young adults I interviewed are highly committed Catholics who go beyond weekly Mass attendance to participate in worship, service, and social activities with other Catholics. As I have already noted, their activities are not always parish centered. They vary in their opinions about Church teaching and would not all fit into the devout Catholic type defined by Smith et al. in *Young Catholic America* (2014). They also vary in the faith journeys that have brought them to a high level of Church engagement. Parishes played an important role—both positive and negative—at some points in their journeys to Catholic engagement, which I sort into three types: Catholic reverts, converts, and persistent Catholics.

Reverts, Converts, and Persistent Catholics

In young adult ministry circles, those who disengage or leave the Church and come back are known as "reverts." Out of the twenty-eight interviewed, five were reverts. They left at different ages and for different reasons, but a common breaking point was college. For example, Jocelyn is a

29-year-old immigrant from Africa who works in the legal system. She dropped out at age 19, as did many of her friends, because of "all the rules." She came back at age 27: "I left the Catholic Church and I went around learning about other churches. I think it is the typical Catholic thing. You have to sometimes stand out and look around and see. I came back because I feel more comfortable in the Church." Sue is a 28-year-old Caucasian woman from the Midwest who works in communications. Growing up, she attended public schools and religious education classes and enjoyed being part of her parish high school youth group. She explained why, without this structured support, she barely went to Mass in college:

> I think people replace religion with other things, like just hanging out, drinking, do[ing] sports, or whatever. . . . I think it's more . . . the way I was raised, that religion is a family thing, a family-oriented thing, so if you don't have that core group to go with or maybe if you had friends to go with, then it would be different—but going by yourself and being disconnected, it's like going to a meeting, not meeting any-body, and just listening to a lecture and leaving.

Sue came to DC for college and, after graduating, started going to Mass again when she found a parish she liked: "I just like the atmosphere. I just feel spiritually lifted, and I think it's important to have balance in your life and kind of be thankful for what you have." She has two sisters who also dropped out in college but have not returned. She explains, "When you fall away, it's hard to get back and [find] a church and [start] that process. They both live in different places than where they were raised, so being proactive and finding a church and going into that atmo-sphere is kind of scary and intimidating."

The reversion process for these young adults involved fits and starts as they tested out parishes, looking for a good fit. The next section on parish shopping describes what this process looks like in more detail. If poten-tial reverts don't find a parish they like, they may try again in a few years, or when they move to a new city, or when they have children and can more easily integrate into the family-centric parish. We don't know how many disengaged Catholics will never return and how many potential reverts are searching parish websites looking for signs that this parish will be right for them.

Two of the young adults in this sample are converts. Amy grew up in the South surrounded by a lot of anti-Catholic prejudice, and she dabbled in various Evangelical churches growing up. In college, she was drawn to the theological richness of the Church and the reverence in worship. She went through RCIA (Rite of Christian Initiation of Adults) her sophomore year. Amy, a 29-year-old Caucasian woman, describes herself as a Catholic evangelist. She listens to Fr. Corapi on Catholic radio every morning and greatly admires him, though this was before Corapi was removed from public ministry by his religious order. Amy shares enthusiastically, "Fr John Corapi says to speak orthodoxy, speak the truth, challenge this age, and you're going to fill your pews and you're going to have converts all over the place. The Church answers today's ills better than anyone else." Stacy, the other convert, couldn't be more different. She grew up Episcopalian, became interested in Latin America in high school, and majored in religion and Latin American studies in college. After graduation, she worked in Latin America and joined the Jesuit Volunteer Corps (JVC). She really liked the JVC community, so in her mid-twenties she did RCIA at a parish in the Arlington diocese. She explains why: "This is kind of a boring answer, but I think it was the focus on the sacramental character of the Eucharist and wanting to participate more fully when I was with my JVC friends." Stacy is the only interviewee who described herself as a feminist. She "has issues" with some Church teachings but does not accept the "cafeteria Catholic" label, because it erroneously reduces Catholicism to a set of narrow laws: "You hear that there can't be divorce, but you don't necessarily focus on the teachings of the poor, and I think in any kind of fundamentalism it is easy to focus on sexual morality." Stacy knows lots of young adults who love the social justice part of the Church but aren't active Catholics, because they don't hear social justice related to the Catholic tradition.

What term should we use for active young adult Catholics who were raised in a Catholic family and never "left" the Church? They used to be the norm, but we have seen from national survey data that a substantial number of Catholics now disaffiliate from the Church, and only a small proportion of those raised Catholic are active in the Church as young adults. While many of their peers, parents, and siblings dropped out, this small group stayed Catholic, and so I call them "persistent" Catholics. Even though they never gave up on the Church, almost all of them struggled at times in this commitment. The sex abuse scandal came up most often as the cause of struggling; intense public negativity against the Church was a critical juncture when some weighed whether to "give up" on it. Several also pointed to the Church's stance against gay marriage, which is very unpopular among their peers. For example, Maddie, a 27-year-old recently married Caucasian, gets really tired of defending herself from anti-Catholic bias: "They assume that since they know you're Catholic, that they know everything about you. They know you're going to get married, and they know you're going to have ten kids, you go to church every Sunday, and you must hate gay people. There are so many presumptions that come with the label, and it's very inaccurate for me." Maddie also talked about living through years of bad Masses:

> I was raised Catholic, and my parents took us every Sunday. You went because that is what you did. It was a fairly miserable church. I got very little out of it. Then I went to college, and I think that is the time you are going to either get people or you're going to lose people, and the school I went to had a strong Newman presence that made it interesting. For the first time I went to Mass and was like, "Oh God, it can be something that isn't miserable," and that is why I stuck with it.

Like Maddie, most of the persistent Catholics experienced a significant shift solidifying their relationship to the Church in young adulthood. I had a long interview with Caitlin at a noisy coffee shop in Arlington. At age 29, Caitlin is a married, stay-at-home mom with children ages 18 months and 6 weeks. In her early twenties, she could never have imagined herself committed to natural family planning. Caitlin began her story like this:

> We were expected to go to church on Sunday. We did most Sundays, but my parents weren't die-hard about it. I went to CCD while in public school, and then I went to a Catholic high school, and I chose a Catholic college but not because it was Catholic. That just wasn't a priority back then. I started off going to church on Sundays and then really fell away in every sense of the term until the very end of college, when I decided to clean up my act and try leading a double life.

For Caitlin, leading a double life meant doing "good" Catholic things like going to Mass, going on retreats, and volunteering, while also living a typical twenty-two-year-old lifestyle in America, which involves being sexually active, getting high, and drinking a lot. At age 25, "the stars aligned" to push her to make big changes. She discovered that the man she was seeing was sleeping with other women, and she was offered a parish youth ministry position. After a lot of prayer during the Lenten season, she decided to take the ministry job and bring her life into alignment with Church teaching, starting with chastity. Caitlin is a persistent Catholic who shifted into a more conservative Catholicism in her mid-twenties.

Natalie is an example of a persistent Catholic who has always been very conservative, but she, too, experienced a shift as a younger adult. Twenty-eight years old and also recently married, Natalie describes her upbringing as "really active in the Church." She attended a conservative Catholic college, where she studied politics. As a young adult, her private prayer life intensified as she began going to daily Mass and Eucharistic adoration, which brought her tremendous peace. Natalie, like Caitlin and Amy, the Catholic evangelist convert, is a proponent of natural family planning and describes herself as orthodox, which is a term used by several of the young adults I interviewed to signal a commitment to neo-traditionalism.

Neo-Traditionalist and Progressive Catholics

In interviews, I heard young adults making distinctions among their peers using terms like "orthodox" or "open" to describe themselves and "hardcore" or "judgmental" to describe what they are not. In these labels, we can hear the echoes of the cultural divide within American Catholicism between those who want a Church of "dynamic orthodoxy" and public piety (neo-traditionalists) and those who want a Church of dialogue, community, and social justice (progressives) (Koneiczny 2013; Baggett 2009; Dillon 1999). Among the twenty-eight interviewees, five are neo-traditionalists who identify wholeheartedly with the Catholicism of Steubenville and Theology of the Body, while the remainder who chose to describe themselves said things like, "I'm not hardcore" and "I'm not one of those crazy Steubenville people." While I can infer from interviews with the latter that they align culturally with progressive Catholics or somewhere on a continuum between progressives and neo-traditionalists, only two interviewees self-identified as progressive. Neo-traditionalism is the dominant public culture of Catholicism in the DC region. However, when

I asked interviewees how they found a parish community, the language of progressive Catholicism, emphasizing community and tolerance, came to the fore.

Parish Shopping and Parish Hopping

Because parishes are defined by geographic boundaries, Catholics are not supposed to choose their parish. By virtue of where they live, they are already part of a parish that will provide their sacramental and catechetical needs. For the twenty-eight young adult Catholics I interviewed, however, the concept of being assigned to a parish is foreign. Reflecting the importance of personal choice, they seek out a parish that "works for me" in a process known colloquially as parish shopping. So what kind of parish works for them? Orthodoxy and piety are important to some young adults, while others want a nonjudgmental atmosphere and steer clear of parishes that are "too much into doctrine." Teresa, a 33-year-old Hispanic woman, summed up the attitude of almost all I spoke with when she said, "I don't come for the sermon, but a sermon could cause me to leave." Architecture, music, intellectual depth, and reverence matter to varying degrees, but by far the most common thing they are looking for is a parish where they can meet other young adult joiners.

St. Raphael Catholic Church, an urban parish in Arlington, is well known as a popular parish for young adults. In sociological terms, St. Raphael is a "magnet church" (Ammerman 2001) because it draws young adults from across the DC region for its 6 p.m. Mass on Sundays. Typically it's standing room only, with the crowd spilling out into the vestibule. Danny, a 26-year-old Asian man, has been attending St. Raphael for two years and is involved in lots of parish activities. He prefers the 6 p.m. Mass even if he can't get a seat: "I'd rather stand with people who look like me than sit with people who don't." Joiners who have attended Mass at St. Raphael describe it as welcoming, friendly, vibrant, open, and tolerant. The parish young adult group meets after the 6 p.m. Mass to plan social events like parties, happy hours, and kayaking trips. St. Raphael also has a young adult bible study and a young adult book club, which is currently reading about John Paul II's Theology of the Body, but these more conservative groups are not connected to the parish's young adult group. St. Raphael, with its abundance of young adults and energetic liturgies, works for many young adults, even some who don't align with the social justice emphasis of this parish—as is the case for Sue, whom we met in the revert section above.

Like many young adults shopping for a parish, Sue looked at parish websites and asked her Catholic friends for suggestions. She has a good friend who goes to Our Lady of Sorrows who "really likes the conservative stuff, so she is pretty Catholic." Even though Sue is also conservative, Our Lady of Sorrows was not a good fit. "It was really formal and conservative. I'm Republican and conservative, but I like a more dynamic church like St. Raphael, which is pretty liberal. Some of the views they establish, I don't necessarily go for, but I just like the atmosphere, and the feeling of being there is much more welcoming than Our Lady of Sorrows, which is more conservative and strict." When I asked Sue what views she didn't agree with at St. Raphael, she explained, "It was a lot of sacrificing and helping the poor, helping the disadvantaged. I'm more of a 'teach a man to fish' as opposed to 'give a man a fish.'" Sue also tried a parish called St. Stephen a few times. "It is kind of in-between St. Raphael and Our Lady of Sorrows, and it's close to my work so it's easier to go there. The Mass is normal. It's not too liberal and not too conservative. It's very straightforward. You know, very Catholic. I don't want to say bland, but neutral I guess."

Sue went to St. Raphael sporadically for a couple of years before she became really involved. She knew there was a parish young adult group but heard it was for people in their late thirties. One Sunday they announced a young adult pizza and beer gathering after Mass, "and I felt like a lot of young adults were going, so I go there and there were like a hundred people there." Excited by the energy in the group, Sue jumped into planning happy hours, retreats, and small faith groups, as long as they were only for young adults, explaining, "I am kind of ageist I guess. I'm kind of picky about that kind of thing." Lately, she has been pulling back from St. Raphael—not attending Mass or young adult events as often. She says she's really busy at work, and it's always the same people who attend.

Sue and Danny have both been very involved in St. Raphael, but their relationship to the parish is quite different. The parish young adult group facilitated Danny's initial entry into the parish, but he is now part of many activities that don't involve young adults exclusively. Danny knows the staff and how things get done in the parish, and he is registered at St. Raphael, something few of young adults I interviewed considered important. For

Danny, St. Raphael is his *home* parish, and he invests significant time and energy into its development. Sue identifies St. Raphael as her parish and is not actively parish shopping, but her ties to St. Raphael are not as strong as Danny's. For Sue, St. Raphael is a more of a *hub* of activity than a home. The parish young adult group provides infrastructure for forming social relationships with Catholics her age. She likes that events are advertised on Facebook so she can see who will attend and assess if they look like people she wants to hang out with in her limited free time. Lately, Sue has been spending more of her free time at diocesan YAM events where she can meet new people. She is committed to the Church and wants to be part of a Catholic social world, but Sue's ties to St. Raphael are tenuous. She is hoping to marry a Catholic man before she turns 30 and will raise her children in the Church, at which point I expect Sue and her family will join a parish, but for now St. Raphael functions as a hub of activity that facilitates relationships with other Catholic young adults.

The interconnected networks of parishes, parachurch organizations, and diocesan YAM offices encourage young adults to move fluidly among these Catholic organizations. Through these networks, parish-based programs advertise to young adults across the DC region to increase participation. Some young adults regularly attend activities at several different parishes, which act as hubs for the Catholic social scene they move within. In contrast to the experience of parish shopping with the intention of seeking a parish home, I call this type of activity "parish hopping." I found several young adults who fit this mode of parish engagement through research at St. Paschal Catholic Church, a Jesuit-run parish in the District. St. Paschal began one of the first young adult groups in the District in the 1970s.

The St. Paschal's Young Adult Community (YAC) is well organized, with a mission statement and large steering committee. The YAC holds a Sunday evening Mass and social café once a month at St. Paschal, which draws around sixty young adults from that parish and beyond. The YAC steering committee runs happy hours, faith sharing groups, softball games, service actions, and retreats for a loosely tied four-hundred-member DC Catholic community connected through email, Facebook, and word-of-mouth. This transparish community could not exist without parish hubs like St. Paschal: the parish provides meeting space, including access to a Jesuit retreat center; website space; and pastoral support from many spiritual leaders connected with the Jesuits. Stacy, who converted to Catholicism after a year in the Jesuit Volunteer Corps, found St. Paschal after attending one of the YAC retreats. She told me the Ignatian meditation group is another place "where random people show up that are sometimes part of the parish and sometimes are not, so I think we have a lot of fluidity in who is a member." Though St. Paschal serves as a home parish for some young adults, it is a hub for many more whose relationship to parishes is often in flux.

I learned the term "parish hopping" from Jacob, a 27-year-old Caucasian who spends a lot of time trying to connect young adults in the region into a strong Catholic network. Jacob is an active member of St. Monica Catholic Church. He attends the parish's young adult bible studies and happy hours, volunteers with the youth sports league, and organizes lots of service events, like the recent diaper drive. When Jacob helps with an event, he always posts the information on his Facebook page and sends it to what he calls the "more robust" young adult groups. "I do my best to outreach to the other parishes. I have some friends at St. Maria Regina. They have a pretty good program. We met through Sue [described above]. I met Sue at a networking happy hour thing a couple of months ago. So I'm just trying to grow the network and get more people connected on any of our given service projects or fundraisers or social events. . . . We need to make sure everyone is connected and sharing ideas and kind of maximizing resources. . . . The more the merrier." Through his extensive outreach, Jacob has extended and strengthened the parish-based networks. He calls his efforts the "seed work": "I got my army of volunteers that I can help mobilize. Just get me an idea, and we can get people over there." The more individuals like Jacob spread the word about Catholic events, the more opportunities young adult Catholics have to connect with others like them.

Stephen's engagement with parishes is a good example of parish hopping and the way parishes function as hubs in a transparish Catholic social world. Stephen has a parish home but also attends events all over the region, because he loves what he calls the social element. Stephen is a single, 25-year-old Caucasian man from the Midwest who came to DC for graduate school. Stephen goes to Mass weekly and confession about twice a month. Here's how he found a parish that is authentic and faithful:

I looked at St. Damien's because it was the closest parish, and there wasn't a ton going on, and what was going on was for people who were a little bit older, like early thirties, late twenties. I was like twenty-three. Then I went to Padre Serra. I went up there because I heard that that was kind of a younger parish. Then I went to St. Monica too. St. Monica, kind of like in its tone and style of liturgy, resonated with me more. . . . Padre Serra, for lack of a better word, was more "Kumbaya," and I like the more-traditional hymns. So St. Monica was more a better fit in that sense, but also the priests were really good.

In a matter of months, Stephen was "conscripted," he jokes, into lots of activities at St. Monica, including young adult service projects and teaching CCD. St. Monica is his home parish without a doubt, but despite all his commitments there, Stephen is active in many aspects of the DC Catholic scene:

What is kind of interesting with this area is that people jump a lot between different groups. It's like Arlington Diocese, Washington, and then St. Monica. I go to a men's group at St. Basil Parish because I work over there. I live in this area, but I am on the listserv for Arlington Diocese. But also, friends and I will go to the Catholic Information Center downtown, where it's kind of its own thing, and then we'll do stuff at St. Monica.

Stephen enjoys going to all kinds of Catholic social gatherings offered through the transparish young adult Catholic scene. Though the examples he provides indicate a preference for neo-traditionalism, he sheepishly admits he goes mostly for the social aspects: "I mean, I recognize that it should be the primary reason to go. . . . I sometimes feel like it's weird in these young adult things. You know, that most of them are single, so you know it's got to be on at least half the people's minds." Stephen met his current girlfriend at a Catholic Information Center event for young professionals.

Most of the twenty-eight young adults I interviewed related to parishes as homes, hubs, or both, as in the case of Stephen. There were a few who also talked about parishes as places they go for the sacraments of Eucharist and confession and for Eucharistic adoration. Stephen, who calls

St. Monica his home parish and goes to many other parishes and diocesan young adult activities, also goes to Mass during the week at a different parish near his home. In other words, he goes to his territorial parish for daily Mass, but this is not the parish he has selected as his home parish. Natalie, a persistent Catholic we met earlier, has selected a parish in Northern Virginia as her home parish, but she likes to visit adoration chapels at other parishes, many of which are open 24/7. Amy, the convert Catholic evangelist we met earlier, doesn't have a home parish and isn't looking for one. As she explains, she goes to selected neo-traditionalist parishes for sacraments and finds her community through the Catholic Information Center:

> I haven't technically joined a parish and it's because I don't like the parish I am technically supposed to belong to, and it's mainly because it's a lot of immigrant community. I don't see a lot of people my age there, but there is a great parish in Old Town Alexandria, Saint Kateri Tekakwitha Catholic Church, which I have attended regularly. But I became a waitress as a second job, which prevented me from going regularly to any one church, so I usually hip hop between St. Agatha Lin in Chinatown at the 7 p.m. Mass and then Saint Kateri Tekakwitha Catholic Church in Alexandria for the daytime Mass. . . . What is nice about the 7:30 p.m. Mass in Chinatown is that they offer confession prior to Mass all the way through the Mass, so I often rely on that. The young folk call that the sinner's Mass because they have confession for so long.

Amy did sign up for St. Kateri's young adult group email list, but she doesn't go to its events. "I have a really great network of Catholic friends here. It might sound terrible, but I feel like I have a full enough life and enough Christian fellowship that I don't really need to seek that out." She does listen to the diocesan Theology on Tap podcasts, but the only group she is active in is the Catholic Information Center. She helps organize the Young Professional Program, which combines lectures and social gatherings, and she attends the monthly Night of Recollection for Women, which includes spiritual talks, adoration, benediction, and confession. Several days a week, Amy is in a parish to receive sacraments or for adoration, but she does not view any of these parishes as a home parish or as hubs of Catholic activity to connect her with other young adults.

For Amy, parishes function as sacrament stations, and the Catholic Information Center provides her with a community of like-minded young adults Catholics. At this point in her life, Amy is single and working two jobs, but she hopes to marry and have a large family. We can anticipate that when she does have a family, she will look for a home parish to raise her children faithfully in the Church.

Conclusion

In this essay, we have heard from young adult Catholics who are active in the Washington, DC, Catholic scene, which is constructed through the work of parish-based young adult groups, diocesan offices for young adult ministry, and parachurch organizations. All these institutions hold programs that further the goals of the USCCB pastoral plan to connect young adults with Jesus Christ, the Church, the Church's mission in the world, and a peer community. However, when it comes to the expectation that the parish will be the center of these connections, the results are mixed. According to *Sons and Daughters of the Light*, "Pastoral care for young adults requires that parishes be a *home* for young adults where they are personally touched in their faith journey" (USCCB 1996, 27). This study reveals that many highly educated, highly committed young adult Catholics in the DC region are relating to parishes in ways that challenge assumptions of parish-centered Catholicism. We have seen that young adults parish shop, sometimes taking a long time to settle into a parish that meets their needs, but they rarely register with the parish. We have seen that even young adults who do select a parish home may be not be participating in the intergenerational parish life and may participate in activities hosted by other parishes and parachurch organizations. We have seen that some young adults do not claim a parish home but are highly engaged in the Church through numerous institutions that allow them to move freely within a regional, transparish young adult Catholic scene. Many young adults move freely among parish-based young adult groups, diocesan young adult ministry, and parachurch organizations.

I have argued that parishes are operating as hubs of activities within this transparish network of young adults. If we think of parishes as hubs, they operate in a similar way to other Catholic institutions (Catholic

Information Center and diocesan young adult ministry). While these hubs do provide sacraments, parishes provide them more regularly than the other institutions. What makes the parish unique in comparison to other young adult Catholic hubs is its intergenerational community, but none of the young adults I interviewed valued the parish as an intergenerational Catholic community at this stage in their lives. Instead, they looked to parishes—along with other hubs—for infrastructure, legitimacy, and support to organize and host young adult–focused events.

There is one other way in which parishes may play a unique role in the lives of young adults. As noted earlier, the DC Catholic region is dominated by neo-traditionalism, promoted through the dioceses and Catholic Information Center. One will not hear anything opposed to Church teaching even in the "open discussions" hosted by the dioceses for young adults on controversial topics, such as sexual orientation. Even the more liberal-leaning parishes in the region must be careful never to post anything that can be construed as contrary to Church teaching on their websites or risk a call from the bishop's office. I found that young adults who are not "hardcore Catholics" congregate in the few moderate-liberal-leaning young adult friendly parishes such as St. Raphael, St. Paschal, and Padre Serra. At these parishes, they face less risk of chastisement when they publically express "less-than-hardcore" Catholic views. At these parishes, they won't be shunned for cohabitating or missing a Holy Day of Obligation. Nor will they be expected to go to confession regularly or support natural family planning. I suspect that these moderate-liberal-leaning parishes serve as a last chance for the "less-than-hardcore" Catholics who would otherwise be estranged from Catholic institutions in the conservative-leaning dioceses of the DC region. Take, for example, the experience of June, a 31-year-old woman who is active at Padre Serra, which she calls her home parish. She was recently married in another parish with a more conservative priest:

> I hadn't gone to confession in like over ten years and I went before my wedding, and the priest said to me, "Do you know that you have been receiving Communion falsely for the past ten years?" I mean, here you are trying to get yourself to confession and it's a big deal you haven't been there in a long time. Maybe you should be praising the person for being

there rather than making them feel bad. If I wasn't actively involved in the Church, and I got a priest like that, I would be like "screw this."

Despite this bad experience with a conservative priest, June isn't leaving the Church, because she has found a young-adult friendly parish where she feels welcome. June hopes to soon have children and raise them in the faith with help from her parish. I heard several versions of June's "last chance" parish story and hope future research will explore whether particular types of parishes retain Catholics who would otherwise be disconnected from the institutional Church.

This essay explores how racially diverse, highly educated, and highly involved young adults Catholics in the region of Washington, DC, relate to parishes. I argue that they relate to parishes in three distinct but overlapping ways: parish as home, parish as hub, and parish as sacrament station. I hope that future research will explore the extent to which these modes of relating to parishes and the development of transparish networks exist in other urban areas and among less-educated young adults. We can further ask to what extent these dynamics are at work more broadly among Catholics who identify as a (numerical) minority within a parish and seek to form peer groups that transcend parish boundaries. For example, my research on Filipino Catholics in the Archdiocese of Los Angeles explores the formation of a diocesan-wide Filipino network facilitated by diocesan staff and supported by parishes with Filipino ministries (Garces-Foley 2009).

The last point of this essay is to suggest that scholars rethink the centrality and functions of the parish in American Catholicism. Based on this study, it would be a mistake to assume that young adults who are "loosely tethered" to DC parishes are disengaged from the Church. We should be wary of using parish commitment as a proxy for institutional commitment to the Church. Also, we should be aware that the regional DC young adult Catholic scene has not come about by accident. Church leaders in parishes, diocesan offices, and parachurch organizations are thrilled to see large numbers of young adults at transparish Catholic events, regardless of parish involvement. These leaders have prioritized engaging young adults through age-specific ministries over socializing this age cohort into parish-centered Catholicism. It remains to be seen how this will affect the integration of young adults into intergenerational parishes when they form families.

References

Ammerman, Nancy. 2001. *Congregation and Community.* New Brunswick, N.J.: Rutgers University Press.

Arnett, Jeffrey Jensen. 2014. *Emerging Adulthood: The Winding Road from the Late Teens Through the Twenties.* New York: Oxford University Press.

Baggett, Jerome P. 2009. *Sense of the Faithful: How American Catholics Live their Faith.* New York: Oxford University Press.

Catholic Diocese of Arlington. n.d. "Catholic Sports Club." Retrieved May 8, 2015. http://www.arlingtondiocese.org/yam/catholicsportsclub.aspx.

Center for Regional Analysis. 2011. *Update from the 2010 Census: Population Change in the Washington, DC Metropolitan Area.* Fairfax, Va.: George Mason University Center for Regional Analysis. Retrieved May 17, 2015. http://cra.gmu.edu/pdfs/researach_reports/recent_reports/Population_Change_in_the_Washington_Metropolitan_Area.pdf.

Clydesdale, Tim, and Kathleen Garces-Foley. 2019. *The Twentysomething Soul: Understanding the Religious and Secular Lives of American Young Adults.* New York: Oxford University Press.

D'Antonio, William V., Michele Dillon, and Mary L. Gautier. 2013. *American Catholics in Transition.* Lanham, Md.: Rowman & Littlefield Publishers.

Dillon, Michelle. 1999. *Catholic Identity: Balancing Reason, Faith, and Power.* Cambridge, UK: Cambridge University Press.

Garces-Foley, Kathleen. 2009. "From the Melting Pot to the Multicultural Table: Filipino Catholics in Los Angeles." *American Catholic Studies* 120 (1): 27–54.

Hoge, Dean R., William D. Dinges, Mary Johnson, and Juan L. Gonzales. 2001. *Young Adult Catholics: Religion in the Culture of Choice.* Notre Dame, Ind.: University of Notre Dame Press.

Howell, Kathryn. 2014. *Growing Up and Aging in Place: Generational Demographics in the Washington, DC Region.* Fairfax, Va.: George Mason University Center for Regional Analysis. Retrieved January 25, 2016. http://cra.gmu.edu/pdfs/studies_reports_presentations/WMSA_Demographics_Apr2014.pdf.

Koneiczny, Mary Ellen. 2013. *The Spirit's Tether: Family, Work, and Religion among American Catholics.* New York: Oxford University Press.

Leege, David C., and Thomas A. Trozzolo. 1983. *Participation in Catholic Parish Life: Religious Rites and Parish Activities in the 1980s.* Notre Dame Study of Catholic Parish Life, Report No. 3. Church Life Research Initiative. Notre Dame, Ind.: University of Notre Dame. Retrieved April 24, 2018. http://icl.nd.edu/initiatives-projects/church-life-research/.

Smith, Christian, Kyle Longest, Jonathan Hill, and Kari Christofferson. 2014. *Young Catholic America Emerging Adults In, Out of, and Gone from the Church.* New York: Oxford University Press.

USCCB (United States Conference of Catholic Bishops). 1996. *Sons and Daughters of the Light: A Pastoral Plan for Ministry with Young Adults*. Washington, DC: United States Conference of Catholic Bishops.

USCCB (United States Conference of Catholic Bishops) Committee for Laity, Marriage, Family Life, and Youth. 2010. *Connecting Young Adults to Catholic Parishes: Best Practices in Catholic Young Adult Ministry*. Washington, DC: United States Conference of Catholic Bishops.

Young Adult Ministry in a Box. n.d. "Introduction." Retrieved May 13, 2015. http://www.youngadultministryinabox.com.

9 Preparing to Say "I Do"

COURTNEY ANN IRBY

Marriages are in crisis. The numbers are low in general, but especially
in the Church. I occasionally hear other priests say, "We should get out
of the marrying business." I think this is odd, because we aren't in the
marrying business. But we *are* in the business of calling people to a
holy life. People wouldn't go to a civil official to do a baptism; likewise,
matrimony is a sacrament that takes place in the Church. Unfortu-
nately, so many people have no idea about the sacrament of marriage.
Couples are critical to the health of the Church, but it's more than just
for the sake of the Church, because the Church exists for the sake of
the world.

—Visiting Priest's Talk on Marriage, Field Notes

As one of the seven sacraments, marriage occupies a special place
within Catholicism. For Catholics, marriage is something people *receive*
from the Church rather than something that individuals can construct
for themselves (USCCB 2009). Unlike most Protestant denominations,
Catholicism maintains a clear distinction between a *civil* wedding and
a *Church* ("valid") wedding. One study found that 70 percent of American
Catholics report either being married "in the Church" or later having their
civil marriage "convalidated" by the Church (Gray, Perl, and Bruce 2007),
indicating the continued centrality of the Catholic Church in individual
believers' marriages. Parishes play an instrumental role in this experience,
mediating between lay Catholics and macro-level Catholic understandings
of marriage. As the local manifestation of the Church, parishes operate
as the site where couples receive the sacrament of marriage and may live
out this new phase of their lives. In practice, this means that US parishes
represent a core context in which American Catholics learn, negotiate, and
relay Catholic messages about marriage.

Parishes' mediating role has been incredibly important as Catholics, along with the rest of Americans, make sense of the changing institution of marriage. For example, people are waiting longer to get married, and a growing proportion are not getting married at all (Cherlin 2009). Among Catholics, the total number of "valid" Church weddings has declined by two-thirds since 1970, despite growth in total numbers of American Catholics (CARA, n.d.). Sociologists explain these broader cultural shifts in family, in part, by the rising view of marriage as a *choice* made in pursuit of personal well-being (Amato et al. 2007; Cherlin 2009; Coontz 2005). The expectation that marriage should be personally fulfilling—accompanied by higher divorce rates—means that "after centuries of being the bedrock of the American family system, marriage is losing its privileged status and becoming one lifestyle choice among many" (Amato et al. 2007, 2). In other words, marriage no longer represents a core milestone of adulthood that people routinely accede to but, rather, one choice among many that people may make as part of their broader efforts to construct a happy and meaningful life (Cherlin 2004; Silva 2013).

Changes in the meaning of marriage illuminate a broader rise in what scholars have called "therapeutic culture" (Aubry and Travis 2015; Bellah et al. 1985; Jenkins 2014; Roof 1999), which privileges logics of "self-knowledge and self-realization" in life decisions (Bellah et al. 1985, 98). From formal authorities (such as therapists and psychologists) to more informal structures (such as self-help literature), individuals can access vast networks to help improve, process, or recover their "true self" (Aubry and Travis 2015; Jenkins 2014; Silva 2013). Characterized by the "constant and creative individual pursuit of self-betterment, expression of inner feelings as the key to growth and recovery, and reliance on expert knowledge and/or intervention" (Jenkins 2014, 4), therapeutic culture has reshaped both family and religion.

As discussed already in this volume, Catholic parishes are key sites of cultural production. In this essay, I explore Catholic parishes' role in cultural production by examining how they operate as meso-level structures that mediate between individuals and broad social change. In particular, I illustrate how therapeutic cultural discourses about self-development and changing marital norms are mediated in and through particular parish practices—in this case, marriage preparation. As Edgell notes, "religious institutions provide moral guidelines that shape family practices, the organization of family life, and our perceptions of the 'good family'" (2011, 636). Rather than consider how cultural frameworks and family practices operate within the *home*, this essay shifts the focus to *parishes*. What does marital discourse in parishes reveal about views on marriage and the locus of religious authority to communicate those views? Toward this end, I compare two moments in time: the development of Catholic marriage preparation in the postwar era (circa 1940s–1960s) and contemporary parish practices in western Washington.

Studying Two Moments in Catholic Marriage Preparation: Data and Methods

This essay draws on two sources of data to compare marriage preparation developed during the postwar era to contemporary parish practices.[1] To study the history of marriage preparation programming, I conducted archival research into two Catholic family movements—Christian Family Movement (CFM) and Cana Conference Movement (CCM)—which helped popularize and spread the practice across the United States.[2]

---

1. The present paper emerges from a larger project that examines shifting landscapes of marriage and religion by studying evangelical Protestant and Catholic premarital counseling. This research was supported by the Women and Leadership Archives and the Society for the Scientific Study of Religion.

2. I relied initially on secondary research by scholars that have studied CCM and CFM to locate archival collections (Burns 1999; Johnson 2001). I visited archives that hold collections of key people that helped establish the movements and set the ideological vision for them. Maryville University Archives (MUA) and Midwest Jesuit Archives (MJA) both have collections of Fr. Edward Dowling, who coined the term "Cana Conference Movement" and helped spread the popularity of the movement. Catholic University of America's Archives (CUAA) has the personal collection of Dr. Alphonse H. Clemens, a Catholic researcher who studied and conducted CCM. The Women and Leadership Archives (WLA) at Loyola University Chicago contains a collection on Pat and Patty Crowley, who were key leaders in CFM both nationally and internationally. Additionally, I visited one archive that houses organizational documents: the Archives of the University of Notre Dame (UNDA) contains organizational documents for both CCM and CFM that includes meeting minutes, newsletters, internal memos, letters, news articles, and even some audio files of CCM events. Finally, I visited one archive of an archdiocese that developed significant programing: Archdiocese of Chicago Archives (ACA) holds collections for Cana Conference Chicago, which was the local diocesan

Archived audio recordings and detailed lecture notes provide a sense of marriage preparation content and organizational vision and mission during the postwar era. Additionally, I analyzed marriage preparation manuals and texts aimed at the general public.[3] Finally, to understand the impact and reception of these movements, I drew on secondary data sources such as empirical research and news publications from the era.[4] Together, these divergent sources of historical data provide a rich picture of clergy and laity's collective efforts to transform Catholic family life in the hope of transforming American culture.

To analyze contemporary practices of Catholic marriage preparation, I conducted ethnographic observations in two parish programs in western Washington. The Pacific Northwest, unlike the Northeast or Midwest, has never been a bastion of Catholicism but instead has been described as the most "unchurched" region in the country (Silk 2005). Catholics comprise 17 percent of Washington residents, falling significantly behind those who claim no religious affiliation, who account for 32 percent (Pew Research Center 2014). Catholic parishes in western Washington, therefore, must actively translate their faith in a setting where religious commitment cannot be taken for granted.

In each parish, I triangulated multiple sources of data, including observations of group classes for couples preparing for marriage, interviews with clerical and lay leaders of parish marriage preparation courses, and

---

office for CCM. This collection provides insights into marriage preparation practices at the diocesan level beyond the active years of the movement.

3. I reviewed five key CCM texts: *Cana Conference Study Week Records, 1949* and *Cana Conference Study Week Records, 1950*, which contain a collection of speeches given at these CCM conferences; *Beginning Your Marriage*, published by Cana Conference of Chicago; *The New Cana Manual*, edited by Walter Imbiorski, who served as assistant director of the Cana Conference of Chicago; and *Cana is Forever: Counsel for Before and After Marriage* by Charles Hugo.

4. While I relied on some journal publications from the era, I gained important information about the demographics and views of those participating in the movements from reviewing unpublished master's theses and doctoral dissertations conducted on these groups from a variety of disciplines. Between the surveys, content analysis, and interviews, I have limited firsthand accounts of people of the era that help reveal some of the reception of the ideas.

content analysis of program materials.[5] Both parishes followed a similar format, with engaged and civilly married couples seeking a "convalidation" attending weekly, two-hour classes that met over four to six weeks.[6] This totaled some twenty hours of fieldwork. To situate these parishes' programming within the broader diocesan structure, I interviewed coordinators of marriage preparation in other urban, suburban, and rural parishes in western Washington.[7] In total, I conducted thirteen interviews, including priests from both parishes; four lay coordinating couples; one religious director, who led the classes I observed; and six lay staff from other parishes.[8] Together, these different types of data allowed me to analyze the extent to which parishes operate as an interactive space where the Church engages with secular expectations of an "individualized marriage" (Cherlin 2004) by teaching people within the parish moralized tools of therapeutic culture.

Two Moments in Time: Parishes' Role in Mediating Cultures of Religion and Marriage

Catholic parishes—like all religious communities—actively negotiate to make sense of their social worlds. In both the postwar and contemporary periods, the Catholic Church constructs a vision of a "sacramental marriage" from religious resources within the faith and in dialogue with broader cultural understandings of love and intimacy. In the following two sections, I analyze how parishes translate broader cultural messages (both religious and secular) to everyday Catholics, examining marriage messages and who has the authority to speak for the Church.

5. In the broader project, I also interviewed couples that participated in the program.

6. According to those leading marriage preparation classes, a significant and frequent minority of participating couples are seeking "convalidations," because they are already civilly married. Regardless of their status as civilly married, these couples seeking to obtain the blessing of the Catholic Church or "get married in the church" were required to participate in marriage preparation.

7. While not explicitly targeting lay leaders, all the people I interviewed outside the two parishes where I conducted observations were lay volunteers or church staff.

8. Since I am comparing contemporary and postwar marriage preparation, I do not focus on the ten interviews with lay couples in this essay, because I do not have similar data from the postwar period.

Speaking to the Laity: Emergence of Catholic Marriage Preparation

The postwar period marked the origins of two key movements in Catholic family life—Christian Family Movement and Cana Conference Movement—that would come to shape how parishes approach marriage preparation. The postwar era may be described nostalgically as an idyllic time for family life and churches (Coontz 1997; Edgell 2006; Marler 1995; Wuthnow 1988), but archival records reveal a different perspective. Fearful of "the forces of materialism, secularism, and relativism" (Burke 1957, vii), Catholic social movements sought to preserve and redeem the place of family and marriage in society. While the CFM and CCM eventually developed different orientations and tactics in their efforts to re-Christianize America and stabilize family life, their origins overlap in working together to establish Catholic marriage preparation programs.

The parish held a central place in each movement's vision to cultivate an engaged laity. CFM brought couples together in the parish to observe their social world and consider small actions that could make a difference in one's community. CCM (which developed from one of these early actions) offered parish programming for Catholic couples to make their homes more holy. Pre-Cana grew out of the realization that many of the insights originally offered to married couples in Cana Conferences would be helpful for engaged couples who existed in a more formative stage.

Arguing that "marriage has become a strictly personal affair with couples almost selfishly seeking their own happiness," priests and laity worked together to design curriculum for Pre-Cana Conferences that "analyze[d] with the couples what married life naturally and properly should be according to God's Plan as revealed in their very natures and in the word He has spoken" (Imbiorski 1957, 72). The format of Pre-Cana varied from single days to a series of evenings or afternoons. All were organized around providing "inspirational and accurate information" (Imbiorski 1957, 72) on marriage from three vantage points: those of priests, married lay couples, and Catholic doctors.

Priests were charged with providing technical and theological details to engaged couples, covering matters such as an "explanation of the Canon Law on marriage, the liturgy of the wedding, [and] the necessity of being spiritually prepared for the reception of the Sacrament of Matrimony" (Farrell 1952, 18). Outlines and recordings of their talks, however, reveal priests' broader conversations on the significance of love. Combining social-scientific, philosophical, and theological discussions, the priests' talks deconstructed "love" for engaged couples. As one priest pondered, "It goes without saying that love is the basis for a happy marriage but what is love?" (Sattler, n.d.) To answer this type of question, written talks and outlines of notes from different priests discuss everything from how love pulls men and women together to fulfill their complementary needs and capacities to explicating how the spiritual virtues associated with conjugal love mirror those of the religious life. Presenting the sacrament of marriage as an opportunity for people to receive both "human love" and "spiritual love," priests' talks balanced a deconstruction of cultural and relational barriers to obtaining a loving marriage alongside their efforts to sacralize marriage. Viewing people as striving to love and be loved, priests warned couples about human barriers that might hinder these goals, such as the potential for disenchantment in marriage and gender differences (Knott 1956). Challenging popular conceptions within the Church that "separated the Sacraments of Holy Orders and Matrimony to a degree where, unconsciously, it was thought that marriage was a second rate vocation," priests discussed spiritual love as a means to bridge the gulf between priests and laity and drew firm boundaries between Catholic and secular visions of a loving marriage (Cana Conference 1950, 1). Explicitly drawing out similarities between marriage and holy orders, various priests' notes describe how married couples are called to embody the religious virtues of poverty, chastity, and obedience, similar to those in religious orders. As one priest described, "Marriage will give you a new reason for holiness; it's your guarantee that love will have a place to take roots in your home" (Imbiorski 1957, 86). From the "natural" elements of gender roles to the "supernatural" call from God to live a deeply spiritual life, priests relied on "love" to justify, motivate, and frame marital actions.

Married lay couples provided the second vantage point on how to prepare and live out the vocation of marriage. Combating "the traditional role of the laity to 'pay, pray, and obey'" (Burns 1999, 5), records of the postwar era indicate that priests often heartily accepted CCM and CFM as lay-driven movements. As one manual notes, "To many of the audience the spectacle of lay people talking about spiritual matters will be a revelation. This will make particularly cogent the emphasis on marriage as a vocation, a complete way of life, with its own possibilities for sanctity arising out of the very nature of the calling, and not in spite of it" (Imbiorski 1957, 100). Yet, despite this excitement, the limited archival records of married couples' talks indicate an ambiguity in their domain and authority to teach engaged couples. Acknowledging "it is a bit more difficult to define the role of the lay couple" (Imbiorski 1957, 98), some worried about their "lack of professional status" and believed their talks must strive to balance a competent discussion of general principles on marriage with only a few illustrations based on their own stories. One sociologist active in conducting CCM at the time, Dr. Alphonse Clemens, worried about the ability of married couples to theorize on marital asceticism, arguing that lay couples are religiously illiterate and not equipped to translate the principles of ascetics to marital life on their own.

Thus, while lauded as grassroots movements aimed at spiritualizing the laity, the lay married couples' perspective appears to have contributed to the larger vision of Pre-Cana by affirming priests' messaging and authority. While the laity could offer a personal dimension to discussions of love and vocation, they were not fully trusted to translate and interpret the theologies and traditions of the faith. Instead, based on the limited remaining archival evidence of the lay couples' talks, their content is markedly similar to the priests. According to one manual, "This will usually overlap what the priest has already said on the subject [the sacrament of marriage], but it will have added validity coming from a married couple who have felt the strength of such grace, and the pervasiveness of such love" (Imbiorski 1957, 103). Couples maintained existing lines of authority in parishes, where religious authority emanated from priest to people.

Moving slightly away from formative education, a doctor provided the final vantage point on marriage. Operating as a form of parish-based sex education, the notes for these sessions often include technical details about male and female anatomy, as well as an overview of physiological development. In addition to providing more biological information, some notes indicate time to discuss the importance of sex within marriage, and all include some treatise on the problems of contraception. Due to the era, however, many discuss the Church's negative view of the rhythm method and instead, following the priests' talks, recommend married couples follow the religious virtue of chastity. Contributing to the larger goal to re-educate couples, the doctors strove to "help the young people shed their false notions about sex and see it as the Church sees it" (Farrell 1952, 19).

Collectively, these three vantage points (of priests, married lay couples, and doctors) presented postwar engaged Catholic couples with an education of what to expect in marriage and how to understand their marriages within a Catholic framework as a spiritualized practice. On the surface, postwar marriage preparation concerned itself primarily with the formation of individuals. Describing the rationale behind marriage preparation, one leader explained, "Your objective should be aimed at assisting couples to form or to deepen sound Christian attitudes with respect to marriage rather than to impart to them theoretical knowledge" (Van Greunsven 1965). Yet despite the apparent "saving souls" approach, marriage preparation at this time emerged from a broader collective moral project that viewed these personal level transformations as a key mechanism for broader social change (Kniss 2003). Believing that "secularism can be routed . . . only by integration from within, not by imposition from without upon an otherwise pagan family pattern of life" (Clemens 1950, 8), marriage preparation represented one arm of the CCM's mission to re-Christianize American society (Cana Conference 1950).

The postwar parish mediated between Catholics as individuals and Catholicism as an authoritative proscription for moral practice. Local parish actors (lay, ordained, and medical) transmitted messages to everyday Catholics about love, family, and marriage within these more traditional, hierarchical conceptions of authority. As a social movement, CCM actions generally targeted local parishes to disseminate their moral vision and, ideally, reshape social life. While the subsequent decades would see a rise in secularism and divorce rates, these postwar family movements did make real impacts on the everyday lives of Catholics. Social historians have noted that Pre-Cana, which was more accessible than marriage counseling and included both men and women (unlike women's magazines), exposed thousands of engaged couples to an emerging view that marriage and love requires hard work, intimacy, and communication (Davis 2010; Moskowitz 2001). In time, marriage preparation programs were established across American dioceses and, following Vatican II (1962–1965), were required by canon law (canon 1063).

A legacy of these family movements, which I explore in the next section, is the increasing importance of Catholic laity as a source of religious authority in parishes. Unlike the postwar era, when CFM and CCM depended on ordained priests to spiritualize the laity, contemporary marriage preparation programs predominately rely on the marital and spiritual insights of lay married couples.

Laity Speaking for Themselves: Contemporary Parish Marriage Preparation Programs

As opposed to the vast network of resources and shared vision that CCM provided to marriage preparation programming during the postwar era, the contemporary Catholic marriage preparation practices I observed operated in a more disjointed manner. Based on my interviews with parish representatives across western Washington, I learned that there was limited diocesan oversight, with each parish constructing a program that fit the local needs of parishioners. Engaged couples had the opportunity to choose between a parish program or a diocesan-wide weekend retreat. Those I spoke with often selected the parochial programs because they were more affordable. For their own part, parishes faced the challenge of developing local curriculum that fulfilled canon law (which requires marriage preparation) and provided engaged couples with a distinctive vision of a sacramental marriage and tangible skills for how to enact it outside church walls. In other words, contemporary Catholic parishes continued to act as a filter between the Catholic Church as an institution and local, lay Catholics as they live out their Catholicism. What differs, however, are the mechanisms through which these messages are delivered on the parish level.

Unlike the postwar marriage preparation practice of having lay doctors and couples support and complement the priest's teachings, the contemporary programs I observed flipped this script. Laity generally coordinated the programs and presented most talks, with clergy now supporting and complementing them. At both sites, the priests generally attended only one class, which they co-led with a laywoman from the church staff to educate couples on the theology and significance of a sacramental marriage. The remainder of the classes and the coordination of the programming fell under the responsibility of laity, with priests "helping out however [they] can," as one interviewee described.[9] In addition to

9. This arrangement of hands-off clergy appears to be a pattern more broadly across the diocese, because in the other five parishes where I interviewed people in charge of marriage preparation, all were laity.

attending less of the programming, the priests' contribution has narrowed to focus more specifically on their presumed domain of expertise. The outlines of the priests' talks during the postwar era subsumed the theological conception of marriage as a vocation within a framework of love and unity. With fewer sessions to speak to the couples, contemporary priests' talks judiciously centered on providing technical theological insights, such as a brief overview of the nature of sacraments with a review of the three elements of form, matter, and minister, or the meaning of a marriage covenant. While these lessons at times referenced ideas of love in passing, for the most part, the nontheological dimensions of marriage were reserved for the laity to communicate. This division of labor did not cut the other way, though: at these and other parishes, the laity were also charged with providing theological insights into marriage.

In some ways, the contemporary reliance on laity to lead marriage preparation and their vested authority to speak on the spiritual vocation of marriage fulfills the legacy of the postwar family movements, which sought to help couples "realize the holiness of their way of living" (Cana Conference 1950, 15). As one laywoman, the parish religious director, explained:

> Our purpose here is to learn to live in God's presence without shame. We can do this by developing certain virtues and habits. To say that marriage is a vocation is a way of saying that it offers us a way to do that. But what does holiness look like in marriage? It's not all about being on your knees. Instead, it involves the mundane tasks of life. It's paying the bills, changing diapers, and numerous other household duties that we do in the spirit for the family unit. It's the attitude with which we work on these things for our family.

Echoing earlier visions of CCM to provide laity with an accessible form of spirituality through marriage, this laywoman sought to reinvigorate the faith lives of engaged couples. In this case, the religious director drew on her position within the parish to inform her understanding of the Church's sacramental vision of marriage.

In general, involvement in marriage preparation resulted from an expressed desire to volunteer and serve the parish. Some couples were literally recruited from the pews; others were matched with this ministry when they expressed interest in being more involved in the parish. As a result, most lay leaders lacked professional credentials in either religion or relationships. Often, the only criteria was for a couple to have been married at least five years. Rather than present themselves as experts, the rotating lay married couples who volunteered to lead an evening of marriage preparation crafted their moral authority from their "ordinary" Catholic marriages. They spoke as fellow—albeit married—parishioners.

The privileging of everyday life experience differs dramatically from the admonition of postwar CCM leaders, who said, "It is a mistake to overdo the 'We're just ordinary folks, not experts' approach" (Imbiorski 1957, 99). Reflecting on their own experiences in marriage preparation and what they wish they had understood as engaged couples themselves, lay couples leading contemporary programs relied on their personal experiences in marriage and within the parish to discern the most useful information in a manner consistent with the Catholic vision of a sacramental marriage. As opposed to the more formal talks found in archival records, the leading couples approached marriage preparation as a casual time to share stories and advice. As one parish team explained in their introductory session:

> For the most part, we won't be teaching, but more acting as a facilitator. Since there is no single road map for marriage, everyone will work together by talking to each other and having discussions. . . . This is an opportunity to just seek out advice. For instance, if you're living apart and have never lived together, then you may not know how to live with each other. Probably one's parents can provide advice on this transition, but it's always good to get more. We love it when couples bring their own interests into the class and how they see things, especially any potential stumbling blocks. The goal is to bring it all forward. The curriculum isn't set in stone. Over the class the goal should be to love each other and think about each other.

Instead of a classroom style with teachers instructing engaged couples on a series of core lessons and concepts, the lay couples facilitating each session worked from a loose outline that combined scripture passages, religious lessons they learned at church, anecdotes from the media, any self-help books they read, and their own marriage. As a result, this created a relaxed environment of casual advice and insights loosely centered on a theme for the week, such as communication, finances, expectations of marriage, or sacramental marriage. Whether discussing how to balance a budget or conflict and communication patterns in marriage, lay leaders urged the attending couples to be self-reflective and open about their personal expectations with their partner.

Undergirding the casual lessons from week to week was the idea that marriage "is a job of struggle" and that to make marriages last, people need to "be committed to love and not just the person." The leadership teams approached the topic of love both hesitantly and confidently. On the one hand, love was acknowledged as integral to the success of marriage, because it keeps the spouses turned toward each other. In one case, comparing a Catholic marriage to an arranged marriage, an interviewed leadership couple explained, "It's important that in marriage people are free to make individual choices because that helps with the romance." On a deeper level, however, the love in marriage is meant to be a reflection of God's love. As the same couple later noted, "God created relationships for us. And marriages exist as our way to access something similar to the Trinity. . . . The trinity exists as three people in love. Marriage is our way to glimpse that relationship." Despite this hopeful confidence that love serves as the basis of marriage, an underlying tension existed, with leaders often insisting on the complexity of love and contending that staying in love requires work. In fact, many of the topics—such as facing one's expectations in marriage, how to balance a budget, and fighting fair—revolve around revealing the necessity of hard work to engaged couples, with the hope that this would lay a foundation of skills for how to address these types of issues. Thus, while love operated as a baseline assumption for all relationships, leaders did not view it as sufficient for the survival of a marriage and instead believed love requires cultivation. As one husband explained, "Marriage takes vigilance, effort, and work all the time. Just like preparing for marriage did. You choose to stick with your choice and stick with your decision. As a result, you receive an ever-deepening love in the grace of God, who will help sustain you in your marriage."

Marriage preparation within many parishes operated under the auspices of religious education or sacramental preparation, which raised tensions surrounding the meaning of a "Catholic" marriage. Priests and lay married couples, for instance, used theological lessons to simultaneously redeem the Catholic identity for those raised Catholic without alienating their partners, who were often not Catholic. In the context of the "unchurched" Pacific Northwest, the majority of couples in the programs I observed were marrying non-Catholics. Often, the fiancé had no religious affiliation. This may help explain why both parishes made efforts to move away from the language of "sacramental marriage" to the more inclusive "faith in marriage." Yet even within this religiously accepting context, priests and lay leaders made many pitches about the relevance and significance of the Catholic Church—and participation in a local parish—for one's marriage. Sometimes this took the form of small comments about the benefits of parochial schools for their children or how useful they found it to be involved in parish ministries. In one of the stronger appeals, a priest challenged the Catholic individuals to be "proud of their faith" by selecting to have a wedding Mass. As he explained:

> There is no greater union than celebrating the Eucharist together. I know some people are concerned about the feelings of their non-Catholic guests, but if you went to an Orthodox or Jewish wedding, you'd think the rituals are beautiful. People won't feel ostracized. Rather, they will appreciate the opportunity to share in your faith. Don't water it down because not everyone is Catholic. You don't need to walk on eggshells. Be proud of our faith. In the event that one partner is not Catholic and you want to honor that, you can have the ceremony without the Eucharist. This is perfectly acceptable and we will work with you.

Marriage preparation is read as an opportunity to bring couples back within the fold, while also reiterating social boundaries between Catholics and non-Catholics and the moral construction of a "good" marriage.

Contemporary Catholic marriage preparation programs craft a casual environment focused on facilitating individual growth and education, consistent with therapeutic culture's emphasis on self-realization. Parishes become sites where individual Catholics may negotiate their personal identities, self-growth, and relationships with others. Rather than conceptualize marriage preparation as part of a larger effort to address "the Christianization of the modern family, planted as it is in a secular environment" (Cana Conference 1950, ix), these parish programs operate predominately at the local level as a means to serve parishioners' transition to marriage. High rates of divorce, secularism, and widespread use of contraception among Catholics have likely diminished religious leaders' hope that marriage preparation will stem this tide. Extending the origins of postwar family movements, Catholic lay couples now act as religious authorities at the parish level, communicating spiritual messages with limited oversight by clergy.

Conclusion

Since its beginning in the postwar era, marriage preparation programming has enabled parishes to mediate the broader cultural schemas of marriage and Catholic theology. Across this period, parishes helped mediate, filter, and translate macro-cultural messages about love, marriage, and family into the lives of Catholics in the pews. While the process of cultural production and transmission has not changed, shifts in the structure of religious authority meant that *who* does the speaking has changed. Laypeople, not just priests, are increasingly empowered to produce local Catholic culture and make sense of Catholic teachings. While in this essay I explored this process of transmission and how an increasing reliance on lay Catholic authority has affected the sacrament of marriage, it is not isolated to this context. Tia Noelle Pratt's essay, for example, shows how this occurs in liturgy, as black Catholics sift and reinterpret traditional practices.

Perhaps surprisingly, the vision of a "good" family has changed little from the postwar era to today. Local Catholic leaders, then and now, broadly present marriage as an institution based on love, requiring hard work, and providing the means for couples' sanctification. In other words, today's engaged couples continue to hear that a good and satisfying marriage is one based on love between partners that motivates them to continuously work on their relationship as part of a larger effort to emulate God's love. Although this occurs within parishes that share a vision similar to those of postwar parishes, the cultural contexts differ. Contemporary marriage preparation programs in Catholic parishes operate within an established therapeutic culture in which individuals regularly engage in self-work (Aubry and Travis 2015; Jenkins 2014; Silva 2013). Unlike CCM's postwar vision, which saw companionate marriage as a means to increase satisfaction within the institution, contemporary leaders have witnessed in their lifetime how "the very features that promised to make marriage such a unique and treasured personal relationship opened the way for it to become an optional and fragile one" (Coontz 2005, 5). Marriage preparation leaders I encountered expressed ambivalence on the topic of love, tending to conceptualize it as a renewable resource that requires careful cultivation. Marriage preparation, therefore, becomes a place where parishes train couples in "marriage work" (Jenkins 2014) by presenting love as a choice that people ultimately will have to choose to make again and again in their relationship.

Moreover, while the primary lessons on how to have a happy and healthy marriage remained fairly consistent, the carrier of that message at the parish level changed. Looking at who can speak on behalf of the Catholic Church reveals a shift in parish-level religious authority. During the postwar, Catholic family movements developed marriage preparation as a way to build a spiritually educated lay populace. Combating the idea of passive laity (Burns 1999), clergy and lay couples joined together to translate spiritual lessons from Catholicism to marriage. In contrast, contemporary marriage preparation programs developed within the religious context that their postwar peers imagined. Catholic family movements laid the groundwork for the reforms of Vatican II (D'Antonio 1995), introducing a democratized religious authority among Catholics inside parishes (Dillon 1999). As opposed to the view that religious and educated elites must translate spiritual issues for the laity, contemporary marriage preparation operates within a religious context that vests laity with interpretative power. The shift to a "reasoned interpretative equality for all church members" (Dillon 1999, 51), coupled with the structural reality of a priest shortage, generates new organizational conditions for marriage preparation.

The contemporary marriage preparation practices I observed are organized and led by lay staff and married couples with limited oversight by priests. Lay leaders, not ordained leaders, translate Catholic teachings and prepare engaged couples for the work of marriage. In doing so, they leverage their "ordinary" Catholic marriages as a way to establish their authority in speaking to engaged couples about how to negotiate married life. Between a therapeutic culture in which everyone learns to monitor and manage their emotional state (Bellah et al. 1985) and the increased openness in Catholic religious authority (Baggett 2009; Dillon 1999), lay Catholic couples transmit everyday knowledge learned generally from personal experience to engaged couples.

Through marriage preparation, parishes collectively engage in meaning-making by transmitting a Catholic vision of marriage to individual parishioners. This allows the Catholic Church to shore up the relevance of the faith tradition and maintain authority to broadly influence peoples' lives. Moreover, the theological view of marriage as a sacrament means that parishes hold a gatekeeping function in laity's sanctification. For sanctification to happen, however, religious education must teach laity about this vision and cultivate a religious mode of being. Marriage preparation programs may not always—or even often—succeed in their attempts to transmit the Church's view of marriage or to stem divorce. But within the context of a hierarchical religious tradition, marriage preparation provides laity with access and authority to participate in local, collective meaning-making through their parishes.

References

Amato, Paul R., Alan Booth, David R. Johnson, and Stacy J. Rogers. 2007. *Alone Together: How Marriage in America is Changing.* Cambridge, Mass.: Harvard University Press.

Aubry, Tim, and Trysh Travis. 2015. "What Is 'Therapeutic Culture,' and Why Do We Need to 'Rethink' It?" In *Rethinking Therapeutic Culture,* edited by Tim Aubry and Trysh Travis, pp. 1–23. Chicago: University of Chicago Press.

Baggett, Jerome P. 2009. *Sense of the Faithful: How American Catholics Live Their Faith.* New York: Oxford University Press.

Bellah, Robert, Richard Madsen, William Sullivan, Ann Swidler, and Steven Tipton. 1985. *Habits of the Heart: Individualism and Commitment in American Life.* Berkeley: University of California Press.

Burke, Edward. 1957. "Foreword." In *The New Cana Manual,* edited by Walter Imbiorski. Chicago: Delaney Publications.

Burns, Jeffrey. 1999. *Disturbing the Peace: A History of the Christian Family Movement, 1949–1974.* Notre Dame, Ind.: University of Notre Dame Press.

CARA (Center for Applied Research in the Apostolate). n.d. "Frequently Requested Church Statistics." http://cara.georgetown.edu/frequently-requested-church-statistics/.

Cherlin, Andrew. 2004. "The Deinstitutionalization of American Marriage." *Journal of Marriage and Family* 66: 848–61.

———. 2009. *The Marriage-Go-Round: The State of Marriage and Family in America Today.* New York: Alfred Knopf.

Coontz, Stephanie. 1997. *The Way We Really Are: Coming to Terms with America's Changing Families.* New York: Basic Books.

———. 2005. *Marriage, A History: From Obedience to Intimacy, or How Love Conquered Marriage.* New York: Penguin Books.

D'Antonio, William V. 1995. "Small Faith Communities in the Roman Catholic Church: New Approaches to Religion, Work, and Family." In *Work, Family, and Religion in Contemporary Society*, edited by Nancy T. Ammerman and Wade C. Roof, pp. 237–59. New York: Routledge.

Davis, Rebecca L. 2010. *More Perfect Unions: The American Search for Marital Bliss*. Cambridge, Mass.: Harvard University Press.

Dillon, Michele. 1999. *Catholic Identity: Balancing Reason, Faith and Power*. New York: Cambridge University Press.

Edgell, Penny. 2006. *Religion and Family in a Changing Society*. Princeton, N.J.: Princeton University Press.

———. 2011. "Religion and Family." In *The Oxford Handbook for the Sociology of Religion*, edited by Peter B. Clarke, pp. 635–50. New York: Oxford University Press.

Gray, Mark, Paul Perl, and Tricia Bruce. 2007. *Marriage in the Catholic Church: A Survey of U.S. Catholics*. Washington, DC: Center for Applied Research in the Apostolate. https://cara.georgetown.edu/publications/marriagereport.pdf.

Imbiorski, Walter, ed. 1957. *The New Cana Manual*. Chicago: Delaney Publications.

Jenkins, Kathleen E. 2014. *Sacred Divorce: Religion, Therapeutic Culture, and Ending Life Partnerships*. New Brunswick, N.J.: Rutgers University Press.

Johnson, Kathryn A. 2001. "Taking Marriage 'One Day at a Time': The Cana Conference Movement and the Creation of a Catholic Mentality." *CUSHWA Center for the Study of American Catholicism*, Working Paper Series 33:1. University of Notre Dame, Notre Dame, Ind.

Kniss, Fred. 2003. "Mapping the Moral Order: Depicting the Terrain of Religious Conflict and Change." In *Handbook of the Sociology of Religion*, edited by Michele Dillon, pp. 331–47. New York: Cambridge University Press.

Marler, Penny L. 1995. "Lost in the Fifties: The Changing Family and the Nostalgic Church." In *Work, Family, and Religion in Contemporary Society*, edited by Nancy T. Ammerman and Wade C. Roof, pp. 23–60. New York: Routledge.

Moskowitz, Eva. 2001. *In Therapy We Trust: America's Obsession with Self-Fulfillment*. Baltimore: John Hopkins University Press.

Pew Research Center. 2014. Religious Landscape Study. Washington, DC: Pew Research Center. http://www.pewforum.org/religious-landscape-study/state/washington/.

Roof, Wade C. 1999. *Spiritual Marketplace: Baby Boomers and the Remaking of American Religion*. Princeton, N.J.: Princeton University Press.

Silk, Mark. 2005. "Religion and Region in American Public Life." *Journal for the Scientific Study of Religion*, 44 (3): 265–70.

Silva, Jennifer. 2013. *Coming Up Short: Working-Class Adulthood in an Age of Uncertainty.* New York: Oxford University Press.

USCCB (United States Conference of Catholic Bishops). 2009. "Marriage: Love and Life in the Divine Plan." A Pastoral Letter of the United States Conference of Catholic Bishops. Washington, DC: United States Conference of Catholic Bishops.

Wuthnow, Robert. 1988. *The Restructuring of American Religion.* Princeton, N.J.: Princeton University Press.

Archival Sources

Cana Conference. 1950. *The Cana Conference Proceedings of the Chicago Archdiocesan Study Week on The Cana Conference, June 28–30, 1949.* Chicago: Cana Conference.

Farrell, John. 1952. *This Is Cana.* St. Meinrad, Ind.: Grail. Reynold Hillenbrand Papers. PMRH Box 120/06, University of Notre Dame Archives.

Knott, John C. 1956. "Director's Outline: Pre-Cana Conference," Alphonse H. Clemens Papers, Clemens 4/4, Catholic University of America's Archives.

Sattler, Henry. n.d. "A Pre-Cana Conference Outline," Alphonse H. Clemens Papers, Clemens 4/4, Catholic University of America's Archives.

Van Greunsven, Norbert J. J. 1965. "Introduction," Alphonse H. Clemens Papers, Clemens 4/4, Catholic University of America's Archives.

Part V: The Practice and Future of a Sociology of Catholic Parishes

The final part of this volume looks to the future. While sociologists can make no guarantees about what the future holds, they do work to systematically gather data over time, pair that data with explanatory theories, and build strong predictions. Part of this future, we hope, involves equipping Catholic parishioners and leaders with tools to assess and understand the sociological elements of their own parishes.

Toward this end, we structured Chapter 10 as a question and answer conversation with a modern sociologist-priest, Fr. John Coleman, SJ. Fr. Coleman shares how he uses sociology and social patterns to better understand and serve his own parish community.

Another element of this future involves building a better framework for a sociology of Catholic parishes. We presented an "embedded field approach" to the study of Catholic parishes in the Introduction. Having now learned about myriad aspects to the study of American parishes throughout these pages, we revisit and expand on this theme in a concluding essay.

Suggested Additional Readings

Coleman, John A. 2013. "Social Movements and Catholic Social Thought: A Sociological Perspective." *Journal of Catholic Social Thought* 10 (2): 259–80.

Dillon, Michele. 2018. *Postsecular Catholicism: Relevance and Renewal.* New York: Oxford University Press.

Eagle, David. 2016. "The Negative Relationship between Size and the Probability of Weekly Attendance in Churches in the United States." *Socius* 2, 1–10.

Gorski, Philip S., David Kyuman Kim, John Torpey, and Jonathan Van Antwerpen, eds. 2012. *The Post-Secular in Question: Religion in Contemporary Society.* New York: Social Science Research Council and New York University Press.

Joas, Hans. 2014. *Faith as an Option: Possible Futures for Christianity.* Stanford, Calif.: Stanford University Press.

Munson, Zaid W. 2009. *The Making of Pro-Life Activists: How Social Movement Mobilization Works.* Chicago: University of Chicago Press.

Summers-Effler, Erika. 2010. *Laughing Saints and Righteous Heroes: Emotional Rhythms in Social Movement Groups.* Chicago: University of Chicago Press.

A Sociologist Looks
      at His Own Parish

A Conversation with John A. Coleman, SJ

JOHN A. COLEMAN, SJ, WITH EDITORS
GARY J. ADLER JR., TRICIA C. BRUCE,
AND BRIAN STARKS

John A. Coleman, SJ, is both a sociologist and a priest. In the mid-1970s, Fr. Coleman completed his doctoral studies at the University of California, Berkeley. During the course of his career, he has been instrumental in helping germinate Catholic research initiatives, including the Center for Applied Research in the Apostolate (CARA) at Georgetown University and the Institute for Advanced Catholic Studies at the University of Southern California. Fr. Coleman has written widely for sociological, theological, pastoral, and public audiences on topics including social thought, civic engagement, environmental activism, Christian ethics, religion and sexuality, and contemporary Catholicism. His scholarship has appeared in numerous journals, edited volumes, and Catholic media, including *America Magazine*, *Commonweal*, the *Journal of Catholic Social Thought*, and the Jesuit quarterly, *Theological Studies*. He has been an associate pastor of Saint Ignatius Parish, adjacent to the campus of the University of San Francisco, since 2009.

Following his involvement in The American Parish Project seminar that birthed this volume, we invited Fr. Coleman to participate in a question and answer dialogue that could tie together sociological research, his current parish setting, and his wealth of pastoral experience. We hope that his responses will demonstrate the usefulness of engaging a "sociological imagination," as C. Wright Mills put it, for Catholic parish life.

You have had a distinguished career as a sociologist. You seem convinced that the tools of social science have something to say about and to the Catholic Church. Is there a moment of experience that confirmed this conviction?

As a young man, I read *Southern Parish* (1951) and *Social Relations in the Urban Parish* (1954) by Joseph Fichter, SJ. I contacted Fichter and sought his advice about pursuing a doctorate in the sociology of religion. I did so at the University of California, Berkeley, under the tutelage of Robert Bellah and Charles Glock. Bellah convinced me that religion was a human universal, although not all religious people found their religion in church. Fichter's work demonstrated that pastors often have little idea of what their people actually believe and that parishes contain vastly different levels of adherence and commitment among parishioners. It also showed that pastors can have great difficulty communicating with their parishioners, and vice versa.

Over the years, I taught courses at Berkeley and later as an endowed professor at Loyola Marymount University on the sociology of American Catholicism and the sociology of American Catholic parishes. This strongly reinforced my conviction that social science has a lot to tell the Catholic Church about the problems and the roles and statuses within parishes and—as in the work of Andrew Greeley, Jay Dolan, and others—about using parishes as a means of accessing individual Catholic behavior rather than as units of analysis in and of themselves.[1]

In my own studies, in mentoring students, and in serving a variety of parishes as a priest, I have observed the impact of sociological factors on the underlying organization and vitality of parish commitment (Baggett 2009). For example, at one point early in my career, I imagined a study of the crucial role of housekeepers in rectories in determining the agenda of parishes and as gatekeepers who, often enough, determined the fate of associate pastors.[2] As a priest, I helped do weekend Masses, weddings, and funerals in many parishes, some of them flourishing and some not. I especially reflected on the notable success of the Oakland Cathedral, where I regularly preached, in bridging African American and progressive well-educated Catholics drawn from across the diocese. At one point, I led a study of paradenominational groups, such as Bread for the World, Habitat for Humanity, and church-based community organizing groups, which convinced me that, while such groups bring added resources for community outreach to parishes, their strength depends on the underlying

1. Cf. the essay in this volume by Tricia Bruce. I used most of the works she cites in her essay in courses I taught on the sociology of Catholic parishes.

2. With parishes now often without housekeepers, they do not have the same power and gate-keeping role they had in the 1960s and early 1970s.

organization and vitality of the parish commitment (Baggett 2000; Wood 2002).

You currently pastor a parish that makes it—in sociological language— an outlier. What would you say are the most unique aspects of your parish? How does this uniqueness add to our understanding of parishes more broadly?

As a large, Jesuit, and part-university parish, Saint Ignatius is atypical but not wholly unique. Many Catholic universities—Jesuit universities among them—have university parishes that draw similarly on the re- sources of a host university while also serving a wider, non-university parish population. A distinctive Jesuit emphasis is found in Saint Ignati- us's mission statement, which reads: "Saint Ignatius is a welcoming and inclusive community. A Jesuit parish, we are called to be companions of Jesus. We come together through word and sacrament to grow in our re- lationship with God and to find the inspiration, desire and strength to be men and women for others. We seek to find God in all things by deepening our faith, listening with discerning and joyful hearts and actively serving the poor and suffering—all for the glory of God" (https://www.stignatiussf .org/overview).

Though 105 years old, Saint Ignatius has been a parish for only twenty- five years. Before becoming a parish, it drew non-USF students to its Sunday Masses but could not perform weddings or baptisms and did not have religious education programs or social outreach. The original Saint Ignatius Church was a parish located in San Francisco's down- town shopping center. An earlier Saint Ignatius College church built in 1878 was destroyed in a 1906 fire resulting from the great earthquake. When the status of corporation sole was first used by US Catholic lead- ers in the 1800s as a protection against lay ownership claims on parish property, the archbishop of San Francisco claimed that he was, there- fore, the rightful owner of the church. The Jesuits (who had raised all the money to buy the property and built the church) contested his claim to Rome. Rome settled in favor of the Jesuits, but the archbishop then declared that since he did not own the church property, Saint Ignatius could no longer be a parish as such. This held from 1867 until 1994, when Archbishop John Quinn allowed the church to become a parish. While Saint Ignatius is an anomaly in San Francisco as not being part of the corporation sole rule, a number of dioceses have begun to re-scind the corporation sole rule and give ownership back to the parish to forestall lawsuits due to clerical sex abuse cases.

With some 1,687 families, Saint Ignatius is a large parish. Its more than two thousand parishioners place it in the upper third of all parishes in terms of size. The typical seating capacity of most parishes is five hundred; Saint Ignatius seats eighteen hundred.[3] While the average number of Masses per weekend is three and a half, Saint Ignatius has six Masses every weekend. Five are sponsored by the parish, and a sixth is sponsored by the campus ministry of the University of San Francisco, which also uses the church for its own university Masses and spiritual events. Some 127 new households joined the parish in 2014.

Because of its large size, Saint Ignatius works intentionally to generate community. We do "nametag Sundays" so people in the pews might get to know one another's names and engage in some interchange. We have greeters at every weekend Mass. Serving its distributed parishioner base, Saint Ignatius hosts "S.I. in the 'Hood," a set of gatherings in parishioners' homes four or five times a year to draw together parishioners in distinct San Francisco neighborhoods.

In terms of demographics, Saint Ignatius mirrors Catholic parishes nationally in many ways. Parishioners are predominantly female (65 percent), although the ratio of female to male among lay leadership is more balanced (55 percent female to 45 percent male). The age range also mirrors national data: 4 percent of lay leaders and 12 percent of parishioners are aged 18–32, 42 percent of lay leaders and 47 percent of parishioners are 35–54, and the remaining 55 percent of lay leaders and 41 percent of parishioners are 55 or older. That said, since Saint Ignatius serves the University of San Francisco's student population as the center for its campus ministry, the number of people at Mass aged 18–32 is, in reality, much larger than 12 percent. Students, however, do not usually register at the parish even if they attend Mass at the parish, and hence don't show up in membership records.

3. All Saint Ignatius percentages reported are from a 2014 parishioner survey, detailed below, that is part of a parish self-study program. National statistics on parishioner demographics can be found in various reports produced by CARA.

Since 89 percent of the parishioners are college graduates or have an advanced degree, Saint Ignatius also has a disproportionately educated constituency (and a higher occupation status) than most parishes. Seven out of ten parishioners (71 percent) are married; 16 percent are single. As a welcoming and inclusive parish, Saint Ignatius also draws some gays and lesbians. The majority of parishioners describe themselves as white, while a quarter are either Hispanic or some other ethnicity. One in ten parishioners are Asian (mainly Filipino or Chinese), and 4 percent are Pacific Islander. Saint Ignatius has only English language liturgies, however.

Saint Ignatius also has more priests than most parishes. The average number of priests on parish staffs nationwide has dwindled: in 2000, only 14 percent of parishes in the United States had more than two priests (these tended to be megaparishes of some three thousand members). Saint Ignatius has three full-time priests, and a fourth who rotates part-time with Saint Ignatius and part-time in a neighboring Jesuit parish. The parish can also draw on twenty-four other Jesuit priests who teach or work at the University of San Francisco to help out with Masses, weddings, and other events.

One way to assess any parish is to look to its financial resources and how the money is spent. In fiscal year 2013–2014, Saint Ignatius took in more than two million dollars. Collections brought in about half of that; the remainder came from sacramental offerings (the bulk from marriage offerings); gifts, donations, and grants; income from the parish book store; advertising in the church bulletin; votive candles; and nonoperating income, such as capital gains and dividend income. Saint Ignatius presently has an endowment of one million dollars for its social outreach programs and more than a half million for church maintenance. The parish now has a one-million-dollar matching grant, which it wants to match to gain revenue for various programs for the church, especially training parishioners to do spiritual direction. The highest cost items annually include salaries and benefits, an archdiocesan "tax," an art gallery, and church maintenance. Other notable expenses include worship supplies and professional consultation. The most expensive other programs are the annual stewardship program and children's faith formation.

While Saint Ignatius may have outlier abundant resources in sixteen paid staff, endowment for church social ministries and church maintenance, and free office and meeting space from the university, many of its issues are found in all parishes: adopting a working mission statement that serves as a touchstone to judge programs, finding ways to expand the number of active volunteers and parishioners, and providing good faith formation and spirituality resources for parishioners to grow in the faith.

How does your perspective as a sociologist shape the way you see your own parish? What do you look at, or for, to understand your parish?

I have been invited on occasion to talk to the parish council and staff on some of the sociological challenges all parishes face in America and to share data on parish life. One was on young adult ministry and data showing that young adult Catholics are less educated in the faith, more individualistic, and more tentative or weak in their affiliation to the church (Bendyna and Perl 2000; Smith et al. 2014). To my chagrin and surprise, of the thirty-four parishes in San Francisco, only two had explicit young adult programs (Mallon 2014). Based on the discovery of this unmet need, two years ago our parish began a group for young adults in their twenties and thirties.

But a parish need not have its own resident sociologist to gain sociological expertise. In 2014, I, along with others, urged Saint Ignatius to take part in a yearlong applied sociology program called Parish Assessment and Renewal (PAR).[4] PAR uses the sociological acumen and organizational analysis of Thomas Sweetser, SJ, to help a parish imagine new ways to organize, do surveys, and find out what is working and what still needs to be done to make the parish more mission centered and vibrant.[5] The goal of the PAR process is to help the parish find new ways to connect with inactive or nonattending parishioners, to help a parish draw up a mission statement, and to translate its goals into action by forming action plans. Sweetser visits a parish that has asked for his help and holds town halls, conducts surveys, asks people how the parish is unique, and clarifies staff

4. Ammerman (2005) notes that only 7 percent of congregations in the United States had paid outside consultants.

5. For an explanation of the PAR process, see Sweetser 2007. Over a forty-year period, Sweetser's PAR project has assessed 235 different (and quite distinct) parishes to help them grow and move to the next level.

job descriptions (relieving some of too many burdens). PAR helps parishes address a multitude of issues found across American parishes.

Almost every parish also faces what is dubbed "the 80–20 ratio," that is, 80 percent of the parish is somewhat nominal, merely coming to Mass and contributing small amounts, versus some 20 percent who contribute and volunteer. PAR has helped us increase our pool of volunteers through personal invitation and by helping people find a category of volunteering that fits their desires. This can also increase financial contributions to the parish.

Another impact of the PAR process (which believes in shared ministry) is a reimagined parish council. There have been widespread complaints about parish councils having merely an advisory role rather than a decision-making function in many parishes. Following Sweetser's advice, at Saint Ignatius the parish council is the ultimate decision maker on issues of budget approval, strategic planning, and capital projects. It has a wide advisory role about programing.

PAR also emphasizes ways for various groups in different ministries to communicate with the parish council, the pastoral staff, and one another. The suggestion is that a parish form five commissions: worship, outreach, community, formation, and administration. Each has eight to nine participants, including one staff member. The idea is to solicit lay input so that staff don't lead the parish alone. The commissions are called on to envision and prioritize goals, funnel information across parish groups, make decisions, link groups, and assess accountability. Sweetser's format allows better communication among staff, parish, and commissions as to what is happening.

Sweetser (2007) also suggests that the parish consider ways to structure ownership and sharing, including a conjoining of roles: a pastor and parish administrator (subject to the pastor) who serves as a kind of parish manager and personnel director. He or she is a partner to the pastor. We followed his advice to do so.

St. Ignatius does have some unique or unusual resources. But the ways PAR increased our clarity about who decides, who must be consulted, how to inform, how to run quality staff meetings, and how to move from maintenance to mission have also benefited hundreds of other American parishes quite different in composition and resources. The establishment of job roles, communication across a wide constituency, expansion of volunteers, and stewardship are not the only issues in a parish, but they remain quite central.

Under canon law, all territorial parishes have a specified catchment area—the geographic space they are responsible for. In what ways does your parish operate as a territory, in the sense of responsibility to a geographic area delimited by the diocese? How does that shape parish ministries and expenditures (or not)?

All Catholic parishes have a defined set of territorial boundaries.[6] Many, however, draw increasingly from across parish boundaries, a kind of de facto congregationalism (Warner 1993). Still, parishes have their main setting in their defined neighborhood. Saint Ignatius was carved out of the territory of some neighboring parishes. Its territorial sweep is not large; parishioners come overwhelmingly from outside Saint Ignatius's parish territory (90 percent). The congregation draws from some seventy-two postal areas in the San Francisco Bay Area.

People are drawn to the church for a number of reasons. Saint Ignatius is a landmark in the city and attracts a steady number of tourists, who come to visit and see the building. The church is lit up at night and can be seen widely throughout San Francisco's skyline. Its 250-feet-tall neoclassical basilica, looming towers, and dome modeled on the dome of Saint Mark in Venice make it more like a cathedral than a parish church. It looms as the most significant and remarkable building on the University of San Francisco campus. *San Francisco Chronicle*'s architectural critic, John King, said of the church's architecture: "This city, yes, is blessed with religious buildings that rise from the landscape to offer spiritual inspiration and/or a topographical marker, depending on your faith. What makes this one shine is the location—uphill on the west side of the city, all the more serenely commanding as a result—and the resonance with which it makes the hubris of its verticality seem downright humane" (2014).

Parishioners are also drawn to the liturgies, music, and homilies. Others graduated from Jesuit high schools or universities and feel a special kinship with a Jesuit parish. The well-regarded faith formation programs for

6. The exception is personal parishes, which are primarily purpose based rather than territorially defined (see Bruce 2017).

children and adults draw still others. Some say that Saint Ignatius was their "last stop" before going away from Catholicism altogether, dissatisfied as they were with their own local parish.

We serve registered parishioners from wherever and also for some services (mainly weddings and funerals or baptisms). We also serve nonregistered alumni of the University of San Francisco or other Jesuit schools. We do weddings, funerals, baptisms, and sick calls even with nonregistered Catholics in our catchment area. We also regularly serve, through Mass and parishioner visits, a retirement home in our catchment area. We are currently considering house-by-house contact with all people (Catholic or not) in our catchment area as a form of outreach, evangelism, and invitation.

Beyond our canonically defined parish territory, we are also connected to the broader diocese in multiple ways. We contribute a large sum (based on annual income from collections) to the Archbishop's Annual Appeal. It is basically a tax that must be paid to the diocese for support of diocesan-wide activities such as Catholic Charities, Catholic Youth Organization, etc. Saint Ignatius's is the second largest such tax in San Francisco, after our neighboring Dominican parish, Saint Dominic. For the sixty-five or so marriages we do each year, we follow diocesan procedures and have the couple fill out a premarriage survey. Couples must also attend an engagement encounter weekend run by the diocese. If the marriage is an interfaith marriage, the priest must also get a dispensation from the marriage tribunal for the marriage. All papers are vetted by the diocese.[7]

Our teen program, moreover, joined with the groups from two neighboring parishes to create a larger group.[8] We make available to them or our young adult group any material from the diocese concerning diocesan-wide programs. We use the diocesan newspaper, *San Francisco Catholic*, to advertise events at the parish, such as any adult faith formation presentation or concert at the parish. As a result, these events also draw nonparishioners to the parish. We cooperate with the diocese on mission appeals and take up special collections. We asked to be one of the churches with a holy door for the Holy Year, which required the bishop's approval. Our priests also attend various diocesan-sponsored retreats or study days.

7. See Courtney Irby's essay on marriage preparation in this volume.

8. See Kathleen Garces-Foley's essay on interparish young adult ministry in this volume.

In this volume, Mark Gray writes about "core" and "periphery" Catholics. How does your parish define, identify, and respond to these types of Catholics?

The idea of core versus periphery Catholics dates back to Joseph Fichter's early work. The distinction is also found in the studies of William D'Antonio and associates. Mass attendance, as D'Antonio, Dillon, and Gautier (2013) show, was 44 percent weekly in 1987 and had fallen to 31 percent nationwide by 2011. Some 26 percent attended Mass less than monthly in 1987; this rose to 47 percent in 2011. In our survey of Saint Ignatius parishioners, we found that only 30 percent said they attended Mass less than once a month, compared to the 47 percent national average. This, of course, misses people who weren't in the pews to take the survey and who might attend less often, but people who *do* attend our church seem to be quite committed. We've also researched this using our database of registered parishioners (though many who come to the church do not register). Of the households that are registered, half are truly active and the rest are more sporadic attenders or givers. That indicates both commitment and room for more.

Another index for us of core versus periphery Catholics shows up in the children's faith formation programs. Many parents simply drop their children off and do not attend Mass themselves. We have tried to contact them and instill the idea that parents are the first teachers in the faith. Sociologists have pointed to parents' own lack of faith formation as one predictor of children's later disaffiliation from Catholicism (Smith et al. 2014). We held one adult faith formation presentation last year on that topic. It might be good for us, as a parish, to take up one of Gray's points about adult Catholics who left the faith for a time and have now returned to self-identifying as Catholic. He notes that between 10 percent and 13 percent of respondents to CARA surveys have said they are "returned Catholics." We are aware anecdotally of such reverts in our parish. Doing interviews on what led them back to the church could illuminate how to get other inactive Catholics to return.

Your huge parish draws a highly educated, socially active, and racially diverse group of parishioners. Yet, as Brett Hoover and Tia Noelle Pratt point out in this book, this can result in multiple subgroups within parish communities that struggle over resources and power or only occasionally overlap. Is this the case in your parish? If not, why not?

To be sure, people who go to our numerous different liturgies do not mingle much or interact with people at other Masses. The young adult group and teenage group tend to go to the 5:00 p.m. Sunday Mass. Parents with children go to the 9:30 a.m. Mass, after which there are catechism classes for the children. Non-Mass events or programs are key to bringing these people together. People from all the different Masses interact in social ministries, such as the shelter meal programs. Members of the parish council and the five commissions (worship, outreach, formation, administration, community) come from different subgroups of the five Masses. Moreover, the worship commission and the director of worship for the parish has meetings that draw together lectors, Eucharistic ministers, ushers, and greeters from all five of the Masses.

"Building Communities: Food, Fun, and Fellowship," Nancy Ammerman's chapter in *Pillars of Faith* (2005), talks about sportive gatherings, outside of worship time, that help build community across disparate groups. Over the last several years, our parish has had a number of these events. We had a large banquet, which filled the University of San Francisco's gym, to celebrate the former pastor's retirement. For the church building's centennial in 2014, we buried a time capsule in the cornerstone of the church to be looked at a hundred years from now. There is a large annual parish picnic on the lawn of the university outside the church every September. All parish volunteers are treated to a buffet each May in celebration of their service. The winter hoedown dance bridges constituencies. In any parish, there will be a tendency toward separate enclaves, but the point of building a wider community is to find multiple ways for the different groups or their representatives to come together.

As Mary Jo Bane writes in this volume, a parish like yours has the potential makings of an "economic lifestyle enclave." What, if anything, does your parish do to resist these tendencies?"

To be sure, Saint Ignatius is, by and large, a middle- to upper-middle-class parish. Our surrounding neighborhood (the parish's geographic boundaries) is also middle- to upper-middle class. Moreover, since 90 percent of the parish comes from outside the parish boundaries, they have resources (cars, free time, etc.) to commute. But some of our parishioners have experienced homelessness. We help support one such man who is a regular at our Masses and adult faith formation programs. A greeter at one of our Masses has been homeless. Few in the parish know this.

I suppose the best way to resist being a lifestyle enclave is to have social outreach or advocacy programs that connect people to the homeless or the poor. Many in the parish are concerned about rising rents in San Francisco and the inability for poorer or working-class people to afford to live in the city. Our shelter meal program and service projects connect us to the poor. Our sister parish in El Salvador reminds us of those outside our lifestyle enclave. We could think more, as Bane suggests, about inter-parish activities to enlarge communities. Many parishioners support a school run by our former pastor that does intense education for poor Hispanic and African American primary school students. Several of our parishioners serve on the board of the school, support it financially, or volunteer as tutors.

But, as my former doctoral student Jerome Baggett puts it, "parishes tend to be much better at steering people toward charitable endeavors than at undertaking long-term projects to fulfill the church's social justice mission" (2009, 175). Recognizing his point that most social outreach programs are aimed at charity rather than social restructuring and advocacy, I urged the parish to begin an explicit social justice advocacy group. Such groups rarely exist in parishes and are often run by a small clique of like-minded people with little connection to or input from the larger parish. We are doing a semester discernment process to determine our focus (whether on immigration reform, ecological issues, or prison reform or working to increase the minimum wage or end human trafficking) with parish input. We'll use a survey of the parish that I am designing, hold a final discernment weekend to choose a topic, and build parish-wide support for explicit advocacy on a social justice issue. In this—as with so much of what we do at the parish level—the sociological perspective will add an essential ingredient in support of our empirically grounded, knowledge-based efforts to serve others for the greater glory of God.

Thank you for these reflections and connections, Fr. Coleman. We are grateful for your input.

References

Ammerman, Nancy. 2005 *Pillars of Faith: American Congregations and Their Partners.* Berkeley: University of California Press.

Baggett, Jerome. 2000. *Habitat for Humanity: Building Private Homes, Building Public Religion.* Philadelphia: Temple University Press.

———. 2009. *Sense of the Faithful: How American Catholics Live the Faith.* New York: Oxford University Press.

Bendyna, Mary, and Paul Perl. 2000. "Young Adult Catholics in the Context of Other Catholic Generations." Working Paper. Center for Applied Research in the Apostolate, Washington, DC.

Bruce, Tricia Colleen. 2017. *Parish and Place: Making Room for Diversity in the American Catholic Church.* New York: Oxford University Press.

D'Antonio, William V., Michele Dillon, and Mary L Gautier. 2013. *American Catholics in Transition.* Lanham, Md.: Rowman & Littlefield Publishers.

Fichter, Joseph. 1951. *The Dynamics of a City Church.* Southern Parish, vol. 1. Chicago: University of Chicago Press.

———. 1954. *Social Relations in the Urban Parish.* Chicago: University of Chicago Press.

King, John. 2014. "Cityscape: 5 Buildings That Embody San Francisco." *San Francisco Chronicle*, October 29, 2014, 18.

Mallon, James. 2014. *Divine Renovation: Bringing Your Parish from Maintenance to Mission.* New London, Conn.: Twenty-Third Publications.

Smith, Christian, Kyle Longest, Jonathan Hill, and Kari Christoffersen. 2014. *Young Catholic America: Emerging Adults In, Out of, and Gone from the Church.* New York: Oxford University Press.

Sweetser, Thomas. 2007. *Keeping the Covenant: Taking the Parish to the Next Level.* New York: Crossroad.

Warner, Stephen. 1993. "Work in Progress: Toward a Paradigm for the Sociological Study of Religion in the United States," *American Journal of Sociology* 48: 1040–1093.

Wood, Richard. 2002. *Faith in Action: Religion, Race, and Democratic Organizing in America.* Chicago: University of Chicago Press.

Conclusion

Parishes as the Embedded Middle of American Catholicism

GARY J. ADLER JR., TRICIA C. BRUCE,
AND BRIAN STARKS

Parishes occupy the embedded middle of American Catholicism. They are small c churches—communities of Catholics—in a centralized, big C Church. In parishes, individual Catholics come together to create a local identity within a global Catholic Church. Parishes mediate between Catholicism as an aggregate of individuals and Catholicism as a global, hierarchical institution. Parishes are durable organizations providing the social structure to reproduce and change Catholicism across generations.

But, as a number of essays in this volume noted, for some time and in various ways, parishes have gone missing for those social scientists and others who study Catholicism. Individuals and institutions have often drawn more interest. Survey reports on individual Catholics come out frequently, garnering attention when they reveal attitudes or behaviors that do not comport with official Catholic teachings. Decades of surveys have dismantled myths about individual Catholics and painted startling new pictures of religious faith as it is practiced (D'Antonio, Dillon, and Gautier 2013; Greeley 1977, 1989, 2001). This approach catches the micro-level of Catholic life. It also imports an individualistic understanding of religion that can distort its communal aspects (Wuthnow 2015). On the other end of the spectrum, studies of Catholic institutions (analyses of the Vatican, the USCCB, and more) highlight the macro-level of American Catholicism (e.g., Burns 1994; Wilde 2007; and Yamane 2005). Macro-research on Catholicism tells us much about religious elites, political power, and the public life of Catholicism but little about local religious communities containing millions of members and the building blocks of larger institutions.

In these pages, contributors showcased the persistent relevance of the *meso*-level of Catholicism, that of parishes. Parishes provide an entry point for sociologists to see how religion works at the point where Catholicism from "below" meets Catholicism from "above." Like other local organizations, parishes are dependent on the fruits and labors of individual members. Likewise, parishes are dependent on the traditions, rules, and meanings of the larger Catholic Church. However, what parishes do and how they do it cannot be induced from the sum of their members nor deduced from a higher-level institutional entity. Parishes merit attention on their own terms, while still accounting for their *embeddedness*—the individuals and institutions to which they are linked. Seeing parishes sociologically means seeing them as the embedded middle.

Toward an Embedded Field Approach

In the Introduction to this volume, we proposed an "embedded field approach" as a way to illuminate the meso-level in sociological studies of Catholicism. Broadly speaking, we suggested that parishes are embedded in and shaped by the social forces of community, geography, and authority. To say that parishes inhabit the middle of Catholicism is to recognize that parishes sit at an intersection of these social forces. This acknowledges the different ways that local parishes use resources, conduct religious rituals, teach religious faith, relate to neighborhoods, and adjust to challenges. These social forces shape and constrain, but never fully determine, what a parish looks like and does at the local level. It is only through understanding the embeddedness of parishes in community, geography, and authority that we can make sense of the patterned similarity we see across parishes—a similarity that coexists with striking diversity, too.

But *which* aspects of community, geography, and authority do parishes relate to, and *how*? The concept of a social field, derived from field theory, offers a helpful way to approach this. For sociologists, the concept of "field" refers to a theoretical space in which all objects of study (in our case, parishes) relate to a set of shared meanings, rules, and challenges as well as to each other (Kniss 2003; Martin 2003). The concept of field is especially useful because, with its roots in the study of electromagnetism, it emphasizes that all objects within a field face the same forces, relate to each other, and even influence the relative position of each other as they themselves change the shape of the field. Field theory brings heuristic elements to clarify complex data that may otherwise appear too diverse or unrelated. Imagine a field as a beanbag chair whose lining sets the broad outlines of a shape, orienting the Styrofoam beads collectively inside.

(Analogies only go so far, of course—we are not suggesting that parishes move only due to outside forces.) Thinking through the concept of a social field illuminates which social forces matter most for understanding how and why entities within the field (people, parishes) behave the way that they do.

Our appreciation for this way of thinking about parishes grew during the seminar that launched this book. The contributors to the original seminar were not asked to take a particular approach to their study of parishes. Nevertheless, our in-person discussions across four days kept returning to similar themes. These themes were not easily classified by static concepts that characterized the existing study of parishes, concepts like "immigrant parishes," "ethnic parishes," or "Vatican II parishes." Those ideal types may be informative but can also be misleading and oversimplified. Instead, the themes we came back to were about social processes: How do parishes deal with change? How do parishes manage diversity or construct culture and community? What makes parishes Catholic?

We expanded this line of thinking after the seminar and formalized it into the shared process approach we articulate here. By focusing on processes that occur *within* parishes as well as *across* a heterogeneous parish population, we forefront the organizational dimension of parishes. Our priority has been to illuminate organizational processes that are more or less shared by parishes across the population before differentiating individual parishes from each other. To this end, we decided not to categorize contributors' essays solely by reference to parishioner demographics (e.g., race, class, region). This approach to categorization, while common, tends to reify micro-level characteristics as the primary defining elements of an organization. Our focus on processes, by contrast, makes a sociology of parishes different from a sociology of Catholics or Catholicism; namely, it puts organizational dynamics at its core.

Many social fields and forces shape parishes as organizations. These include theological trends, religious authority structures, economic crises, demographic transitions, and subcultural communities. Any one of these can provide parishes with meanings, opportunities, and resources (or constraints). In the United States, the organizational form of the congregation is especially important in this regard, as Nancy Ammerman pointed out in her essay. US Catholic parishes, not unlike Jewish synagogues or

Islamic mosques, have come to share many features of Protestant churches. But congregations are not the only field shaping parishes.

An example can illustrate how field theory uncovers the meso-level of parish life. Imagine a simple Cartesian plane with two dimensions: an x-axis and a y-axis. Using coordinates, we could plot any parish as a point along those dimensions. Each point stands in relation to all other points. For example, we might be interested in how parishes deal with religious authority. We could think of the social field of "religious authority" as a space structured by differing modes of religious authority. We might theorize, based on previous research (Baggett 2009; Dillon 1999; Konieczny 2013), that the field of religious authority in twenty-first-century US parishes is characterized by two dimensions: styles of interpretive authority within the Catholic tradition and levels of lay religious involvement. Parishes could be plotted by their emphases on autonomous interpretation versus obedience to hierarchical doctrine (dimension one) and the centrality of lay member involvement/leadership in parish life (dimension two).

We may plot the parishes described by Tia Noelle Pratt in this volume near the center of the first dimension, as they "own" some elements of Catholic doctrine, "sifting out" others. These parishes may land farther along dimension two, as the laity incorporate distinctive liturgical styles in Mass. Meanwhile, the parishes studied by Courtney Ann Irby appear on the hierarchical end of dimension one, as they comply with Church regulations for sacramental marriage preparation, and also high on the second dimension's axis, given their contemporary reliance on lay leadership in marriage preparation. Finally, some parishes that young adults encountered in Kathleen Garces-Foley's essay emphasized personal adoption of justice and civic engagement aspects of Church tradition (the opposite end of dimension one) but channeled only limited lay involvement into parish life (low on dimension two), partly as a consequence of their engagement with nonparish Catholic organizations.

What would this simple analysis of just a few parishes reveal? Importantly, it would change our initial impulse to think of Pratt's parishes only as "urban parishes" or "black parishes" or of Irby's as "West Coast parishes." Those identities would certainly be part of an understanding of these parishes. But they are insufficient for understanding a specific dimension of parishes: religious authority. Such an approach also unsettles an artificial binary of "liberal" versus "conservative" parishes, which congeals together many meanings that obfuscate the complexity of actual parish practice (Sullivan 2016). What would you learn about how a parish involves laypeople's religious experience by focusing on that binary? Not much. Moreover, an analysis like this would show that while all parishes deal with lay religious involvement, they do so in surprising (and surprisingly different) ways. Pratt's parishes relied on laypeople to personalize worship services, while Garces-Foley's parishes struggled to generate meaningful spaces of belonging for young adults. The relative nonconcern by some parishes for young adults only makes sense when you pay attention to another social field: nonparish Catholic organizations that already cater to this sector. A simple analysis like this—starting with just a few parish cases—helps us understand diversity among parishes by emphasizing their position vis-à-vis a shared social force (in this case, religious authority).

The heuristic of an embedded field approach is useful for understanding the organizational dynamics of parishes for a number of reasons. Here, we identify five. First, the embedded field approach pulls away from a rationalist, voluntarist assumption that parishes are the way they are because of the purposeful decisions of individual actors, whether lay members, priests, or bishops. Of course the decisions and purposes of individual actors matter in parish life, but they are enacted amid (and shaped by) larger forces. Second, this approach suggests that even if we study only *one* parish, we need to account for its relationship to other parishes and to the social forces in which all parishes are embedded. Third, this approach acknowledges numerous shaping forces at play—not solely theology, resources, ethnicity, or location. Catholic authority will not always be the most salient field. Fourth, this approach reminds us that there are many ways to "be a parish." Many parishes (and priests and laypeople) may claim their own way as the "best" or "most faithful" way.

A fifth and final advantage to an embedded field approach is that it makes the social shaping of parishes more overt. Parishes are prisms of myriad elements of social life. Parishes are places where residential segregation may facilitate parish segregation, where therapeutic culture may shape sacramental preparation, where political attitudes take root, where parts of individual Catholics' identities are built. To put it plainly, parishes are embedded in society, and society is embedded in parishes. It is their quality of embeddedness—as one layer among many—that makes them especially interesting. We amplify a question posed by sociologist Mary Ellen Konieczny, who participated in our seminar: "What would scholars learn about parishes if we looked at them first from the point of view of their embeddedness in a larger but still local organizational structure and culture?" (2018, 17).

What does all this mean for the future of a sociology of parishes? Distilling lessons from the essays in this volume, we offer three admonitions.

1. *Seeing parishes sociologically means comparing assumptions with reality.*

Several times throughout this volume, we heard the name and story of an early American priest-sociologist, Joseph Fichter. Fr. Fichter's sociological study of a parish was silenced when Church leaders found out that parishioner behavior did not mirror what they professed during Mass. Micro-level actions did not match macro-level pronouncements; studying the parish had revealed this gap.

While jarring and consequential at the time, this is in fact one of the greatest benefits of any sociological study of parishes: its capacity to tell the story like it is. Sociologists are not in the business of toeing a company line or skewing data to favor a hoped-for outcome. Deploying the aforementioned tools of social science, sociologists paint a picture of what *is*. That picture is clarified by participants in the sustained, peer-reviewed conversation known as social science. While priests, bishops, lay leaders, and parishioners get understandably absorbed by the day-to-day workings of parish life, sociology requires us to pause, measure, analyze, and compare what we *think* is happening to what actually *is* happening. Often, that comparison will surprise us.

This volume was full of surprises revealed through careful parish study. Mary Jo Bane, for example, showed us that US parishes do not evenly incorporate the kind of racial and economic diversity that exists in America more broadly or the inclusion preached about in sermons. Mark Gray pointed out that weekly Mass attenders (American Catholicism's "core") are much more likely than less-frequent attenders (the "periphery") to place importance on religious practice. Growth in the periphery means that fewer Catholics will see practice as a core component in their own religious identities. Elsewhere, Gary Adler highlighted the paradox of growing political involvement by Catholic parishes alongside increased restraint on roles for women, gays, and lesbians. Kathleen Garces-Foley revealed that parishes can operate as hubs in a style of (non)membership that is in tension with the common, family-based structure of parish organizational life. Even more surprises came from Courtney Ann Irby, who disclosed the difficulty of delivering sacramental preparation through minimally trained lay leaders. How all this happens tells an unexpected story, with implications for congregations and organizations more broadly.

The sociology of parishes should compare assumptions with reality, grounding lived experience within a sociological framework. This better understanding helps us understand what models for parish life exist in real life and which are possible. By way of example, recent public attention to the "Benedict Option" (Dreher 2017)—promoting withdrawal into religiously homogenous communities as a strategy to resist social change—led one journalist to profile the "intentional community" of a Catholic parish in Hyattsville, Maryland (Gjelton 2017). But just a bit of sociological data from the US Census and CARA quickly reveals that this parish is an outlier: it is embedded in a highly educated, high-income area and is served by three times the number of priests for an average US parish. Put simply, if the "Benedict Option" were the parish model of the future, not many parishes could fit the bill. The sociology of parishes can introduce (and test) a multitude of models for parish life.

All this means that the sociology of parishes may produce findings that aren't what certain audiences expect (or wish) to hear. This can generate a sense of fear on the part of practitioners and an animosity toward sociology as problem identifiers and sociologists as problem makers. As Tricia Bruce pointed out in her essay, this tension has its roots in the earliest sociological studies of the parish. But sociology (and the sociologist) need not be read as problematic: research reveals areas for growth and change. A lack of knowledge does not make something less real on the ground. While hardly a benign endeavor, parish studies may be usefully paired with theology and pastoral practice to support desired outcomes.

Reinserting parishes in the middle of studies about American Catholicism—between individual behavior on the ground and structured institutions from the top—lends a powerful tool to reveal gaps (or congruence) between ideas and reality. Absent this middle level, we can be less certain as to how and where individual Catholics and an elusive "Catholic Church" converge.

2. *The sociology of parishes must work in conversation—and tension—with the study of congregations.*

These pages repeat a theme that looks like two sides of a coin. On the one side, parishes are embedded in a field of congregations, sharing commonality across multiple spheres of social life. On the other side, parishes are distinctive, special, and even "exceptional" when we compare them to other congregations. Both characteristics stem from the act of placing parishes in their contexts: alongside non-Catholic congregations and embedded within Catholicism.

A shorthand way to get at the common qualities of parishes and non-Catholic congregations would be to fill in the blank for this statement: "Parishes are an example of how congregations _____." To illustrate, Tia Noelle Pratt provides an example of how congregations actively negotiate shared traditions to generate spaces of meaning and welcome for racial minorities. Brett Hoover shows us how congregations embed broader power dynamics and racial inequalities observed across society.

But, as the essays in this book also remind us, parishes display distinctive characteristics that challenge commonly held understandings of congregations. To illustrate how they are different, sociologists need to identify when and where parishes *don't* fit a common mold. How are parishes different from other congregations, even within the shared social field of local American religious life? Seeing Catholic parishes as *exceptional* means asking a somewhat different set of questions.

Here, too, the preceding pages lend several clues. We learned that parishes are much larger, on average, than other congregations. Parishes are more likely to be multiracial and are increasingly comprised of Hispanic Americans. An embedded field approach suggests that there are social forces explaining these differences. Within Catholicism, parishes are linked to distant networks of authority: dioceses and the global Church. Parishes are not merely the products of de facto community building but require formal, canonical decrees to come into being. Parishes encompass both geographic territory and the cultural work of a community (who may or may not mirror proximate neighborhoods). Parishes serve "core" Catholics who attend Mass regularly but also "periphery" Catholics who do not. This means that the demographic composition of parishes is due in part to settlement patterns, not just intentional outreach. And, unlike many congregations, parish leadership is neither entirely organic nor democratic. Catholic laws, oaths, and rules regarding the authority to preach and celebrate Mass and whether priests can get married all affect the availability of clergy, with consequences for parish size. In short, parishes are not (always, in all ways) like other congregations, nor other organizations, nor other sites of social life. The exceptional qualities of parishes—their nonconformity to the congregational form—mean that they require specialized study in their own right.

In fact, this is where the language of embedded field theory first emerged in our discussions, as we talked about how parishes so obviously belong to the field of congregations but also are embedded within the Catholic tradition. This creates another set of forces, meanings, and comparisons. We recognize, moreover, that this quality of embeddedness is not unique to Catholic parishes; Southern Baptist congregations (who participate in the Southern Baptist Convention and are asked but not required to uphold its guidelines) are not the same as congregations embedded within the United Methodist Church (who discuss their denomination as "the connection"). Highlighting the different meanings, elements, and forces at play in the "congregational field" and the "Catholic field" (compared to the "Southern Baptist field" and so on) helps us recognize the myriad ways that parishes are shaped by society. The political field and newly resonant culture wars surrounding immigration, for example, shape Hispanic Catholic parishes as well as other non-Catholic Latino and multiracial congregations.[1]

Reclaiming parishes as an embedded middle in studies of Catholicism means acknowledging both commonality and exceptionalism and seeking to understand the forces that explain both patterns. It is not enough to look only at parishes' broad similarities without paying attention to their

1. Multiple social fields and forces are relevant not just to Catholic parishes (and other denominations) but even to nondenominational congregations, which have seen large growth in recent decades. Because all these organizations find themselves embedded within multiple social fields, future researchers of parishes (and other congregations) might usefully explore how immigration forces, technological shifts, or even trends in pop culture shape the patterning of parishes and other congregations. In this book, we have focused on particular fields and forces that we believe are especially relevant and important for parish research, but future parish research could take researchers in creative directions beyond what we can currently imagine.

differences, too (and rooting those similarities and differences in theoretical explanations of the forces behind the patterns).

3. The sociology of parishes requires methodological breadth and strength.

Sociologists are trained in social science methods to gather data, minimize bias, and identify patterns. Systematic methods of data collection and analysis are what separate sociology from, for example, anecdotes or quick-turnaround journalism. For social scientists, methodology is not an afterthought but the basis of new discovery and reassessment of "known" facts. The sociology of parishes must be rooted in sound social scientific methods.

From the first studies of parishes until today, both qualitative and quantitative methodologies have played their role (Lane 1996). But contemporary declines in survey response rates and the move toward "big data" blur the boundaries of confidentiality and risk inaccuracy. Case studies presented with insufficient comparison may misrepresent what's typical or miss variation across examples. Private funding, too, raises pressing questions about the norms of data ownership and transparency. Facing these and more challenges, the methods used to study parishes must broaden and strengthen.

One way to renew the methodology used for the study of parishes is to look to what has worked well in similar research. We need not start from scratch. We learned from Nancy Ammerman that parish studies can borrow and benefit from the research methods ("tools") used in congregational studies. Ammerman and many of her collaborators demonstrate numerous ways to situate parishes within their ecological settings, demographics, physical spaces, symbolic use, and stories. These approaches played out in subsequent essays when, for example, Brett Hoover walked us through scenes at Queen of Heaven parish or when John Coleman explained how he researched his own parish.

Another source of renewal can come from bringing parishes back into studies of civic organization, religious life, and American Catholicism more generally. This may require supplementing existing projects with additional methods or "going big" with a new, well-funded project. Often, surges in useful sociological insight about parishes have been tied to large, multiple-year infusions of resources into well-designed research projects.

Tricia Bruce's essay detailed how this occurred with the founding of CARA after Vatican II, with the Notre Dame study in the 1980s, and with congregational surveys in the late 1990s and 2000s. Each of these moments was characterized by methodologically sophisticated research projects with strong bases in the academic study of sociology. It seems reasonable to suggest that we have arrived at another such moment in which a focused application of appropriate resources could transform our understanding of parishes, especially at a time of major demographic change in the United States.

Any such project should, we advise, keep the following two criteria in mind. First, it should engage experts in a number of methodologies, especially those with expertise in recent methodological developments. This volume intentionally showcased diverse methodological approaches from a wide array of data sources. Adler, Gray, and Bane used quantitative tools and pre-existing data sources to depict broad-scale trends over time. Pratt, Hoover, and Garces-Foley drew on qualitative data to expose processes likely unseen by a survey. Irby and Bruce worked with historical data to trace change over time.

Even so, as Carol Ann MacGregor has written, "data on parishes is much harder to acquire than other types of data" (2018, 24) and tends not to be easily linkable to other data.[2] We know of several university researchers who have independently, with great time investment, digitized Catholic sources to make them more accessible. A common parish data source, perhaps housed on the Association of Religion Data Archives (ARDA)—the leading research repository for social scientists interested in religion—would help rectify this. Data inaccessibility severely limits research on parishes and exacerbates a parochialism that prevents parishes from being seen by non-Catholics and social scientists as social institutions worth studying.

Research on parishes would also benefit from more *types* of data. Creative new mechanisms for data collection—online and mobile among them—may increase participation, if paired with adequate guards against measurement error. Large-scale projects now incorporate visual, aural, and social network data in addition to traditional survey and ethnographic

2. MacGregor (2018) provides an array of interesting questions that could be answered if the social science infrastructure of research on Catholicism were expanded.

data. This can advance our ability to embed organizations in their ecologies, contextualized by data from multiple demographic, economic, and governmental sources. A good deal of social science research today is multilevel, "nesting" lower groupings of social life into higher ones (MacGregor 2018). Nesting would reveal how individual parishioners are embedded in parishes and how parishes are embedded in communities and dioceses. Each level has its own dynamics that, together, tell a richer and more accurate story than told by one level alone.

The second criteria to remember when designing parish studies is that its participants and audience go beyond scholars of religion. As this volume has shown, parish research cuts across myriad facets of social life. Parishes provide opportunities for scholars of family, immigration, civic organizations, education, race/ethnicity, and more to analyze core issues in their specialties. Parish studies can also be conducted in consultation with Catholic officials, researchers, and funders. This kind of bridging can generate a more robust and impactful study of parishes.

Such partnerships (and funding relationships) can, of course, raise suspicions about weakened methodological design, suppressed findings, or limitations on data access. Proprietary research funded or conducted by Catholic organizations is needed to serve the targeted purposes of pastoral funders. But the current dependence of many Catholic leaders on data that are not widely used by social scientists—even those who study Catholicism—indicates that something is amiss. Financial and data transparency has received greater attention by social scientists in the past decade; one upshot is that the sociological study of religion is relatively evenhanded in its analysis of religion (Smilde and May 2015). Well-funded, readily accessible research conducted to the highest standards would deepen accuracy and creative insight. Involvement by academic researchers would also introduce knowledge about parishes to non-Catholic scholars. University-based research projects could train young scholars in the methods and theories of social science, while advancing knowledge about parishes.

There should be a productive tension between the work of the academy, with its interests in careful theoretical exploration, and the work of pastoring, with its interest in building faith and designing pragmatic responses to life on the ground. This relationship (the "dual-constituency value proposition," as Bruce called it in her essay) could find better balance when it comes to social science. Church leaders today may be less familiar with social science tools than they were immediately following Vatican II and increasingly suspicious of their potential for harm. As Bruce suggests, the current system may continue to be hobbled by fear. Nevertheless, we see productive ways, through greater contact and dialogue, in which this pattern can change. We hope this book is one of them.

Next Steps in a Sociology of American Parishes

American Catholicism is changing. Seeing changes in American Catholics and in the US Catholic Church requires studying its core unit of organization and community: parishes. We contend that parishes occupy the embedded middle between American Catholics as individuals and Catholicism as a collective Church. With this perspective, what topics might social scientists focus on from here?

Without a doubt, sociological parish research can investigate large-scale demographic change. American Catholics are increasingly diverse racially, as are parishes. To what extent do parishes embed American diversity? This means pushing ahead on the kinds of questions that Mary Jo Bane raises in this volume, analyzing the intersection of racial, ethnic, and economic diversity. Within parishes, how does racial diversity shape power dynamics and community leadership? Brett Hoover modeled an ethnographic approach to these questions. These issues are urgent, as they challenge Catholic and civic norms about inclusion and equality.

American Catholics are also moving closer to a relative periphery of religious involvement. Mark Gray documented this trend and suggested some consequences. In this light, how do parishes facilitate, encourage, or obstruct different styles of religious involvement? How are parish communities formed when members are spread across so many services and led by fewer priests? The answers to these questions bear implications for those who lead and organize parishes in response to Catholics' needs and behaviors.

How parishes organize essential activities appears to be changing as well. Waves of parish closures in older dioceses have led to different configurations, combining existing parish communities (Seitz 2011). Pratt hinted at the hardship of this, as Catholics navigate multiple cultures, memories, and physical spaces. What do parish closures mean for the role of religion in civic ecologies? And how do new parishes in new (nonurban) places bridge or separate Catholics from proximate communities? Do parishes still tie people to place? These questions connect back to the role of geography, a constituent element in the Catholic and sociological understanding of a parish.

Many other questions remain unasked and underexplored, akin to what scholars of religious mystics call the *via negativa*. What have parish studies (including this volume) *not* addressed? More can be pursued, for example, on specific processes within Latino-serving parishes. As Hosffman Ospino and colleagues have identified, Latino Catholicism is minimally researched and (too often) pastorally neglected. Latino-serving parishes tend to have weaker economic bases, be underresourced by dioceses, and bring together different patterns of worship and theological preference. If—or because—an era of wide-reaching, countercultural, "brick-and-mortar" American Catholicism is over, how do today's parishes change and influence the lives of this fastest-growing demographic group? Of particular interest to sociologists may be how Latino-serving parishes facilitate (or inhibit) engagement, equality, and justice. The younger average age of Latino Catholics parallels questions about generational change. Catholic young adults are the most ethnically diverse segment of the Catholic population. Their affiliation and belief patterns differ drastically from those of older generations. What changes might this portend, alongside segmented work careers and loose connections to communal organizations?

Still other parishes—and other people—sit at the margins or wholly outside the purview of current scholarship on American Catholic parishes. Meaningful transformations in rural parishes, for example, have generally escaped scholarly attention. Some are experiencing large influxes of Catholic immigrants; others, population decline. How do rural parishes participate in communal integration, protect the vulnerable, or mediate the effects of economic uncertainty?

The Catholic Church may be at a turning point regarding the inclusion, support, and advancement of women and LGBT persons at the parish level. Despite resistance to transformative theological change (Chaves 1997), American Catholics have been relatively ahead of the curve in support for social inclusion and rights for these groups (Smith 2015). How do parishes promote, resist, or ignore social changes affecting a broad cross section of Americans, not to mention cohere a diversity of Catholic opinion? What happens on the ground in terms of sacramental inclusion, leadership roles, and ministry for socially marginalized groups?

Finally, writing this volume made us far more aware of potential collaborators beyond academic social scientists. While our initial and persistent aim has been to reengage sociologists, we see great possibility (and need) for connecting with others beyond our own discipline. There are many religious studies scholars, theologians, and ministerial officials who employ social scientific methods and ideas in their work. While their questions and intended audience may be different, they, too, benefit from a more robust sociological investigation of parishes. Too few of these persons and projects are known to sociologists. Our own volume contributors exemplify this bridging potential, bringing familiarity with Catholic organizations and ideas that sociologists might not otherwise have. This is only the beginning. The best sociology of parishes develops not in isolation, but in conversation.

Many are invested in the present and future of American Catholic parishes. The stakes are high; the rewards, rich. By embedding parishes in the middle of studies of American Catholicism, we hope that this volume may meaningfully advance future work, because seeing parishes means seeing the (re)making of local Catholicism.

References

Baggett, Jerome P. 2009. *Sense of the Faithful: How American Catholics Live Their Faith*. New York: Oxford University Press.

Burns, Gene. 1994. *The Frontiers of Catholicism: The Politics of Ideology in a Liberal World*. Berkeley: University of California Press.

Chaves, Mark. 1997. *Ordaining Women: Culture and Conflict in Religious Organizations*. Cambridge, Mass.: Harvard University Press.

D'Antonio, William V., Michele Dillon, and Mary L. Gautier. 2013. *American Catholics in Transition*: Lanham, Md.: Rowman & Littlefield Publishers.

Dillon, Michele. 1999. *Catholic Identity: Balancing Reason, Faith, and Power*. New York: Cambridge University Press.

Dreher, Rod. 2017. *The Benedict Option: A Strategy for Christians in a Post-Christian Nation*. New York: Sentinel.

Gjelten, Tom. "Catholics Build 'Intentional' Community of Like-Minded Believers." *National Public Radio*. April 10, 2017. https://www.npr.org/2017/04/10/522714982/catholics-build-intentional-community-of-like-minded-believers?utm_campaign=storyshare&utm_source=twitter.com&utm_medium=social.

Greeley, Andrew M. 1977. *The American Catholic: A Social Portrait*. New York: Basic Books.

———. 1989. *Religious Change in America*. Cambridge, Mass.: Harvard University Press.

———. 2001. *The Catholic Imagination*. Berkeley: University of California Press.

Kniss, Fred. 2003. "Mapping the Moral Order: Depicting the Terrain of Religious Conflict and Change." In *Handbook of the Sociology of Religion*, edited by Michele Dillon, pp. 331–47. New York: Cambridge University Press.

Konieczny, Mary. Ellen. 2013. *The Spirit's Tether: Family, Work, and Religion among American Catholics*. New York: Oxford University Press.

———. 2018. "Studying Catholic Parishes: Moving Beyond the Parochial." *American Catholic Studies* 129 (1): 14–21.

Lane, Ralph. 1996. "The Sociology of the Parish: Fichter's Work and Beyond." *Sociology of Religion* 57 (4): 345–49.

MacGregor, Carol Ann. 2018. "The Parish as the 'Missing Middle' Unit of Analysis in Catholic Studies. *American Catholic Studies* 129 (1): 22–27.

Martin, John Levi. 2003. "What Is Field Theory?" *American Journal of Sociology* 109 (1): 1–49.

Seitz, John. 2011. *No Closure: Catholic Practice and Boston's Parish Shutdowns*. Cambridge, Mass.: Harvard University Press.

Smilde, David, and Matthew May. 2015. "Causality, Normativity, and Diversity in 40 Years of US Sociology of Religion: Contributions to Paradigmatic Reflection." *Sociology of Religion* 76 (4): 369–88.

Smith, Mark A. 2015. *Secular Faith: How Culture Has Trumped Religion in American Politics*. Chicago: University of Chicago Press.

Sullivan, Susan Crawford. 2016. "Whither Polarization? (Non) Polarization on the Ground." In *Polarization in the US Catholic Church: Naming the Wounds, Beginning to Heal*, edited by Mary Ellen Konieczny, Charles C. Camosy, and Tricia C. Bruce, pp. 46–58. Collegeville, Minn.: Liturgical Press.

Wilde, Melissa. 2007. *Vatican II: A Sociological Analysis of Religious Change*. Princeton, N.J.: Princeton University Press.

Wuthnow, Robert. 2015. *Inventing American Religion: Polls, Surveys, and the Tenuous Quest for a Nation's Faith*. New York: Oxford University Press.

Yamane, David. 2005. *The Catholic Church in State Politics: Negotiating Prophetic Demands and Political Realities*. Lanham, Md.: Rowman & Littlefield.

Acknowledgments

Somewhere between the casinos and cuisine of a late summer 2011 conference in Las Vegas, we (Gary, Tricia, and Brian) shared our first conversations about a mutual interest in advancing a more robust sociology of Catholicism and better-connected network of scholars. Our first collective action involved organizing and presenting a session devoted to the sociology of Catholic parishes at the Association for the Sociology of Religion annual meeting. The unfolding conversations were both fruitful and unfinished, signaling that we were on to something. The American Parish Project (TAPP) was born.

We gratefully acknowledge the Institute for Advanced Catholic Studies (IACS) of the University of Southern California, the Louisville Institute, the McGrath Institute for Church Life at the University of Notre Dame, and the Oak Ridge Association of Universities for supporting The American Parish Project as it expanded nationally to incorporate more voices. We thank Nancy Ammerman, Jerome Baggett, Mary Ellen Konieczny, and R. Stephen Warner for their participation and sage advice in a 2014 consultation. A subsequent national call for papers invited research on the social science of US Catholic parishes, generating a promising set of proposals. Support from the IACS enabled us to gather sixteen scholars from various social science disciplines and career stages for a multiday workshop. Thank you to attendees Nancy Ammerman, Mary Jo Bane, Kristin Geraty Bonacci, John Coleman, Maureen Day, Kathleen Garces-Foley, Mark Gray, Brett Hoover, Courtney Irby, Mary Ellen Konieczny, Aprilfaye Manalang, Kristy Nabhan-Warren, and Tia Noelle Pratt. A special thanks goes to Maureen Day, who compiled a record of our dialogue and worked subsequently with Brian, Tricia, and Gary to compose a summary report sent to leaders in all US dioceses.

Moving from workshop to edited volume, we are especially grateful for the support extended by Angela Alaimo O'Donnell and John C. Seitz, coeditors of the Fordham University Press book series Catholic Practice in North America. Thank you also to Fordham University Press editor Fredric Nachbaur and to helpful anonymous reviewers of the manuscript. We offer a special thank-you to each of our volume contributors. Tricia, Brian, and Gary extend thanks also to Maryville College, Kennesaw State University, and the Pennsylvania State University, respectively, as well as to our families. We hope that this volume adds another stepping stone on the path to a more robust sociology of Catholicism.

Contributors

GARY J. ADLER JR. is assistant professor of sociology at Pennsylvania State University. His research on culture, organizations, and religion has been published in numerous journals, including *Social Problems*, *Social Science and Medicine*, *Journal for the Scientific Study of Religion*, and *Sociology of Religion*. He is the author of *Empathy Beyond US Borders: The Challenges of Transnational Civil Engagement* (Cambridge University Press, 2019) and editor of *Secularism, Catholicism, and the Future of Public Life* (Oxford University Press, 2015). From 2012 to 2015, he was the founding director of research for the Institute for Advanced Catholic Studies and a research scientist in the School of Religion at the University of Southern California.

NANCY T. AMMERMAN is professor emerita of sociology of religion in the Sociology Department of the College of Arts and Sciences and in the School of Theology at Boston University. She is a leading voice in congregational studies and has served as president of the Society of the Scientific Study of Religion and the Association of the Sociology of Religion. Her books include *Sacred Stories, Spiritual Tribes: Finding Religion in Everyday Life* (Oxford University Press, 2013), *Everyday Religion: Observing Modern Religious Lives* (Oxford University Press, 2006), *Pillars of Faith: American Congregations and their Partners* (University of California Press, 2005), and *Bible Believers: Fundamentalists in the Modern World* (Rutgers University Press, 1987).

MARY JO BANE is the Thornton Bradshaw Professor of Public Policy and Management Emerita at the Harvard Kennedy School. Her research interests center on poverty and inequality and how Catholic teaching and Catholic parish life address these issues. She is the author of numerous books and articles on poverty, education, families, and welfare and once served as assistant secretary for Families and Children in the federal Department of Health and Human Services.

TRICIA C. BRUCE is the author of *Parish and Place: Making Room for Diversity in the American Catholic Church* (Oxford University Press, 2017) and *Faithful Revolution: How Voice of the Faithful Is Changing the Church* (Oxford University Press, 2011) as well as the coeditor of *Polarization in the US Catholic Church: Naming the*

Wounds, Beginning to Heal (Liturgical Press, 2016). She holds appointments with the Center for the Study of Religion and Society at the University of Notre Dame and the University of Texas at San Antonio and has led research for the United States Conference of Catholic Bishops' Secretariat of Cultural Diversity in the Church. She is a former Congregational Studies fellow, research assistant professor with the Center for Applied Research in the Apostolate (CARA) at Georgetown University, and associate professor of sociology at Maryville College.

JOHN A. COLEMAN, SJ, is associate pastor at St. Ignatius Church in San Francisco and a Jesuit from the Province of California. He was formerly the Charles Casassa Professor of Social Values at Loyola Marymount University in Los Angeles and professor at the Jesuit School of Theology and the Graduate Theological Union in Berkeley, California. He is the editor of *Christian Political Ethics* (Princeton University Press, 2007), *Globalization and Catholic Social Thought: Present Crisis, Future Hope* (Orbis, 2005), and *One Hundred Years of Catholic Social Thought: Celebration and Challenge* (Orbis, 1991).

KATHLEEN GARCES-FOLEY is professor of religious studies at Marymount University. Her research interests include multiracial churches, young adults and religion, and contemporary death practices. She is the coauthor of *The Twentysomething Soul: Understanding the Religious and Secular Lives of American Young Adults* (Oxford University Press, 2019), author of *Crossing the Ethnic Divide: The Multiethnic Church on a Mission* (Oxford University Press, 2007), and editor of *Death and Religion in a Changing World* (Routledge, 2006).

MARK M. GRAY is research associate professor and senior research associate at the Center for Applied Research in the Apostolate (CARA) at Georgetown University. He has published on a wide number of topics related to Catholic parishes, religious switching, Catholic schools, and politics in two books and journals such as the *Journal for the Scientific Study of Religion* and *Review of Religious Research*. He has designed, led, or participated in CARA research projects including the National Survey of Catholic Parishes, Emerging Models of Pastoral Leadership, and CARA Catholic Polls.

BRETT C. HOOVER is associate professor of theological studies at Loyola Marymount University in Los Angeles. He teaches pastoral theology, congregational studies, and American Catholicism at the graduate and undergraduate levels. A former Congregational Studies fellow, his research has focused on ethnographic accounts of the relationship between different cultural groups in culturally diverse Catholic parishes in the United States. He is the author of *The Shared Parish: Latinos, Anglos, and the Future of U.S. Catholicism* (New York University Press, 2014).

COURTNEY ANN IRBY is assistant professor of sociology at Illinois Wesleyan University, having completed her PhD at Loyola University Chicago in the Department of Sociology. Her research considers the changing norms and meaning associated with how people form intimate relationships, including constructions of gender and sexuality. Her dissertation examined how religious groups mediate cultural changes in marriage by comparing Catholic and evangelical Protestant marriage preparation programs. Her articles have appeared in *Gender & Society*, *Critical Research on Religion*, *Sociology of Religion*, and *Sociology Compass*.

TIA NOELLE PRATT is a sociologist of religion specializing in the Roman Catholic Church in the United States. Specifically, she focuses on systemic racism in the US Catholic Church, African American Catholic identity, and millennial-generation Catholics. She is currently a scholar-in-residence at the Aquinas Center in Philadelphia, Pennsylvania and President of TNPratt & Associates, LLC.

BRIAN STARKS is associate professor of sociology at Kennesaw State University and former director of the Catholic Social and Pastoral Research Initiative at the University of Notre Dame. He completed his PhD at Indiana University in 2005 with support from the National Science Foundation. His research on the impact of religion (and Catholic identity) on parental values, politics, generosity, and more has been published in journals including *Social Forces*, *Journal for the Scientific Study of Religion*, and *Sociology of Religion*. He has served as researcher and consultant on studies of religious educators, religious giving, and Catholic parishes with Hispanic ministry and as principal investigator for a national study of Catholic campus ministry commissioned by the United States Conference of Catholic Bishops' Secretariat on Catholic Education.

Index

ACSS. *See* American Catholic
  Sociological Society
African Americans: black Church
  and, 133–34; Black History Month
  and, 148, 149; in black parishes, 18,
  38, 50. *See also* Black Catholic
  identity
age cohorts: Catholic population, 156;
  of core and periphery, 104, 105;
  culture relating to, 173; by
  generation, 171. *See also* young
  adult Catholics; youth
The American Catholic Parish (Dolan),
  33
*American Catholics in the Protestant
  Imagination* (Carroll), 36
American Catholics in Transition
  (D'Antonio, Dillon, and Gautier),
  157–58, *158*
*American Catholic Sociological
  Review*, 26
American Catholic Sociological
  Society (ACSS), 25
The American Parish Project, 16
Ammerman, Nancy, 34; *Pillars of
  Faith* by, 227; *Studying Congregations*
  by, 49
Appleby, Scott, 123, 124
Archdiocese of Washington, 176,
  178–79
Archives of the University of Notre
  Dame (UNDA), 198n2
Asian Americans, 38, 73, 113, 119, 120,
  221; immigration and, 153
assimilation, 119–20
Association of Religion Data Archive,
  36, 241
authority, 7; Catholic individuals and,
  29–30; community, geography,
  and, 1–3, 232–33; lived behavior

and, 28–30; organizations and, 14;
  parish size and, 60–61; power and
  process in parish life, 12–13, 56–58;
  religious authority, as social field,
  234; structures, 56–58

Baggett, Jerome, 37, 228
Balswick, Jack O., 31
Baptismal Rite, 139
baptisms, 17
Bischoff, Kendra, 161, *162*
bishops, 32, 35, 40, 56, 175–76
black Catholic identity: community
  and, 133; conclusion on, 148–50; at
  Holy Nativity, 117–18, 124–25;
  identity work at black parishes,
  134–35; liturgical styles and, 135–37,
  138; "owning" of, 134–35; parish
  culture production and, 135–36,
  149–50; religious experience and,
  132–34; Roman Catholic Church
  and, 133–34, 144–46, 149–50; at
  St. Bernadette Soubirous, 144–49;
  at St. John Vianney, 138–44,
  148–49; sifting process and, 135–37,
  140–42, 144–50
black Church, 133–34
Black History Month, 148, 149
black parishes, 18, 38, 50. *See also*
  black Catholic identity
Bourdieu, Pierre, 5
Bruce, Tricia C., 25n1, 35

Cana Conference Movement (CCM),
  198–99, 198n2, 199n3, 201–10
Cannon, Lynn Weber, 122–23
CARA. *See* Center for Applied
  Research in the Apostolate
Carroll, Michael, 34, 36
Castelli, Jim, 33

social surveys: data from, 70–71, 231;
by GfK Custom Research, 100,
100n8; on young adult Catholics,
173–76. *See also* Census Bureau;
Center for Applied Research in the
Apostolate; General Social Survey;
National Congregations Study
society: of organizations, 13–14;
parishes embedded in, 235–43
socioeconomic class: economic
inequality and, 154–55; income gap
and, 18, 154; in Latino parishes,
154–68, 156, 158, 160, 162, 163, 164;
lifestyle enclave and, 227–28;
parish life and, 227–28; race
relating to, 154–55; rich and poor
parishes compared with total
population, 157–59, 158
Sociological Abstracts, 36
sociology: of congregations, 17, 47–63,
233–34; embedded field approach
to, 15–19, 215, 231–45, 239n1; future
of, 236–43; of parishes, 4–7, 15–19,
23, 25–41, 236–43; parish studies
and, 217–24; re-introducing, 4–7;
religion and, 4–5, 26, 29; Second
Vatican Council and, 4, 4n2
The Sociology of the Parish (Nuesse and
Harte), 28, 40
Sons and Daughters of the Light, 175,
191
Southern Parish. See *Dynamics of a
City Church*
speaking in tongues, 83
spirited liturgical style, 136–37, 138
The Spirit's Tether (Konieczny), 37
spirituality, in marriage, 201–3,
206–9
Stark, Rodney, 95–96
Studying Congregations (Ammerman),
49
Study of Latino Faith Communities, 36
suburban parishes, 11. *See also* Queen
of Heaven; St. Martin de Porres
Sweetser, Thomas P., 31–32, 222–23,
222n5
Swidler, Ann, 50n3
symbols, 50, 132, 134–35

Takayama, K. Peter, 122–23
teens, 103, 104, 225, 227

theological orientation: conservative
parishes, 80–84; for Hispanics,
80–84; in local parish culture,
79–84, 80, 82; NCS on, 80–81;
neo-traditionalists, 184–85, 189,
190, 192; progressives, 184–85
Theology on Tap, 179–80, 190
therapeutic culture, 197, 200, 207–11
tongues, speaking in, 83
tradition: for Catholic individuals,
9–11; community and, 9–11;
culture and, 50; identity and,
9–11
traditional liturgical style, 136, 138
transparency, 242
trends, 17, 35, 67; Catholic population
relating to, 95; continuity as,
72–75; on demographics, 32, 75–79,
76, 77, 153; on diversity, 153; on
economic inequality, 154–55; how
to see, 69–72; in local parish
culture, 79–84; in organizational
composition, 73, 75–79; in parish
membership boundaries, 86–90,
87, 89, 164–66; politics and, 84–86;
social surveys and, 70–71; what has
changed in, 75–90

UNDA. *See* Archives of the University
of Notre Dame
uniracial congregation, 78
uniracial Hispanic parishes, 78–82
United States Conference of Catholic
Bishops (USCCB), 32, 175–76
urban parishes, 11, 37, 96. *See also* Holy
Nativity; Saint Ignatius Parish
USCCB. *See* United States Conference
of Catholic Bishops

Vatican II. *See* Second Vatican Council
"view from the pew" data, 72

Warner, R. Stephen, 47
Washington, DC: Archdiocese of
Washington, 176, 178–79;
demographics of young adults in,
178; Diocese of Arlington in, 176,
178–79, 189; Latinos and Hispanics
in, 178–79; young adult Catholics
in, 173–74, 176–80, 184–93
Weber, Max, 12

well-being, 48
WLA. *See* Women and Leadership
  Archives
women: as congregational leaders, 60;
  excluded from parish membership,
  86–89, *87, 89*; preaching by, 88
Women and Leadership Archives
  (WLA), 198n2
worship: in charismatic Catholicism,
  83–84; in megachurches, 60; styles,
  83–84 (*see also* liturgical styles)

YAC. *See* St. Paschal's Young Adult
  Community
Yamane, David, 37
Young, Barry, 31
young adult Catholics, 18–19, 171, 222,
  235; CARA on, 176; Catholic
  identity for, 174–75; Catholic
  Information Center and, 190–91,
  192; converts, 180, 182, 184, 188,
  190; data and interviews with,
  174–78; demographics, in DC, 178;
  diversity of, 178–79, 193; education
  and, 173; Latino and Hispanic,
  178–79; NCYAMA, 175–76;
  neo-traditionalist, 184–85, 189,
  190, 192; Notre Dame Study of

Catholic Parish Life on, 175; parish
  participation and, 174–75, 180–85;
  parish shopping and parish hopping
  by, 185–91; persistent Catholics,
  180, 182–84; politics and, 185–86,
  192–93; programs for, 175–76,
  178–80; progressives, 184–85;
  reverts, 180–84; at St. Monica
  Catholic Church, 188; at
  St. Paschal's YAC, 187–88; at
  St. Raphael Catholic Church,
  185–87; social surveys on, 173–76;
  Sons and Daughters of the Light and,
  175, 191; in Theology on Tap,
  179–80, 190; USCCB, 175–76; in
  Washington, DC, 173–74, 176–80,
  184–93; young adult ministry, DC,
  178–79, 187
*Young Adult Catholics: Religion in the
  Culture of Choice* (Hoge et al.), 174
Young Catholic America (Smith et al.),
  180
youth, 171; children's programs, 226;
  National Study of Youth and
  Religion, 174; retention, 97, 97n3;
  teens, 103, *104*, 225, 227

Zech, Charles, et al., 35

CATHOLIC PRACTICE IN NORTH AMERICA

John C. Seitz, series editor

CPSIA information can be obtained
at www.ICGtesting.com
Printed in the USA
LVHW091514161219
640665LV00001B/74/P

9 780823 284344